SUPER 10

CBSE Class 10
Science

2023 Exam Sample Papers

with 2021-22 Previous Year Solved Papers, CBSE Sample Paper & 2020 Topper Answer Sheet

DISHA
Publication Inc

In the interest of student community

Circulation of softcopy of Book(s) in pdf or other equivalent format(s) through any social media channels, emails, etc. or any other channels through mobiles, laptops or desktops is a criminal offence. Anybody circulating, downloading, storing, softcopy of the Book on his device(s) is in breach of the Copyright Act. Further Photocopying of this book or any of its material is also illegal. Do not download or forward in case you come across any such softcopy material.

DISHA Publications Inc.
45, 2nd Floor, Maharishi Dayanand Marg,
Corner Market, Malviya Nagar, new Delhi -110017
Tel: 49842349/ 49842350

© Copyright DISHA Publication Inc.

All Rights Reserved. No part of this publication may be reproduced in any form without prior permission of the publisher. The author and the publisher do not take any legal responsibility for any errors or misrepresentations that might have crept in.
We have tried and made our best efforts to provide accurate up-to-date information in this book.

Typeset By
DISHA DTP Team

Buying books from DISHA

Just Got A Lot More Rewarding!!!

We at DISHA Publication, value your feedback immensely and to show our apperciation of our reviewers, we have launched a review contest.

To participate in this reward scheme, just follow these quick and simple steps:
- Write a review of the product you purchase on Amazon/Flipkart.
- Take a screenshot/photo of your review.
- Mail it to *disha-rewards@aiets.co.in*, along with all your details.

Each month, selected reviewers will win exciting gifts from DISHA Publication. Note that the rewards for each month will be declared in the first week of next month on our website.

https://bit.ly/review-reward-disha.

Write To Us At
feedback_disha@aiets.co.in

Contents

- Latest Syllabus Issued by CBSE for Academic Year (2022-2023) — i-iii
- CBSE Sample Paper 2022-23 with solutions — SQP 1–12
  (Issued by CBSE on 16th Sept. 2022)
- CBSE Solved Paper 2022 (Term II & I) — 2022-1–16
- CBSE Topper-2020 Answer Sheet — TS-1–22

10 Sample Papers with Blue Print

- Sample Paper-1 — Sc-1-Sc-6
- Sample Paper-2 — Sc-7-Sc-12
- Sample Paper-3 — Sc-13-Sc-18
- Sample Paper-4 — Sc-19-Sc-24
- Sample Paper-5 — Sc-25-Sc-30
- Sample Paper-6 — Sc-31-Sc-36
- Sample Paper-7 — Sc-37-Sc-42
- Sample Paper-8 — Sc-43-Sc-48
- Sample Paper-9 — Sc-49-Sc-54
- Sample Paper-10 — Sc-55-Sc-60

SOLUTIONS TO SAMPLE PAPERS 1-10 — Sc-61-Sc-102

Latest Syllabus Issued by CBSE for Academic Year (2022-2023)

COURSE STRUCTURE
CLASS X
(Annual Examination)

Time: 03 Hours **Max. Marks: 80**

Unit No.	Unit	Marks
I	Chemical Substances-Nature and Behaviour	25
II	World of Living	25
III	Natural Phenomena	12
IV	Effects of Current	13
V	Natural Resources	05
	Total	80
	Internal assessment	20
	Grand Total	100

Theme: Materials

Unit I: Chemical Substances - Nature and Behaviour

Chemical reactions: Chemical equation, Balanced chemical equation, implications of a balanced chemical equation, types of chemical reactions: combination, decomposition, displacement, double displacement, precipitation, endothermic exothermic reactions, oxidation and reduction.

Acids, bases and salts: Their definitions in terms of furnishing of H+ and OH– ions, General properties, examples and uses, neutralization, concept of pH scale (Definition relating to logarithm not required), importance of pH in everyday life; preparation and uses of Sodium Hydroxide, Bleaching powder, Baking soda, Washing soda and Plaster of Paris.

Metals and nonmetals: Properties of metals and non-metals; Reactivity series; Formation and properties of ionic compounds; Basic metallurgical processes; Corrosion and its prevention.

Carbon compounds: Covalent bonding in carbon compounds. Versatile nature of carbon. Homologous series. Nomenclature of carbon compounds containing functional groups (halogens, alcohol, ketones, aldehydes, alkanes and alkynes), difference between saturated hydro carbons and unsaturated hydrocarbons. Chemical properties of carbon compounds (combustion, oxidation, addition and substitution reaction). Ethanol and Ethanoic acid (only properties and uses), soaps and detergents.

Theme: The World of the Living

Unit II: World of Living

Life processes: 'Living Being'. Basic concept of nutrition, respiration, transport and excretion in plants and animals.

Control and co-ordination in animals and plants: Tropic movements in plants; Introduction of plant hormones; Control and co-ordination in animals: Nervous system; Voluntary, involuntary and reflex action; Chemical co-ordination: animal hormones.

Reproduction: Reproduction in animals and plants (asexual and sexual) reproductive health - need and methods of family planning. Safe sex vs HIV/AIDS. Child bearing and women's health.

Heredity and Evolution: Heredity; Mendel's contribution- Laws for inheritance of traits: Sex determination: brief introduction: (topics excluded - evolution; evolution and classification and evolution should not be equated with progress).

Theme: Natural Phenomena

Unit III: Natural Phenomena

Reflection of light by curved surfaces; Images formed by spherical mirrors, centre of curvature, principal axis, principal focus, focal length, mirror formula (Derivation not required), magnification.

Refraction; Laws of refraction, refractive index.

Refraction of light by spherical lens; Image formed by spherical lenses; Lens formula (Derivation not required); Magnification. Power of a lens.

Functioning of a lens in human eye, defects of vision and their corrections, applications of spherical mirrors and lenses.

Refraction of light through a prism, dispersion of light, scattering of light, applications in daily life (excluding colour of the sun at sunrise and sunset).

Theme: How Things Work

Unit IV: Effects of Current

Electric current, potential difference and electric current. Ohm's law; Resistance, Resistivity, Factors on which the resistance of a conductor depends. Series combination of resistors, parallel combination of resistors and its applications in daily life. Heating effect of electric current and its applications in daily life. Electric power, Interrelation between P, V, I and R.

Magnetic effects of current : Magnetic field, field lines, field due to a current carrying conductor, field due to current carrying coil or solenoid; Force on current carrying conductor, Fleming's Left Hand Rule, Direct current. Alternating current: frequency of AC. Advantage of AC over DC. Domestic electric circuits.

Theme: Natural Resources

Unit V: Natural Resources

Our environment: Eco-system, Environmental problems, Ozone depletion, waste production and their solutions. Biodegradable and non-biodegradable substances.

Note for the Teachers:

1. The chapter Management of Natural Resources (NCERT Chapter 16) will not be assessed in the year-end examination. However, learners may be assigned to read this chapter and encouraged to prepare a brief write up to any concept of this chapter in their Portfolio. This may be for Internal Assessment and credit may be given Periodic Assessment/Portfolio).

2. The NCERT text books present information in boxes across the book. These help students to get conceptual clarity. However, the information in these boxes would not be assessed in the year-end examination.

A Foundation Series with 3 Goals
Bring Concept Clarity, Sharpen Problem Solving & Build a Strong Foundation.

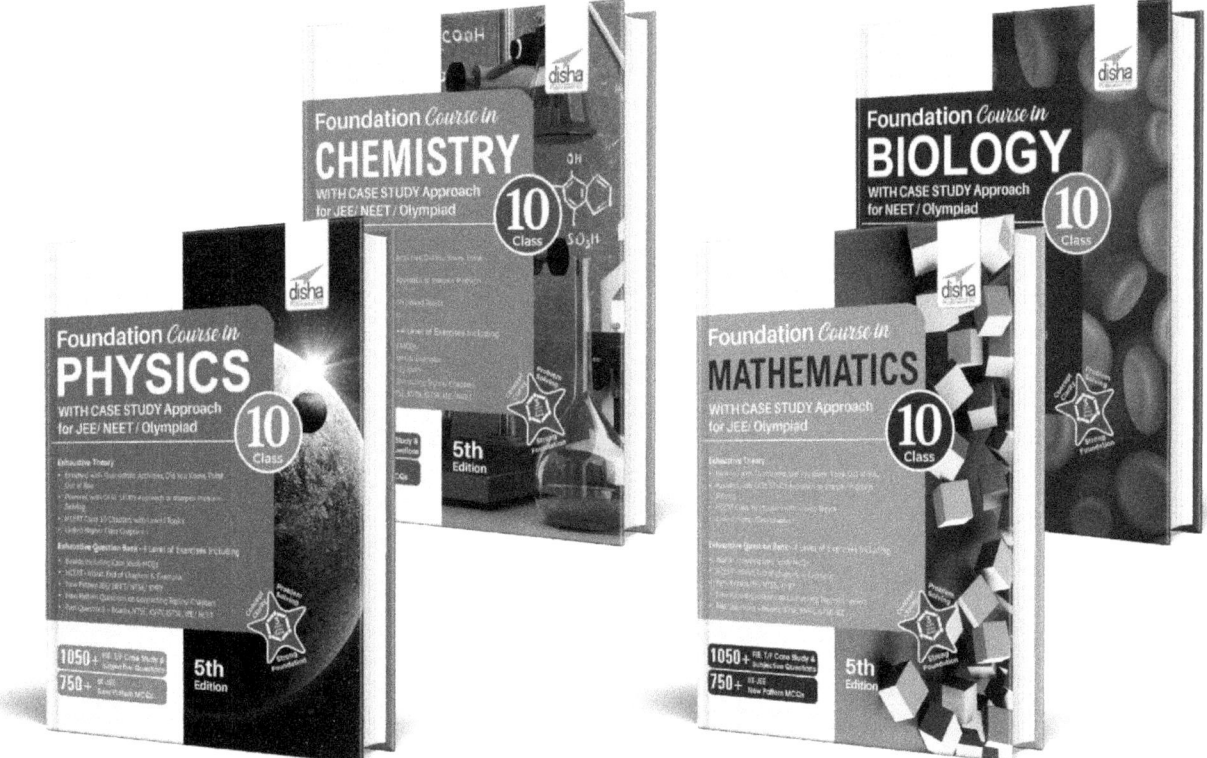

The theory is followed by the Exercise part which covers in total **1800 questions divided into 4 levels of fully solved exercises,** which are graded as per their level of difficulty.

- **Exercise 1: Master Boards: MCQs**, FIB, True-False, Assertion–Reason, Passage, Matching, Very Short, Short & Long Answer Type Questions including Past Years Board Qns. This Exercise also includes – Reasoning Based, HOTS and Case Based MCQs.
- **Exercise 2: Master the NCERT:** All Textbook & Exemplar Questions
- **Exercise 3: Foundation Builder:** Question Bank on NCERT chapter including MCQs 1 Correct, MCQs>1 Correct, Passage, Assertion-Reason, Multiple Matching and Numeric/ Integer Type Questions with past years – NTSE, JSTSE & KVPY considering Syllabus and Level of difficulty.
- **Exercise 4: Foundation Builder+ :** Question Bank on Connecting Topics/ Chapters including MCQs 1 Correct, MCQs>1 Correct, Passage, Assertion-Reason, Multiple Matching and Numeric/ Integer Type Questions with past years – NTSE, JSTSE & KVPY considering Syllabus and Level of difficulty.

The book adheres to the latest syllabus set by the NCERT, going beyond by incorporating those topics which will assist the students to scale-up in the next classes to achieve their academic dreams of Medicine or Engineering.

CBSE SAMPLE QUESTION PAPER (THEORY)
SESSION : 2022-2023

Time Allowed : 3 Hours **Max. Marks : 80**

General Instructions

1. This question paper consists of 39 questions in 5 sections.
2. All questions are compulsory. However, an internal choice is provided in some questions. A student is expected to attempt only one of these questions.
3. **Section A** consists of 20 objective type questions carrying 1 mark each.
4. **Section B** consists of 6 Very Short Answer type questions carrying 02 marks each. Answers to these questions should in the range of 30 to 50 words.
5. **Section C** consists of 7 Short Answer type questions carrying 03 marks each. Answers to these questions should in the range of 50 to 80 words.
6. **Section D** consists of 3 Long Answer type questions carrying 05 marks each. Answer to these questions should be in the range of 80 to 120 words.
7. **Section E** consists of 3 source-based/case-based units of assessment of 04 marks each with sub-parts.

SECTION-A
Select and write one most appropriate option out of the four options given for each of the Questions 1 to 20

1. The change in colour of the moist litmus paper in the given set up is due to

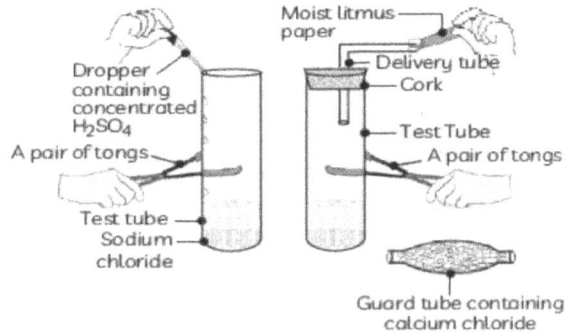

   (i) presence of acid
   (ii) presence of base
   (iii) presence of H⁺ (aq) in the solution
   (iv) presence of Litmus which acts as an indicator

   (a) (i) and (ii) (b) Only (ii)
   (c) Only (iii) (d) Only (iv)

2. In the redox reaction $MnO_2 + 4HCl \rightarrow MnCl_2 + 2H_2O + Cl_2$
   (a) MnO_2 is reduced to $MnCl_2$ & HCl is oxidized to H_2O
   (b) MnO_2 is reduced to $MnCl_2$ & HCl is oxidized to Cl_2
   (c) MnO_2 is oxidized to $MnCl_2$ & HCl is reduced to Cl_2
   (d) MnO_2 is oxidized to $MnCl_2$ & HCl is reduced to H_2O

3.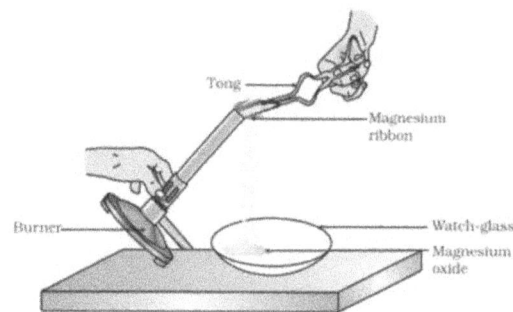

Which of the following is the correct observation of the reaction shown in the above set up?
(a) Brown powder of Magnesium oxide is formed
(b) Colourless gas which turns lime water milky is evolved
(c) Magnesium ribbon burns with brilliant white light
(d) Reddish brown gas with a smell of burning Sulphur has evolved.

4. With the reference to four gases CO_2, CO, Cl_2 and O_2, which one of the options in the table is correct?

Option	Acidic oxide	Used in treatment of water	Product of respiration	Product of incomplete combustion
(a)	CO	Cl_2	O_2	CO
(b)	CO_2	Cl_2	CO_2	CO
(c)	CO_2	O_2	O_2	CO_2
(d)	CO	O_2	CO_2	CO_2

5. On placing a copper coin in a test tube containing green ferrous sulphate solution, it will be observed that the ferrous sulphate solution
(a) turns blue, and a grey substance is deposited on the copper coin.
(b) turns colourless and a grey substance is deposited on the copper coin.
(c) turns colourless and a reddish–brown substance is deposited on the copper coin.
(d) remains green with no change in the copper coin.

6. Anita added a drop each of diluted acetic acid and diluted hydrochloric acid on pH paper and compared the colors. Which of the following is the correct conclusion?
(a) pH of acetic acid is more than that of hydrochloric acid.
(b) pH of acetic acid is less than that of hydrochloric acid.
(c) Acetic acid dissociates completely in aqueous solution.
(d) Acetic acid is a strong acid

7. The formulae of four organic compounds are shown below. Choose the correct option

(a) A and B are unsaturated hydrocarbons
(b) C and D are saturated hydrocarbons
(c) Addition of hydrogen in presence of catalyst changes A to C
(d) Addition of potassium permanganate changes B to D

8. In the given transverse section of the leaf identify the layer of cells where maximum photosynthesis occurs.

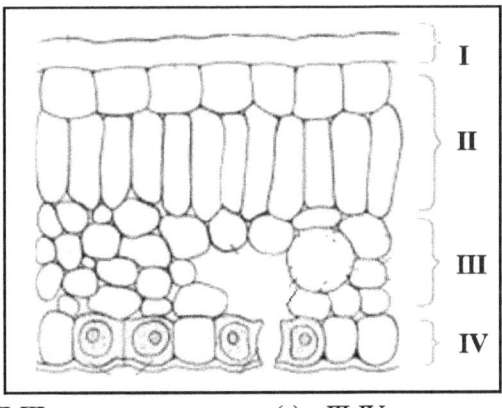

(a) I, II (b) II, III (c) III, IV (d) I, IV

9. Observe the experimental setup shown below. Name the chemical indicated as 'X' that can absorb the gas which is evolved as a byproduct of respiration.

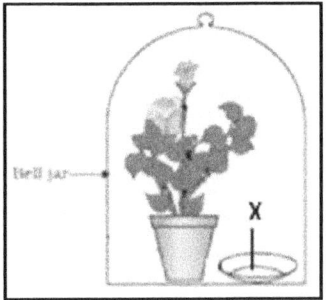

(a) NaOH (b) KOH (c) $Ca(OH)_2$ (d) K_2CO_3

10. If a tall pea plant is crossed with a pure dwarf pea plant then, what percentage of F1 and F2 generation respectively will be tall?
(a) 25%, 25% (b) 50%, 50% (c) 75%, 100% (d) 100%, 75%

11. Observe the three figures given below. Which of the following depicts tropic movements appropriately?

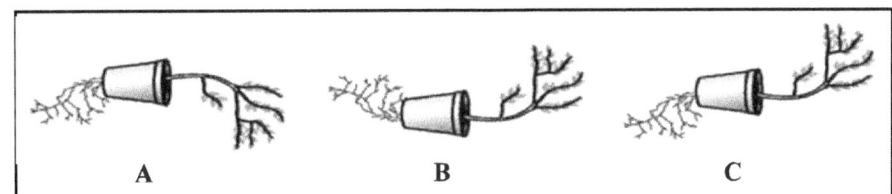

(a) B and C (b) A and C (c) B only (d) C only

12. The diagram shown below depicts pollination. Choose the options that will show a maximum variation in the offspring.

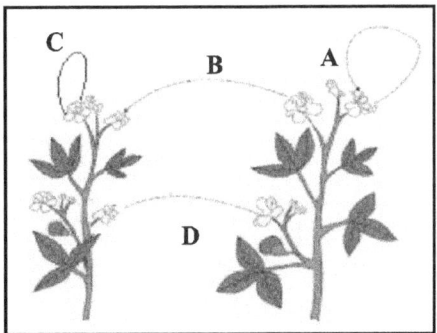

(a) A, B and C (b) B and D (c) B, C and D (d) A and C

13. A complete circuit is left on for several minutes, causing the connecting copper wire to become hot. As the temperature of the wire increases, the electrical resistance of the wire
    (a) decreases.
    (b) remains the same.
    (c) increases.
    (d) increases for some time and then decreases.
14. A copper wire is held between the poles of a magnet.

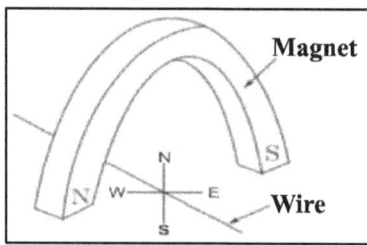

The current in the wire can be reversed. The pole of the magnet can also be changed over. In how many of the four directions shown can the force act on the wire?
    (a) 1   (b) 2   (c) 3   (d) 4
15.

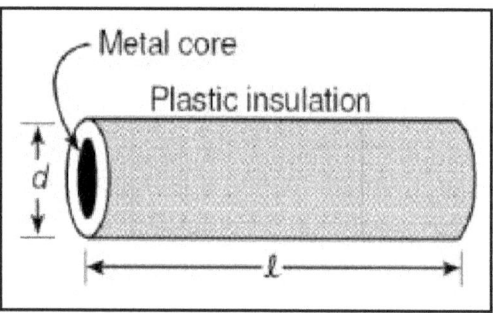

Plastic insulation surrounds a wire having diameter d and length l as shown above. A decrease in the resistance of the wire would be produced by an increase in the
    (a) length l of the wire
    (b) diameter d of the wire
    (c) temperature of the wire
    (d) thickness of the plastic insulation
16. Which of the following pattern correctly describes the magnetic field around a long straight wire carrying current?
    (a) straight lines perpendicular to the wire.
    (b) straight lines parallel to the wire.
    (c) radial lines originating from the wire.
    (d) concentric circles centred around the wire.

Directions: Q.No. 17–20 are Assertion - Reasoning based questions: These consist of two statements – Assertion (A) and Reason (R). Answer these questions selecting the appropriate option given below:
(a) Both A and R are true and R is the correct explanation of A
(b) Both A and R are true and R is not the correct explanation of A
(c) A is true but R is false
(d) A is False but R is true

17. **Assertion:** Silver bromide decomposition is used in black and white photography.
    Reason: Light provides energy for this exothermic reaction.
18. **Assertion:** Height in pea plants is controlled by efficiency of enzymes and is thus genetically controlled.
    Reason: Cellular DNA is the information source for making proteins in the cell.
19. **Assertion:** Amphibians can tolerate mixing of oxygenated and deoxygenated blood.
    Reason: Amphibians are animals with two chambered heart

SECTION-B
Q. no. 21 to 26 are Very Short Answer Questions.

20. **Assertion:** On freely suspending a current – carrying solenoid, it comes to rest in Geographical N-S direction.
    Reason: One end of current carrying straight solenoid behaves as a North pole and the other end as a South pole, just like a bar magnet.

21. A clear solution of slaked lime is made by dissolving $Ca(OH)_2$ in an excess of water. This solution is left exposed to air. The solution slowly goes milky as a faint white precipitate forms. Explain why a faint white precipitate forms, support your response with the help of a chemical equation.

    OR

    Keerti added dilute Hydrochloric acid to four metals and recorded her observations as shown in the table given below:

Metal	Gas Evolved
Copper	Yes
Iron	Yes
Magnesium	No
Zinc	Yes

    Select the correct observation(s) and give chemical equation(s) of the reaction involved.

22. How is the mode of action in beating of the heart different from reflex actions? Give four examples.
23. Patients whose gallbladder are removed are recommended to eat less oily food. Why?
24. Name the substances other than water, that are reabsorbed during urine formation. What are the two parameters that decide the amount of water that is reabsorbed in the kidney?
25.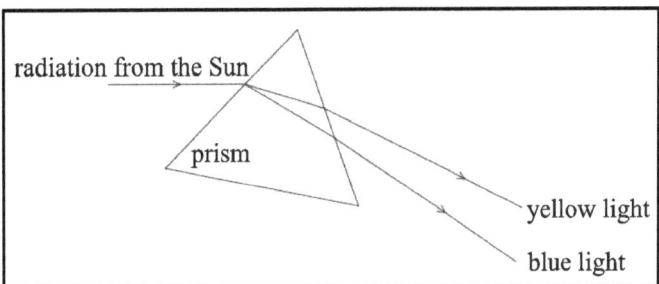

    State the phenomena observed in the above diagram. Explain with reference to the diagram, which of the two lights mentioned above will have the higher wavelength?

    OR

    How will you use two identical prisms so that a narrow beam of white light incident on one prism emerges out of the second prism as white light? Draw the diagram.

26. A lot of waste is generated in neighborhood. However, almost all of it is biodegradable. What impact will it have on the environment or human health?

SECTION-C
Q.no. 27 to 33 are Short Answer Questions.

27. (i) $A + BC \longrightarrow AC + B$

    (ii) $AB + CD \longrightarrow AC + BD$

    Identify the types of reaction mentioned above in (i) and (ii). Give one example for each type in the form of a balanced chemical equation.

28.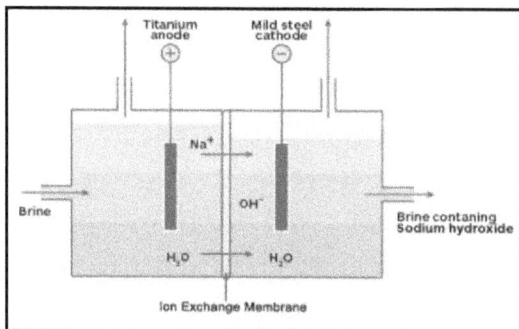
    (a) Identify the gasses evolved at the anode and cathode in the above experimental set up.
    (b) Name the process that occurs. Why is it called so?
    (c) Illustrate the reaction of the process with the help of a chemical equation.
29. The leaves of a plant were covered with aluminium foil, how would it affect the physiology of the plant?

    OR

    How is lymph an important fluid involved in transportation? If lymphatic vessels get blocked, how would it affect the human body? Elaborate.
30. Rohit wants to have an erect image of an object using a converging mirror of focal length 40 cm.
    (a) Specify the range of distance where the object can be placed in front of the mirror. Justify.
    (b) Draw a ray diagram to show image formation in this case.
    (c) State one use of the mirror based on the above kind of image formation.
31. (a) A lens of focal length 5 cm is being used by Debashree in the laboratory as a magnifying glass. Her least distance of distinct vision is 25 cm.
        (i) What is the magnification obtained by using the glass?
        (ii) She keeps a book at a distance 10 cm from her eyes and tries to read. She is unable to read. What is the reason for this?
    (b) Ravi kept a book at a distance of 10 cm from the eyes of his friend Hari. Hari is not able to read anything written in the book. Give reasons for this?
32. A student fixes a white sheet of paper on a drawing board. He places a bar magnet in the centre and sprinkles some iron filings uniformly around the bar magnet. Then he taps gently and observes that iron filings arrange themselves in a certain pattern.
    (a) Why do iron filings arrange themselves in a particular pattern?
    (b) Which physical quantity is indicated by the pattern of field lines around the bar magnet?
    (c) State any two properties of magnetic field lines.

    OR

    A compass needle is placed near a current carrying wire. State your observations for the following cases and give reasons for the same in each case-
    (a) Magnitude of electric current in wire is increased.
    (b) The compass needle is displaced away from the wire.
33. Why is damage to the ozone layer a cause for concern? What are its causes and what steps are being taken to limit this damage?

SECTION-D
Q.no. 34 to 36 are Long Answer Questions.

34. Shristi heated Ethanol with a compound A in presence of a few drops of concentrated sulphuric acid and observed a sweet smelling compound B is formed. When B is treated with sodium hydroxide it gives back Ethanol and a compound C.
    (a) Identify A and C
    (b) Give one use each of compounds A and B.
    (c) Write the chemical reactions involved and name the reactions.

OR

(a) What is the role of concentrated Sulphuric acid when it is heated with Ethanol at 443 K. Give the reaction involved.

(b) Reshu by mistake forgot to label the two test tubes containing Ethanol and Ethanoic acid. Suggest an experiment to identify the substances correctly? Illustrate the reactions with the help of chemical equations

35. (a) Why is it not possible to reconstruct the whole organism from a fragment in complex multicellular organisms?

(b) Sexual maturation of reproductive tissues and organs are necessary link for reproduction. Elucidate.

OR

(a) How are variations useful for species if there is drastic alteration in the niches?

(b) Explain how the uterus and placenta provide necessary conditions for proper growth and development of the embryo after implantation?

36.

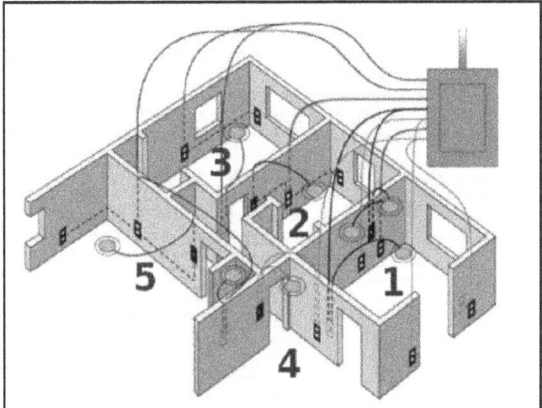

The diagram above is a schematic diagram of a household circuit. The house shown in the above diagram has 5 usable spaces where electrical connections are made. For this house, the mains have a voltage of 220 V and the net current coming from the mains is 22A.

(a) What is the mode of connection to all the spaces in the house from the mains?

(b) The spaces 5 and 4 have the same resistance and spaces 3 and 2 have respective resistances of 20Ù and 30Ù. Space 1 has a resistance double that of space 5. What is the net resistance for space 5.

(c) What is the current in space 3?

(d) What should be placed between the main connection and the rest of the house's electrical appliances to save them from accidental high electric current?

SECTION-E

Q.no. 37 to 39 are case - based/data -based questions with 2 to 3 short sub - parts. Internal choice is provided in one of these sub-parts.

37. Read the following case/passage and answer the questions.

Two students decided to investigate the effect of water and air on iron object under identical experimental conditions. They measured the mass of each object before placing it partially immersed in 10 ml of water. After a few days, the object were removed, dried and their masses were measured. The table shows their results.

Student	Object	Mass of Object before Rusting in g	Mass of the coated object in g
A	Nail	3.0	3.15
B	Thin plate	6.0	6.33

(a) What might be the reason for the varied observations of the two students?

(b) In another set up the students coated iron nails with zinc metal and noted that, iron nails coated with zinc prevents rusting. They also observed that zinc initially acts as a physical barrier, but an extra advantage of using zinc is that it continues to prevent rusting even if the layer of zinc is damaged. Name this process of rust prevention and give any two other methods to prevent rusting.

OR

(b) In which of the following applications of Iron, rusting will occur most? Support your answer with valid reason.

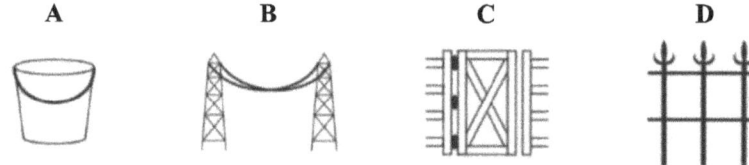

A - Iron Bucket electroplated with Zinc
B - Electricity cables having iron wires covered with aluminium
C - Iron hinges on a gate
D - Painted iron fence

38. Read the following case/passage and answer the questions.

Pooja has green eyes while her parents and brother have black eyes. Pooja's husband Ravi has black eyes while his mother has green eyes and father has black eyes.

(a) On the basis of the above given information, is the green eye colour a dominant or recessive trait? Justify your answer.
(b) What is the possible genetic makeup of Pooja's brother's eye colour?
(c) What is the probability that the offspring of Pooja and Ravi will have green eyes? Also, show the inheritance of eye colour in the offspring with the help of a suitable cross.

OR

(d) 50% of the offspring of Pooja's brother are green eyed. With help of cross show how this is possible.

39. Read the following case/passage and answer the questions.

The above images are that of a specialized slide projector. Slides are small transparencies mounted in sturdy frames ideally suited to magnification and projection, since they have a very high resolution and a high image quality. There is a tray where the slides are to be put into a particular orientation so that the viewers can see the enlarged erect images of the transparent slides. This means that the slides will have to be inserted upside down in the projector tray.

To show her students the images of insects that she investigated in the lab, Mrs. Iyer brought a slide projector. Her slide projector produced a 500 times enlarged and inverted image of a slide on a screen 10 m away.

(a) Based on the text and data given in the above paragraph, what kind of lens must the slide projector have?
(b) If v is the symbol used for image distance and u for object distance then with one reason state what will be the sign for $\dfrac{v}{u}$ in the given case?
(c) A slide projector has a convex lens with a focal length of 20 cm. The slide is placed upside down 21 cm from the lens. How far away should the screen be placed from the slide projector's lens so that the slide is in focus?

OR

(c) When a slide is placed 15 cm behind the lens in the projector, an image is formed 3 m in front of the lens. If the focal length of the lens is 14 cm, draw a ray diagram to show image formation. (not to scale)

SOLUTIONS

1. **(c)** Only iii (1 mark)
2. **(b)** MnO_2 is reduced to $MnCl_2$ & HCl is oxidized to Cl_2 (1 mark)
3. **(c)** Magnesium ribbon burns with brilliant white light (1 mark)
4. **(b)** CO_2, Cl_2, CO_2, CO (1 mark)
5. **(d)** Ferrous sulphate solution remains green with no change in the copper coin. (1 mark)
6. **(a)** Only i (1 mark)
7. **(c)** Addition of hydrogen in presence of catalyst changes A to C (1 mark)
8. **(b)** II,III (1 mark)
9. **(b)** (1 mark)
10. **(d)** (1 mark)
11. **(d)** C only (1 mark)
12. **(b)** B and D (1 mark)
13. **(c)** increases (1 mark)
14. **(b)** 2 (Either North or South) (1 mark)
15. **(b)** diameter d of the wire
16. **(d)** The field consists of concentric circles centred around the wire. (1 mark)
17. **(c)** A is true but R is false (1 mark)
18. **(a)** Both A and R are true and R is the correct explanation of A (1 mark)
19. **(c)** A is true but R is false (1 mark)
20. **(a)** Both A and R are true and R is the correct explanation of A (1 mark)
21. Calcium hydroxide reacts with Carbon dioxide present in the atmosphere to form Calcium carbonate which results in milkiness/white ppt / Formation of Calcium carbonate (2 marks)

    $Ca(OH)_2 + CO_2 \rightarrow CaCO_3 + H_2O$

    OR

    $Fe + HCl \rightarrow FeCl_2/FeCl_3 + H_2$ (No deduction for balancing/states)
    $Zn + HCl \rightarrow ZnCl_2 + H_2$

22.

Beating of heart	Reflex actions
Involuntary actions are the actions which are not controlled by our will	Reflex actions are the sudden action in response to something.
They to dnot need any kind of stimulus to work.	They required stimulus for its action.
These actions are regulated by the brain.	These actions are regulated by the spinal cord.
They do not involve skeletal muscle.	They do involve skeletal muscle.
These actions are performed throughout one's life.	These actions are produced in response to an event of an emergency.
This action may be quick or slow.	Reflex action are always quick.

23. Gallbladder stores bile which helps in emulsification of lipids. In the absence of stored bile, emulsification of fats will be negligible/ affected/ less and thus fat digestion will be slow. Hence there are such diet restrictions. (2 marks)

24. Glucose, amino acids, salts (any 2, 1 mark each) and a major amount of water are selectively re-absorbed as the urine flows along the tube.

    The amount of water reabsorbed depends on how much excess water there is in the body and on how much of dissolved waste there is to be excreted. (2 marks)

25. Dispersion- The splitting of white light into seven colours on passing through a prism.

    Velocity is directly proportional to wavelength given constant frequency. So yellow will have greater wavelength than blue as the velocity of yellow light is greater than blue. (2 marks)

    OR

    Angle of deflections of the two prisms need to be equal and opposite. While the first prism splits the light in the seven colours due to different angles of deflection, the second prism combines the spectrum along a single ray and the colours again combine to give white light as the emergent light. (2 marks)

    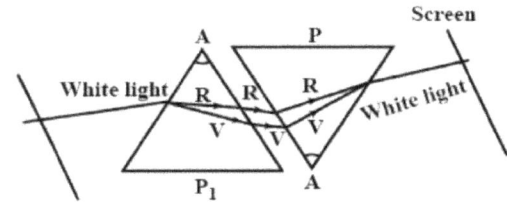

26. Excess generation of biodegradable wastes can be harmful as - Its decomposition is a slow process leading to production of foul smell and gases. It can be the breeding ground for germs that create unhygienic conditions. (2 marks)

27. (i) Displacement - . M
    - $Fe(s) + CuSO_4(aq) \rightarrow FeSO_4(aq) + Cu(s)$ (1 mark)
    - $Zn(s) + CuSO_4(aq) \rightarrow ZnSO_4(aq) + Cu(s)$
    - $Pb(s) + CuCl_2(aq) \rightarrow PbCl_2(aq) + Cu(s)$

    (Any one of the reaction or other displacement reaction.)

    (ii) Double displacement. (1 marks)

    $Na_2SO_4(aq) + BaCl_2(aq) \rightarrow BaSO_4(s) + 2NaCl(aq)$

    (Any one of the reaction or other double displacement reaction.)

    (3 marks)

28. (a) Anode: Chlorine; Cathode: Hydrogen
    (b) Chlor alkali process as the products obtained are alkali, chlorine gas and hydrogen gas Electric current
    (c) $2NaCl(aq) + 2H_2O(l) \longrightarrow 2NaOH(aq) + Cl_2(g) + H_2(g)$
    (3 marks)

29. No photosynthesis will occur so no glucose will be made. Also no respiration will take place as no Oxygen will be taken in.

    No transpiration will occur so there would be no upward movement of water or minerals from the soil as there will be no transpirational pull.

    Temperature regulation of leaf surface will be affected.

    OR

    Lymph carries digested and absorbed fat from the intestine and drains excess fluid from extracellular space back into the blood. Blockage of lymphatic system will lead to water retention and poor fat absorption in the body. (3 marks)

30. (a) The object has to be placed at a distance between 0 - 40 cm. This is because image is virtual, erect and magnified when the object is placed between F and P.

    (b)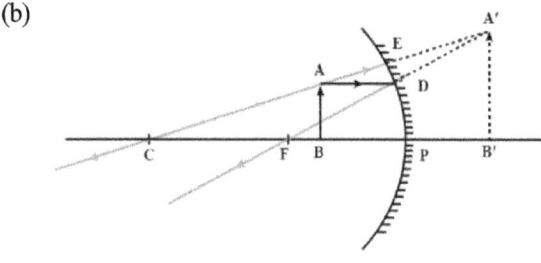

    (c) Used as shaving mirror or used by dentists to get enlarged image of teeth (3 marks)

31. (a) Given image distance = v = –25 cm, focal length = f = 25 cm, magnification = m = ?

    From lens formula, $\dfrac{1}{f} = \dfrac{1}{v} - \dfrac{1}{u} = \dfrac{1}{u} = \dfrac{1}{v} - \dfrac{1}{f}$

    $\dfrac{1}{u} = \dfrac{1}{-25} - \dfrac{1}{5} = \dfrac{-1-5}{25} = \dfrac{-6}{25}$

    Object distance $= u = \dfrac{-25}{6}$ cm.

    We know that, $m = \dfrac{v}{u} = \dfrac{-25 \times 6}{-25} = 6.$

    (b) This is because the least distance of distinct vision is 25 cm. (3 marks)

32. (a) When iron filings are placed in a magnetic field around a bar magnet, they behave like tiny magnets. The magnetic force experienced by these tiny magnets make them rotate and align themselves along the direction of field lines.
    (b) The physical property indicated by this arrangement is the magnetic field produced by the bar magnet.
    (c) Magnetic field lines never intersect, magnetic field lines are closed curves. (3 marks)

    OR

    (a) The deflection in the compass needle increases as Magnetic field of the current carrying conductor is directly proportional to current flowing through it.
    (b) The deflection in the needle decreases as the magnetic field is inversely proportional to the perpendicular distance from the wire. (3 marks)

33. Damage to the ozone layer is a cause for concern because the ozone layer shields the surface of earth from harmful UV radiations from the sun which cause skin cancer in human beings.

    Synthetic chemicals like chlorofluorocarbons (CFCs) which are used as refrigerants and in the fire - extinguishers are the main reason for the depletion of the ozone layer.

    Steps taken to limit this damage - Many developing and developed countries have signed and are obeying the directions of UNEP (United Nations Environment Programme) to freeze or limit the production and usage of CFCs at 1986 levels. (3 marks)

34. (a) A. Ethanoic acid/ Or any other carboxylic acid, C- Sodium salt of ethanoic acid/ any other carboxylic acid/ sodium ethanoate.
    (b) Use of A- dil solution used as vinegar in cooking/ preservative in pickles
    Use of B. making perfumes, flavoring agent
    (c) $CH_3COOH + C_2H_5OH \xrightarrow{Conc\ H_2SO_4}$
    $CH_3COOC_2H_5 + H_2O$
    $CH_3COOC_2H_5 + NaOH \longrightarrow CH_3COONa + C_2H_5OH$
    (5 marks)

    OR

    (a) Sulphuric acid acts as dehydrating agent
    $C_2H_5OH \xrightarrow{Conc\ H_2SO_4,\ 443K} C_2H_4 + H_2O$
    (b) By reaction with sodium carbonate/ bicarbonate 1M with the samples, ethanol will not react whereas ethanoic acid gives brisk effervescence
    $2CH_3COOH + Na_2CO_3 \rightarrow 2CH_3COONa + H_2O + CO_2$

OR

$CH_3COOH + NaHCO_3 \rightarrow CH_3COONa + H_2O + CO_2$

(5 marks)

35. (a) The reason is that many multi-cellular organisms are not simply a random collection of cells. Specialised cells are organised as tissues, and tissues are organised into organs, which then have to be placed at definite positions in the body. Therefore, cell-by-cell division would be impractical.

(b) Sexual maturation of reproductive tissues is a necessary link for reproduction because of the need for specialised cell called germ-cells to participate in sexual reproduction. The body of the individual organism has to grow to its adult size, the rate of general body growth begins to slow down, reproductive tissues begin to mature.

A whole new set of changes in the appearance of the body takes place like change in body proportions, new features appear. This period during adolescence is called puberty.

There are also changes taking place that are different between boys and girls. In girls, breast size begins to increase, with darkening of the skin of the nipples at the tips of the breasts. Also, girls begin to menstruate at around this time. Boys begin to have new thick hair growth on the face and their voices begin to crack. (5 marks)

OR

(a) If the niche were drastically altered, the population could be wiped out. However, if some variations were to be present in a few individuals in these populations, there would be some chance for them to survive. Variation is thus useful for the survival of species over time.

(b)
- The lining of the uterus thickens and is richly supplied with blood to nourish the growing embryo.
- The embryo gets nutrition from the mother's blood with the help of placenta. It is embedded in the uterine wall.
- It contains villi on the embryo's side of the tissue. On the mother's side are blood spaces, which surround the villi.
- This provides a large surface area for glucose and oxygen to pass from the mother to the embryo. The developing embryo will also generate waste substances which can be removed by transferring them into the mother's blood through the placenta.

(1 mark)

- The child is born as a result of rhythmic contractions of the muscles in the uterus. (5 marks)

36. (a) All spaces are connected in parallel.

(b) Let Resistance of Space 5 and 4 be R ohms respectively

Resistance of Space 1 = 2 R ohms

Resistance of Space 2 = 30 ohms

Resistance of Space 3 = 20 ohms

Current = 22 A

V = 220 V

Total Resistance = V/I

$$\frac{1}{R_1} + \frac{1}{R_2} + \frac{1}{R_3} + \frac{1}{R_4} + \frac{1}{R_5} = \frac{1}{R_{eq}}$$

$$\frac{1}{2R} + \frac{1}{30} + \frac{1}{20} + \frac{1}{R} + \frac{1}{R} = \frac{1}{R_{eq}}$$

$$\frac{30 + 2R + 3R + 60 + 60}{60R} = \frac{1}{R_{eq}}$$

$$\frac{150 + 5R}{60R} = \frac{1}{R_{eq}}$$

$$Req = \frac{60R}{150 + 5R} = \frac{\cancel{220}^{10}}{22}$$

$60R = 10(150 + 5R)$

$60R = 1500 + 50R$

$10R = 1500$

$R = 150 \, \Omega$ (5 marks)

37. (a) Rusting occurs in both A and B so there is an increase in mass.

As the surface area of B is more, extent of rusting is more

(b) Galvanization

Oiling/ greasing/ painting/ alloying/ chromium plating or any other (4 marks)

OR

(b) C - Iron hinges on a gate -

Iron is in contact with both atmospheric oxygen and moisture/ water vapour. (4 marks)

38. (a) Yes, green eye colour is recessive as it will express only in homozygous condition

(b) BB, Bb

(c) bb*Bb

	B	b
b	Bb	bb
b	Bb	bb

Genetic cross

50% of the offsprings can have green eye colour (0.5)

(4 marks)

OR

(c) Brother is heterozygous(Bb) and wife is green(bb)
(1 mark)

Wife bb*Bb brother

	B	b
b	Bb	bb
b	Bb	bb

50% of the offsprings can have green eye colour as per the cross shown. (4 marks)

39. (a) Convex Lens
(b) Negative as the image is real and inverted.
(c) $1/f = 1/v - 1/u$
$1/20 = 1/v - 1/-20$
$1/v = 1/20 - 1/21$
$= (21 - 20)/420$
$= 1/420$
$v = 420$ cm (2 marks)

OR

(c)

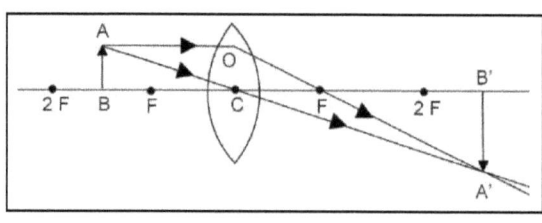

(2 marks)

All India 2022
CBSE Board Solved Paper
Term-II

Time Allowed : 2 Hours   *Maximum Marks : 40*

General Instructions:

Read the following instructions carefully and strictly follow them.
   (i) This question paper contains **15** questions. All questions are compulsory.
   (ii) This question paper is divided into **three** sections viz. Section **A**, **B** and **C**.
   (iii) Section A - Question numbers **1** to **7** are short answer type questions. Each question carries **two** marks.
   (iv) Section B - Question numbers **8** to **13** are also short answer type questions. Each question carries **three** marks.
   (v) Section C - Question numbers **14** and **15** are case based questions. Each question carries **four** marks.
   (vi) Internal choices have been provided in some questions. Only one of the alternatives has to be attempted.

SECTION - A

1. In the following food chain, only 2J of energy was available to the peacocks. How much energy would have been present in Grass? Justify your answer.
   GRASS → GRASS HOPPER → FROG → SNAKE → PEACOCK   **2**

   OR

   (a) What is meant by garbage? List two classes into which garbage is classified.
   (b) What do we actually mean when we say that the "enzymes are specific in their action"?

2. (a) Name the poles P, Q, R and S of the magnets in the following figures 'a' and 'b' :   1/2+1/2+1 = 2

   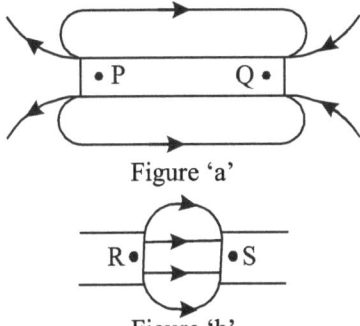

   Figure 'a'

   Figure 'b'

   (b) State the inference drawn about the direction of the magnetic field lines on the basis of these diagrams.

   OR

   When is the force experienced by a current - carrying straight conductor placed in a uniform magnetic field.   1+1 = 2
   (i) Maximum;
   (ii) Minimum ?   **3**

3. Name the reproductive parts of an angiosperm. Where are these parts located? Explain the structure of its male reproductive part.   **2**

   OR

   What is puberty? Mention any two changes that are common to both boys and girls in early teenage years.

4. (a) Name the reproductive and non-reproductive parts of bread mould (Rhizopus).
   (b) List any two advantages of vegetative propagation.   **2**

5. In the following figure showing a germinating gram seed, name the parts labelled as A, B and C :   1/2×4 = 2

   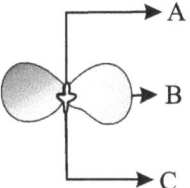

   Why is part 'B' considered to be important during germination ?

6. A part of modern periodic table is given below. On its basis, answer the following questions: 1/2×4 = 2

Group No.→ Period ↓	1	2	13	14	15	16	17	18
2		A				B		
3	E			D			F	C

   (a) Write the molecular formula of the compound formed by the combination :
       (i) A and F   (ii) E and B
   (b) Which of the element is a
       (i) noble gas?   (ii) metalloid?

7. Write the chemical formula of two consecutive homologous of organic compounds having functional group – OH. What happens to the (i) boiling point and (ii) solubility of organic compounds of a homologous series as the molecular mass increases.   1/2×4 = 2

SECTION - B

8. (a) We do not clean ponds or lakes, but an aquarium needs to be cleaned regularly. Why? **1 + 2**
   (b) Why is ozone layer getting depleted at the higher levels of the atmosphere? Mention one harmful effect caused by its depletion.

9. (a) List the factors on which the resistance of a uniform cylindrical conductor of a given material depends. **2+1**
   (b) The resistance of a wire of 0.01 cm radius is 10 Ω. If the resistivity of the wire is 50×10^{-8} Ω m, find the length of this wire.

OR

   (a) What is the meaning of electric power of an electrical device? Write its SI unit. **1½**
   (b) An electric kettle of 2kW is used for 2h. Calculate the energy consumed in
      (i) kilowatt hour and **1½**
      (ii) joules.

10. In the given circuit determine the value of:
    (i) total resistance of the circuit **1½**
    (ii) current flowing through the ammeter. **1½**

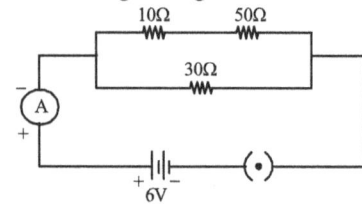

11. A green stemmed tomato plant denoted by (GG) is crossed with a tomato plant with purple stem denoted by (gg). **3**
    (i) What colour of the stem would you expect in their F1 progeny?
    (ii) In what ratio would you find the green and purple coloured stem in plants of F2 progeny?
    (iii) What conclusion can be drawn for the above observations?

12. Consider the following organic compounds: **3**

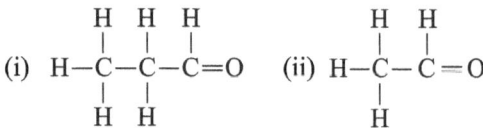

    (a) Name the functional group present in their compounds.
    (b) Write the general formula for the compounds of this functional group.
    (c) State the relationship between these compounds and draw the structure of any other compound having similar functional group.

OR

    (a) Draw the electron dot structure for ethyne. **1+2 = 3**
    (b) List two differences between the properties exhibited by covalent compounds and ionic compounds.

13. (a) State Newland Law of Octaves. **1 + 1 + ½ + ½ = 3**
    (b) With an example, explain Dobereiner's Triads.
    (c) List one limitation each of both the attempts mentioned in 'a' and 'b'.

SECTION - C

This section has 02 case based questions (14 and 15). Each case is followed by **03** sub-questions (a, b and c). Part (a) and (b) are compulsrory. However an internal choice has been provided in Part (c).

14. A student was asked to perform an experiment to study the force on a current carrying conductor in a magnetic field. He took a small aluminum rod AB, a strong horse shoe magnet, some connecting wires, a battery and a switch and connected them as shown. He observed that on passing current, the rod gets displaced. On reversing the direction of current, the direction of displacement also gets reversed. On the basis of your understanding of this phenomenon, answer the following questions: **4**

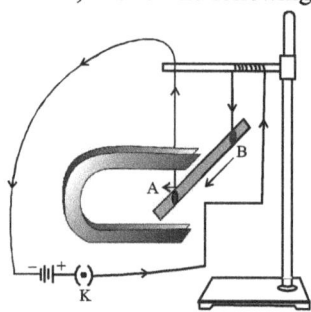

    (a) Why does the rod get displaced on passing current through it?
    (b) State the rule that determines the direction of the force on the conductor AB.
    (c) (i) In the above experimented set up, when current is passed through the rod, it gets displaced towards the left. What will happen to the displacement if the polarity of the magnet and the direction of current both are reversed?
        (ii) Name any two devices that use current carrying conductors and magnetic field.

OR

Draw the pattern of magnetic field lines produced around a current carrying straight conductor held vertically on a horizontal cardboard. Indicate the direction of the field lines as well as the direction of current flowing through the conductor.

15. Mendel blended his knowledge of Science and mathematics to keep the count of the individuals exhibiting a particular trait in each generation. He observed a number of contrasting visible characters controlled in pea plants in a field. He conducted many experiments to arrive at the laws of inheritance.
    (a) If only one pair of contrasting characters like tall and short plants is taken, plants obtained in F1 generation are not of medium height. Why?
    (b) Name the recessive traits in above case.
    (c) Mention the type of the new combinations of plants obtained in F2 progeny along with their ratio, if F1 progeny was allowed to self pollinate. **1+1+2 = 4**

OR

If 1600 plants were obtained in F2 progeny, write the number of plants having traits:
(i) Tall with round seeds
(ii) Short with wrinkled seeds
Write the conclusion of the above experiment.

Solutions

1. Energy present in Grass = 20000 J
   Justification : According to the ten percent law of energy in a food chain, only ten % of energy is transferred to the next trophic level. Thus, the energy keeps on decreasing by 10% of each level.
   Explanation
   Energy available to grass = 20000 J **[1 Mark]**
   Energy available to grass hopper
   = 10% of 20000 = 2000 J
   Energy available to frog = 10% of 2000 = 200 J
   Energy available to snake = 10% of 200 = 20 J
   Energy available to peacock = 10% of 20 = 2 J **[1 Mark]**
   hence, justified.

   OR

   (a) The household waste or rubbish produced in our day-to-day life is called garbage. For example, spoilt food, vegetable peels, leaves, wood, glass, paper, plastic, etc. **[1 Mark]**
   Garbage is classified into the following two types:
   (i) Biodegradable garbage-
       E.g.,-spozlt food, vegetable peels etc. **[½ Mark]**
   (ii) Non-Biodegradable garbage-
       E.g.,-plastic, metal, cans, etc. **[½ Mark]**

2. (a) In figure (a) P – North Pole : Q – South Pole
       (b) R – North Pole : S – South Pole
       [½ + ½ Mark]
   (b) Magnetic field lines always starts from North Pole and end at South Pole. **[1 Mark]**

   > **Note**
   > *All magnetic field lines are closed curves. They come out of the magnet from the side of north pole and go into it on the side of the south pole. They continue inside the magnet.*

   OR

   The force experienced by a current-carrying straight conductor placed in a uniform field is
   (i) maximum when the conductor is placed perpendicular to the magnetic field. **[1 Mark]**
   (ii) minimum when the conductor is placed parallel to the magnetic field. **[1 Mark]**

3. The male reproductive part of an angiospermic plants is stamen and female is called carpel. It is located in the flower. Male reproductive part consist of two parts-
   [1 Mark]

   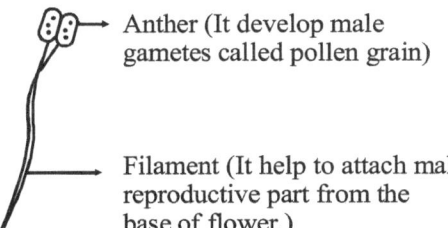

   Anther (It develop male gametes called pollen grain)
   Filament (It help to attach male reproductive part from the base of flower.) **[1 Mark]**

   OR

   – Puberty is the phase in humans, when a boy or girl reach to their sexual maturity. **[1 Mark]**
   – Two changes that are common to both boys and girls in early teenage years are–
   (i) Releasing of hormones. **[1 Mark]**
   (ii) Growth of public hair, facial hair and increasing in height.

4. (a) Reproductive part of bread mould is sporangium. While non-reproductive part of bread mould is hyphae. **[1 Mark]**
   (b) Advantages of vegetative propagation are:
   (i) Produces identical quality as the parent. **[1 Mark]**
   (ii) Plants do not have seed viablities, hence can be reproduce.

5.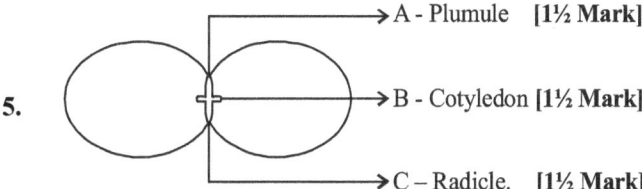
   → A - Plumule **[1½ Mark]**
   → B - Cotyledon **[1½ Mark]**
   → C – Radicle. **[1½ Mark]**

   Cotyledons store food reserves in the seed, Hence it supply nutrition to the developing embryo. **[½ Mark]**

6. (a)
   (i) Element 'A' belongs to group 2nd therefore it must be divalent and element 'F' belongs to group 17 therefore it must be monovalent. Hence molecular formula should be

   $\overset{+2}{A} \overset{-1}{F}$

   ∴ $A_1 F_2$ or we can write it as $A F_2$ **[½ Mark]**
   (ii) Element 'E' belongs to the group 1 therefore it should be monovalent and element 'B' belongs to group 16th therefore it must be divalent. Hence molecular formula should be

   $\overset{+1}{E} \overset{-2}{B}$

   ∴ $E_2 B_1$ or $E_2 B$ **[½ Mark]**
   (b)
   (i) Element 'C' is a noble gas. **[½ Mark]**
   (ii) Element 'D' is a metalloid. **[½ Mark]**

7. In a homologous series the consecutive members differ by $-CH_2$ unit. For alcohol functional group the consecutive homologous are
   (a) CH_3OH **[½ Mark]**
   (b) CH_3CH_2OH **[½ Mark]**
   (i) Boiling point increases with increase in the molecular mass in the homologous series. **[½ Mark]**
   (ii) Solubility in water decreases with increase in the molecular mass in the homologous series. **[½ Mark]**

In alcohol homologous series, as the size of alkyl group increases, solubility in water decreases due to increase in non-ionic interactions (van der Waal interaction).

8. (a) Ponds and Lakes are natural ecosystems as they contain decomposers which act as a cleaning agents, whereas an aquarium is an artificial ecosystem, which do not contain decomposers that clean it. Hence It need to be clean periodically. **[1 Mark]**
   (b) Ozone Layer getting depleted at the higher levels of the atmosphere due to effect of chlorofluorocarbons (CFCs). Its harmful effect is skin cancer. **[2 Marks]**

CFCs are used as refrigerants and in fire extinguisher.

9. (a) The factors on which the resistance of a conductor depends are
   (i) Length of the conductor (l): Resistance (R) of a conductor is directly proportional to length
   i.e., $R \propto l$
   (ii) Area of cross-section (A): Resistance (R) of a conductor is inversely proportional to area of cross-section i.e., $R \propto \dfrac{1}{A}$
   (iii) Material of the conductor: Resistance of a conductor depends on material of the conductor.
   i.e., $R \propto \dfrac{l}{A}$ or, $R = \rho \dfrac{l}{A}$
   Here, ρ = resistivity or specific resistance of the conductor which depends on the material of the conductor. **[2 Marks]**

Resistance of a conductor depends on temperature also.
$R_t = R_0(1 + \alpha t)$
α = temperature coefficient of resistance
R_0 = resistance at 0°C
R_t = resistance at t°C

(b) According to question, resistance $R = 10\Omega$, radius of the wire $r = 0.01$ cm $= 0.01 \times 10^{-2}$m $= 1 \times 10^{-4}$m, resistivity $\rho = 50 \times 10^{-8} \Omega$ m, length of the wire $l = ?$
using formula, $R = \rho \dfrac{l}{A} = \rho \dfrac{l}{\pi r^2}$

$10 = \dfrac{50 \times 10^{-8} \times l}{3.14 \times (1 \times 10^{-4})^2} \Rightarrow l = \dfrac{3.14 \times 10 \times 10^{-8}}{50 \times 10^{-8}}$

$= \dfrac{3.14}{5} = 0.628$ m **[1 Mark]**
$\therefore l = 62.8$ cm

OR

(a) Consider a current I flowing through a resistor or device of resistance R. Let the potential difference across it be V. Let t be the time during which a charge Q flows across. Therefore, the appliance supply energy = VQ in time t.
Hence electric power of an electric device = energy per unit time,

$P = V\dfrac{Q}{t} = VI = I^2R \; [\because V = IR]$

or, $P = V^2/R$ **[1 Mark]**
The SI unit of electric power is watt (w)
1 watt = 1 volt × 1 ampere = 1VA **[½ Mark]**
(b) (i) The commercial unit of electric energy is kilowatt hour (kwh) commonly known as unit.
1 kwh = 1000 watt × 3600 second = 3.6×10^6 watt second
= 3.6×10^6 J
As per question, electric kettle of 2 kw = 2000 watt and used for 2h = 2 × 3600 second
$\therefore$ Energy consumed in kilowatt hour
= 2000 × 2 × 3600
= $4 \times 3.6 \times 10^6$ J
= 4 kilowatt hour. **[1 Mark]**
(ii) Energy consumed in joules = $4 \times 3.6 \times 10^6$ J
= 144×10^5 Joules **[½ Mark]**

10. (i) In the given circuit diagram, resistances of 10 Ω and 50 Ω are in series and resistance of 30 Ω connected in parallel with them.
Therefore total resistance of the circuit (R)

$\dfrac{1}{R} = \dfrac{1}{10+50} + \dfrac{1}{30} = \dfrac{1+2}{60} = \dfrac{3}{60}$

$\therefore R = \dfrac{60}{3}\Omega = 20 \; \Omega$ **[1½ Marks]**

(ii) Current flowing through the ammeter,

$I = \dfrac{V}{R} = \dfrac{6}{20} = 0.3A$ **[1½ Marks]**

11. (i) Green stem   Purple Stem   **[1 Mark]**
   Parent – GG   gg
   ↓   ↓
   gamete – G   g

   f_1 Gen –   Gg   (green stem)

   (i) f_1 progeny must be like their dominant parent with green stemmed tomato plant.

(ii) f_2 Gen

Phenotype ratio → $\underbrace{GG : Gg : Gg}_{\text{green stem}} : \underbrace{gg}_{\text{purple stem}}$

Hence, the Ratio for green stem and purple stem is 3:1 respectivily.

(iii) The above observation show law of dominances. **[1 Mark]**

> **Note**
> Law of dominance state that when parents with pure, contrasting traits are crossed together, only one form of trait appear in next generation.

12. (a) Aldehyde functional group (–CHO) is present in both the compounds (i) and (ii). **[1 Mark]**
    (b) General Formula : $C_n H_{2n+1} CHO$ **[1 Mark]**
    (c) These two compounds are homologous compound of (–CHO) functional group series. They differ by –sdCH$_2$ unit from each other. Another compound of the same functional group can be written as follows.
    $CH_3 CH_2 CH_2 CHO$

    Structural formula:  **[1 Mark]**

    OR

    (a) Ethyne HC ≡ CH
    Electron dot structure:

     **[1 Mark]**

    (b)

Covalent Compounds	Ionic Compounds
(i) Covalent compounds generally have low melting and boiling point.	(i) Ionic compounds have high melting and boiling point because of the presence of strong electrostatic attraction between the ions.
(ii) Covalent compounds are generally soluble in organic solvent and insoluble in water.	(ii) Ionic compounds are soluble in water and generally insoluble in organic solvent.

[2 Marks]

13. (a) Newland arranged the then known elements in the order of increasing atomic masses. He found that every eighth element had properties similar to that of the first element. He called it the 'law of octaves'. **[1 Mark]**
    (b) Döbereiner arranged the elements with similar properties into groups having three elements in each group known as triad. Döbereiner showed that when the three elements in a triad are arranged in the order of increasing atomic masses, the atomic mass of the middle element was roughly the average of the atomic masses of the other two elements.
    Li   6.9
    Na   23.0
    K   39.0

    Atomic mass of Na = $\dfrac{6.9 + 39.0}{2} = 22.95 \approx 23.0$

    which is approximately equal to the atomic mass of Na. **[1 Mark]**
    (c) **Limitation of Law of octaves:** Law of octaves applicaple only up to calcium, after calcium every eighth element did not possess properties similar to that of the first. **[½ Mark]**
    limitation of Döbereiner Triad: Döbereiner could identify only three triads from the elements khown at that time. Hence this system was not very usefull. **[½ Mark]**

> **Note**
> Drawback of Newland's law of octaves is that he placed some unlike elements under the same note. For example, he placed Co and Ni, with F, Cl, Br which have very different properties than these elements. Therefore, this law worked well with lighter elements only.

14. (a) The rod get displaced on passing current through it because a force is exerted on the rod when it is placed in a magnetic field. **[1 Mark]**
    (b) Fleming's left hand rule determines the direction of the force on the conductor AB.
    According to this rule, stretch the thumb, forefinger and middle finger of your left hand such that they are mutually perpendicular. If the first finger points in the direction of magnetic field and the second finger in the direction of current, then the thumb will point in the direction of motion or the force acting on the conductor. **[1 Mark]**
    (c) (i) If the polarity of the magnet and the direction of current both are reversed, the rod gets displaced towards the right. **[1 Mark]**
    (ii) Two devices that use current carrying conductors and magnetic field are electric motor and electric generator. **[1 Mark]**

OR

Pattern of magnetic field lines produced around a current carrying straight conductor held vertically.
Also indicated the direction of field lines as well as the direction of current flowing through the conductor.

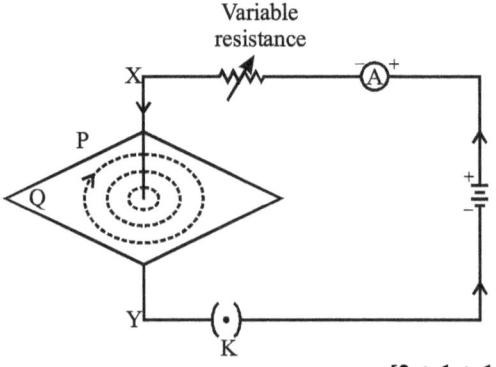

[2 + 1 + 1 Marks]

15. (a) If only one pair of contrasting characters is taken. f_1 generation either shows tall or short characterstic, as it follows law of dominance where only dominant character expres itself. **[1 Mark]**
(b) Short plant have recessive trait. **[1 Mark]**

(c)
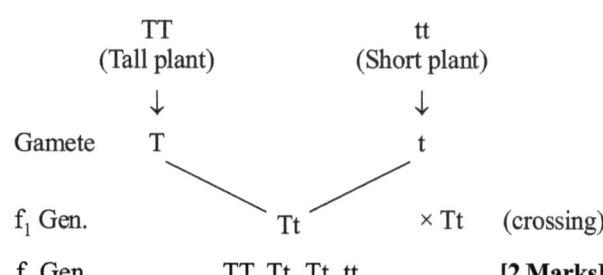

f_1 Gen.   Tt   × Tt   (crossing)

f_2 Gen.   TT, Tt, Tt, tt   **[2 Marks]**
Phenotype Ratio → 3 : 1

OR

f_2 proreny for dihybrid cross are

(i) Tall with round seeds – 9 = $\frac{9}{16}$ of 1600 = 900

[1 Mark]

(ii) Short with wrinkled seed – 1 = $\frac{1}{16}$ of 1600 = 100

[1 Mark]

- As it follow dihybrid cross, hence, f_2 generation is having phenotype ratio 9 : 3 : 3 : 1.
- It shows law of independent assortments. **[2 Marks]**

 *Note*

A monohybrid cross results in a phenotypic ratio of 3:1.
A dihybrid cross result in a phenotypic ratio of 9:3:3:1.

All India 2022
CBSE Board Solved Paper
Term-I

Time Allowed : 90 Min. *Maximum Marks : 40*

General Instructions:
Read the following instructions very carefully and strictly follow them :
(i) This question paper contains **60** questions out of which **50** questions are to be attempted. All questions carry equal marks.
(ii) The question paper consists three Sections – Section A, B and C.
(iii) Section – **A** consists of **24** questions. Attempt any **20** questions from Q. No. **1** to **24**.
(iv) Section – **B** also consists of **24** questions. Attempt any **20** questions from Q. No. **25** to **48**.
(v) Section – **C** consists of three Case Studies containing **12** questions and **4** questions in each case. Attempt any **10** from Q. No. **49** to **60**.
(vi) There is only one correct option for every Multiple Choice Question (*MCQ*). Marks will not be awarded for answering more than one option.
(vii) There is no negative marking.

SECTION - A

Section-A consists of **24** questions (Q. No. **1** to **24**). Attempt any **20** questions from this section. The first attempted 20 questions would be evaluated.

1. A student took Sodium Sulphate solution in a test tube and added Barium Chloride solution to it. He observed that an insoluble substance has formed. The colour and molecular formula of the insoluble substance is:
   (a) Grey, Ba_2SO_4
   (b) Yellow, $Ba(SO_4)_2$
   (c) White, $BaSO_4$
   (d) Pink, $BaSO_4$

2. Which of the following oxide(s) is/are soluble in water to form alkalies?
   (i) Na_2O (ii) SO_2 (iii) K_2O (iv) NO_2
   (a) (i) and (iii)
   (b) (i) only
   (c) (ii) and (iv)
   (d) (iii) only

3. Study the diagram given below and identify the gas formed in the reaction.

   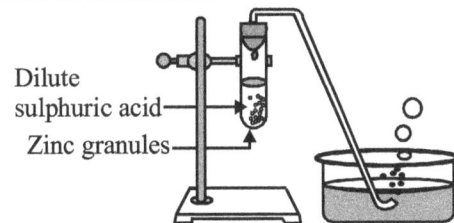

   (a) Carbon di-oxide which extinguishes the burning candle.
   (b) Oxygen due to which the candle burns more brightly.
   (c) Sulphur dioxide which produces a suffocating smell.
   (d) Hydrogen which while burning produces a popping sound.

4. Sodium reacts with water to form sodium hydroxide and hydrogen gas. The balanced equation which represents the above reaction is:
   (a) $Na(s) + 2H_2O(l) \rightarrow 2NaOH(aq) + 2H_2(g)$
   (b) $2Na(s) + 2H_2O(l) \rightarrow 2NaOH(aq) + H_2(g)$
   (c) $2Na(s) + 2H_2O(l) \rightarrow NaOH(aq) + 2H_2(g)$
   (d) $2Na(s) + H_2O(l) \rightarrow 2NaOH(aq) + 2H_2(g)$

5. Which of the options in the given table are correct?

Option	Natural Source	Acid Present
(i)	Orange	Oxalic acid
(ii)	Sour milk	Lactic acid
(iii)	Ant sting	Methanoic acid
(iv)	Tamarind	Acetic acid

   (a) (i) and (ii)
   (b) (i) and (iv)
   (c) (ii) and (iii)
   (d) (iii) and (iv)

6. $C_6H_{12}O_6(aq) + 6O_2(aq) \rightarrow 6CO_2(aq) + 6H_2O(l)$
   The above reaction is a/an
   (a) displacement reaction
   (b) endothermic reaction
   (c) exothermic reaction
   (d) neutralisation reaction

7. Which of the following statements about the reaction given below are correct?
   $MnO_2 + 4HCl \rightarrow MnCl_2 + 2H_2O + Cl_2$
   (i) HCl is oxidized to Cl_2
   (ii) MnO_2 is reduced to $MnCl_2$
   (iii) $MnCl_2$ acts as an oxidizing agent
   (iv) HCl acts as on oxidizing agent
   (a) (ii), (iii) and (iv)
   (b) (i), (ii) and (iii)
   (c) (i) and (ii) only
   (d) (iii) and (iv) only

8. Select from the following the statement which is true for bases.
   (a) Bases are bitter and turn blue litmus red.
   (b) Bases have a pH less than 7.
   (c) Bases are sour and change red litmus to blue.
   (d) Bases turn pink when a drop of phenolphthalein is added to them.

9. Study the following table and choose the correct option:

	Salt	Parent Acid	Parent Base	Nature of Salt
(a)	Sodium Chloride	HCl	NaOH	Basic
(b)	Sodium Carbonate	H_2CO_3	NaOH	Neutral
(c)	Sodium Sulphate	H_2SO_4	NaOH	Acidic
(d)	Sodium Acetate	CH_3COOH	NaOH	Basic

10. It is important to balance the chemical equations to satisfy the law of conservation of mass. Which of the following statements of the law is <u>incorrect</u>?
    (a) The total mass of the elements present in the reactants is equal to the total mass of the elements presents in the products.
    (b) The number of atoms of each element remains the same, before and after a chemical reaction.
    (c) The chemical composition of the reactants is the same before and after the reaction.
    (d) Mass can neither be created nor can it be destroyed in a chemical reaction.

11. Consider the following statements in connection with the functions of the blood vessels marked A and B in the diagram of a human heart as shown.

    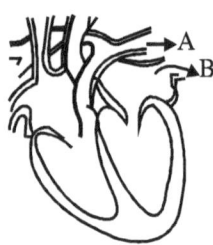

    (i) Blood vessel A – It carries carbon dioxide rich blood to the lungs.
    (ii) Blood vessel B – It carries oxygen rich blood from the lungs.
    (iii) Blood vessel B – Left atrium relaxes as it receives blood from this blood vessel.
    (iv) Blood vessel A – Right atrium has thick muscular wall as it has to pump blood to this blood vessel.
    This correct statements are
    (a) (i) and (ii) only   (b) (ii) and (iii) only
    (c) (ii), (iii) and (iv)   (d) (i), (ii) and (iii)

12. In living organisms during respiration which of the following products are <u>not</u> formed if oxygen is not available?
    (a) Carbon dioxide + Water
    (b) Carbon dioxide + Alcohol
    (c) Lactic acid + Alcohol
    (d) Carbon dioxide + Lactic Acid

13. The correct statements with reference to single celled organisms are
    (i) Complex substances are not broken down into simpler substances.
    (ii) Simple diffusion is sufficient to meet the requirement of exchange of gases.
    (iii) Specialised tissues perform different functions in the organism.
    (iv) Entire surface of the organism is in contact with the environment for taking in food.
    (a) (i) and (iii)   (b) (ii) and (iii)
    (c) (ii) and (iv)   (d) (i) and (iv)

14. Which one among the following is not removed as a waste product from the body of a plant?
    (a) Resins and Gums   (b) Urea
    (c) Dry Leaves   (d) Excess Water

15. Which of the following statements are correct in reference to the role of A (shown in the given diagram) during a breathing cycle in human beings?

    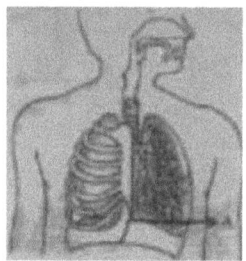

    (i) It helps to decrease the residual volume of air in lungs.
    (ii) It flattens as we inhale.
    (iii) It gets raised as we inhale.
    (iv) It helps the chest cavity to become larger.
    (a) (ii) and (iv)   (b) (iii) and (iv)
    (c) (i) and (ii)   (d) (i), (ii) and (iv)

16. Which one of the following conditions is true for the state of stomata of a green leaf shown in the given diagram?

    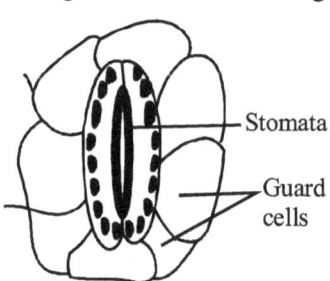

    (a) Large amount of water flows into the guard cells.
    (b) Gaseous exchange is occurring in large amount.
    (c) Large amount of water flows out from the guard cells.
    (d) Large amount of sugar collects in the guard cells.

17. In which of the following is a concave mirror used?
    (a) A solar cooker
    (b) A rear view mirror in vehicles
    (c) A safety mirror in shopping malls
    (d) In viewing full size image of distant tall buildings.

18. A student wants to obtain magnified image of an object AB as on a screen. Which one of the following arrangements shows the correct position of AB for him/her to be successful?

(a)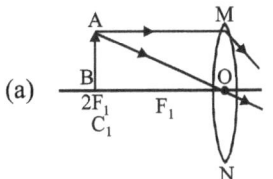
(b)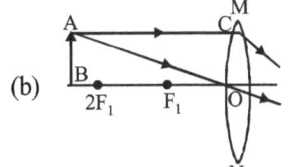
(c)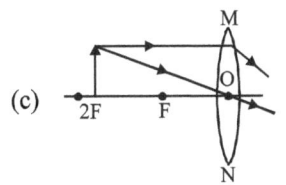
(d)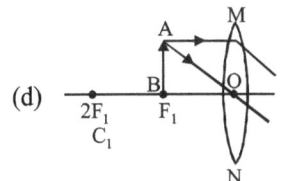

19. The following diagram shows the use of an optical device to perform an experiment of light. As per the arrangement shown, the optical device is likely to be a:
    (a) Concave mirror
    (b) Concave lens
    (c) Convex mirror
    (d) Convex lens

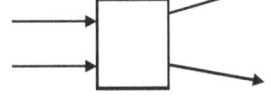

20. A ray of light starting from air passes through medium A of refractive index 1.50, enters medium B of refractive index 1.33 and finally enters medium C of refractive index 2.42. If this ray emerges out in air from C, then for which of the following pairs of media the bending of light is least?
    (a) air-A   (b) A-B   (c) B-C   (d) C-air

21. Which of the following statements is **not true** for scattering of light?
    (a) Colour of the scattered light depends on the size of particles of the atmosphere.
    (b) Red light is least scattered in the atmosphere.
    (c) Scattering of light takes place as various colours of white light travel with different speed in air.
    (d) The fine particles in the atmospheric air scatter the blue light more strongly than red. So the scattered blue light enters our eyes.

22.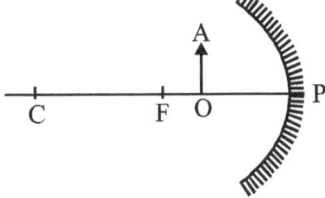

For the diagram shown, according to the new Cartesian sign convention the magnification of the image formed will have the following specifications:
(a) Sign - Positive, Value - Less than 1
(b) Sign - Positive, Value - More than 1
(c) Sign - Negative, Value - Less than 1
(d) Sign - Negative, Value - More than 1

23.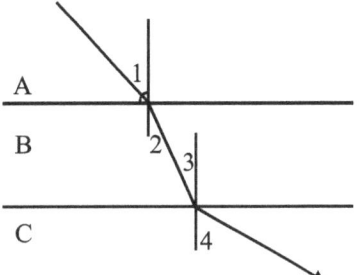

A ray of light is incident as shown. It A, B and C are three different transparent media, then which among the following options is true for the given diagram?
(a) $\angle 1 > \angle 4$
(b) $\angle 1 < \angle 2$
(c) $\angle 3 = \angle 2$
(d) $\angle 3 > \angle 4$

24. In the diagram given below, X and Y are the end colours of the spectrum of white light. The colour of 'Y' represents the

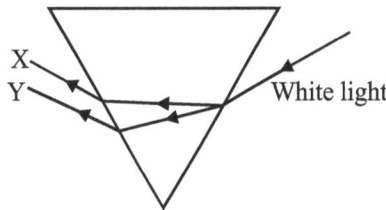

(a) Colour of sky as seen from earth during the day.
(b) Colour of the sky as seen from the moon.
(c) Colour used to paint the danger signals.
(d) Colour of sun at the time of noon.

SECTION - B

Section-B consists of **24** questions (Q. No. 25 to 48). Attempt any **20** questions from the section. The first attempted **20** questions would be evaluated.

25. Which one of the following reactions is categorised as thermal decomposition reaction?
    (a) $2H_2O(l) \rightarrow 2H_2(g) + O_2(g)$
    (b) $2AgBr(s) \rightarrow 2Ag(s) + Br_2(g)$
    (c) $2AgCl(s) \rightarrow 2Ag(s) + Cl_2(g)$
    (d) $CaCO_3(s) \rightarrow CaO(s) + CO_2(g)$

26. Consider the pH value of the following acidic samples:

S. No.	Sample	pH Value
1.	Lemon Juice	2.2
2.	Gastric Juice	1.2
3.	Vinegar	3.76
4.	Dil. Acetic acid	3.0

The decreasing order of their H^+ ion concentration is
(a) $3 > 4 > 1 > 2$
(b) $2 > 1 > 3 > 4$
(c) $2 > 1 > 4 > 3$
(d) $3 > 4 > 2 > 1$

27. Study the experimental set up shown in given figure and choose the correct option from the following:

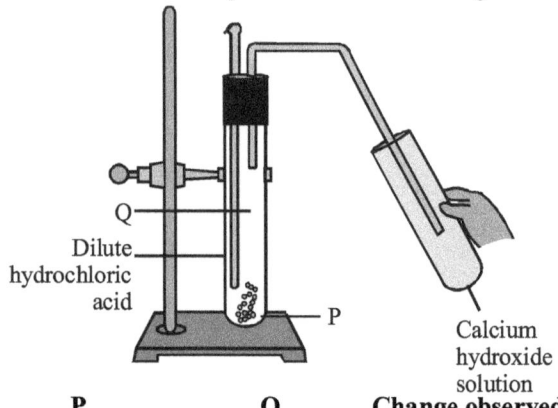

	P	Q	Change observed in calcium hydroxide solution
(a)	K$_2$CO$_3$	Cl_2 gas	No change
(b)	KHCO$_3$	CO$_2$ gas	No change
(c)	KHCO$_3$	H$_2$ gas	Turns milky
(d)	K$_2$CO$_3$	CO$_2$ gas	Turns milky

28. Which one of the following structures correctly depicts the compound CaCl_2?

   (a) $Ca^{2+}[\ddot{C}\!l\!:]^{2-}$ (b) $[:\ddot{C}a:]^{2+}[:\ddot{C}\!l\!:]_2$
   (c) $Ca^{2+}[\ddot{C}\!l\!:]_2$ (d) $[:\ddot{C}a:]^+[:\ddot{C}\!l\!:]_2^-$

29. The pair(s) which will show displacement reaction is/are
   (i) NaCl solution and copper metal
   (ii) AgNO$_3$ solution and copper metal
   (iii) Al_2(SO$_4$)$_3$ solution and magnesium metal
   (iv) ZnSO$_4$ solution and iron metal
   (a) (ii) only (b) (ii) and (iii)
   (c) (iii) and (iv) (d) (i) and (ii)

30. Which of the following salts do not have the water of crystalisation?
   (i) Bleaching Powder (ii) Plaster of Paris
   (iii) Washing soda (iv) Baking soda
   (a) (ii) and (iv) (b) (i) and (iii)
   (c) (ii) and (iii) (d) (i) and (iv)

Question No. **31-35** consists of two statements - **Assertion (A)** and **Reason (R)**. Answer these questions selecting the appropriate option given below:
   (a) Both (A) and (R) are true and (R) is the correct explanation of (A).
   (b) Both (A) and (R) are true but (R) is not the correct explanation of (A).
   (c) (A) is true, but (R) is false.
   (d) (A) is false, but (R) is true.

31. **Assertion (A)** : Sodium hydrogen carbonate is used as an ingredient in antacids.
    Reason (R) : NaHCO$_3$ is a mild non-corresive basic salt.

32. **Assertion (A)** : Burning of Natural gas is an endothermic process.
    Reason (R) : Methane gas combines with oxygen to produce carbon dioxide and water.

33. **Assertion (A)** : Nitrogen is an essential element for plant growth and is taken up by plants in the form of inorganic nitrates or nitrites.
    Reason (R) : The soil is the nearest and richest source of raw materials like Nitrogen, Phosphorus and other minerals for the plants.

34. **Assertion (A)** : Sun appears reddish at the time of Sunrise and Sunset.
    Reason (R) : Distance travelled by sunlight in the atmosphere is lesser during sunrise and sunset as compared to noon.

35. **Assertion (A)** : Hydrochloric acid helps in the digestion of food in the stomach.
    Reason (R) : Hydrochloric acid creates an acidic medium to activate protein digesting enzymes.

36. A student was asked to write a stepwise procedure to demonstrate that carbon dioxide is necessary for photosynthesis. He wrote the following steps. The wrongly worded step is –

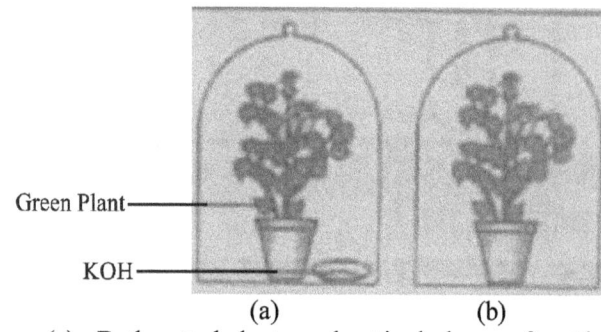

   (a) Both potted plants are kept in dark room for at least three days.
   (b) Bottom of the bell jars is sealed to make them air tight.
   (c) Both potted plants are kept in sunlight after the starch test.
   (d) A leaf from both the plants is taken to test the presence of starch.

37. Respiratory structures of two different animals a fish and a human being are as shown.
    Observe (a) and (b) and select one characteristic that holds true for both of them.

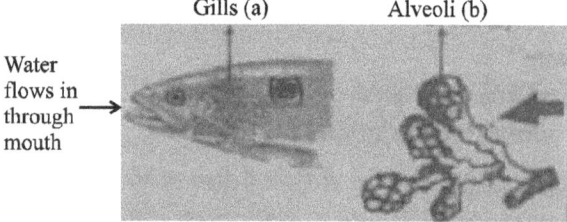

   (a) Both are placed internally in the body of animal.
   (b) Both have thin and moist surface for gaseous exchange.
   (c) Both are poorly supplied with blood vessels to conserve energy.
   (d) In both the blood returns to the heart after being oxygenated.

38. Observe the diagram of an activity given below. What does it help to conclude, when the person exhales into the test-tube?

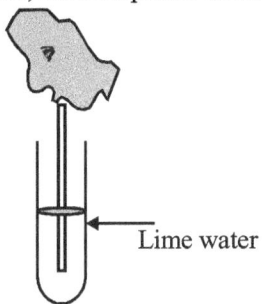

(a) Percentage of carbon dioxide is more in inhaled air.
(b) Fermentation occurs in the presence of oxygen.
(c) Percentage of carbon dioxide is more in the exhaled air.
(d) Fermentation occurs in the presence of carbon dioxide.

39. If a lens can converge the sun rays at a point 20 cm, away from its optical centre, the power of this lens is –
(a) + 2D   (b) – 2D   (c) + 5D   (d) – 5D

40. The radius of curvature of a converging mirror is 30 cm. At what distance from the mirror should an object be placed so as to obtain a virtual image?
(a) Infinity
(b) 30 cm
(c) Between 15 cm and 30 cm
(d) Between 0 cm and 15 cm

41. The length of small intestine in a deer is more as compared to the length of small intestine of a tiger. The reason for this is –
(a) Mode of intake of food.
(b) Type of food consumed.
(c) Presence or absence of villi in intestines.
(d) Presence of absence of digestive enzymes.

42. Identify the two components of Phloem tissue that help in transportation of food in plants
(a) Phloem parenchyma & sieve tubes
(b) Sieve tubes & companion cells
(c) Phloem parenchyma & companion cells
(d) Phloem fibres and sieve tubes

43. A converging lens forms a three times magnified image of an object, which can be take on a screen. If the focal length of the lens is 30 cm, then the distance of the object from the lens is
(a) – 55 cm   (b) – 50 cm
(c) – 45 cm   (d) – 40 cm

44.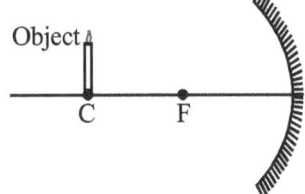

Which of the following statements is not true in reference to the diagram shown above?
(a) Image formed is real.
(b) Image formed is enlarged.
(c) Image is formed at a distance equal to double the focal length.
(d) Image formed is inverted.

45.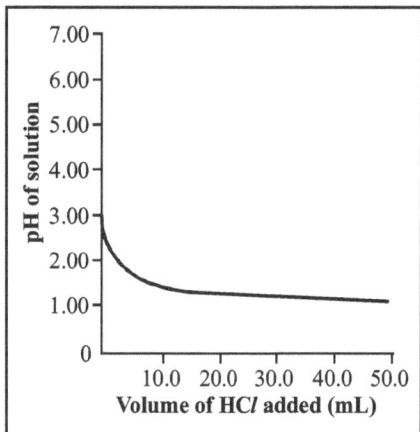

In the diagram shown above n_1, n_2 and n_3 are refractive indices of the media 1, 2 and 3 respectively. Which one of the following is true in this case?
(a) $n_1 = n_2$ (b) $n_1 > n_2$
(c) $n_2 > n_3$ (d) $n_3 > n_1$

46. The refractive index of medium A is 1.5 and that of medium B is 1.33. If the speed of light in air is 3×10^8 m/s, what is the speed of light in medium A and B respectively?
(a) 2×10^8 m/s and 1.33×10^8 m/s
(b) 1.33×10^8 m/s and 2×10^8 m/s
(c) 2.25×10^8 m/s and 2×10^8 m/s
(d) 2×10^8 m/s and 2.25×10^8 m/s

47. An object of height 4 cm is kept at a distance of 30 cm from the pole of a diverging mirror. If the focal length of the mirror is 10 cm, the height of the image formed is
(a) + 3.0 cm   (b) + 2.5 cm
(c) + 1.0 cm   (d) + 0.75 cm

48. 50.0 mL of tap water was taken in a beaker. Hydrochloric acid was added drop by drop to water. The temperature and pH of the solution was noted. The following graph was obtained. Choose the correct statements related to this activity.

(i) The process of dissolving an acid in water is highly endothermic
(ii) The pH of the solution increases rapidly on addition of acid.
(iii) The pH of the solution decreases rapidly on addition of acid.
(iv) The pH of tap water was around 7.0.
(a) (i) and (ii)   (b) (i) and (iii)
(c) (iii) and (iv)   (d) (ii) and (iv)

SECTION - C

Section-C consists of **three** cases followed by questions. There are a total of **12** questions (Q. No. **49** to **60**) in this Section. Attempt any **10** questions from this section. The first attempted 10 questions would be evaluated.

Case-I :

A student, took four metals P, Q, R and S and carried out different experiments to study the properties of metals. Some of the observations were:
- All metals could not be cut with knife except metal R.
- Metal P combined with oxygen to form an oxide M_2O_3 which reacted with both acids and bases.
- Reaction with water.

  P – with Did not react either with cold or hot water but reacted steam

  Q – Reacted with hot water and the metal started floating

  R – Reacted violently with cold water

  S – Did not react with water at all

Based on the above observations answer the following:

49. Out of the given metals, the one which needs to be stored used Kerosene is
    (a) P   (b) R
    (c) S   (d) Q

50. Out of the given metals, the metal Q is
    (a) Iron   (b) Zinc
    (c) Potassium (d) Magnesium

51. Metal which forms amphoteric oxides is
    (a) P   (b) Q
    (c) R   (d) S

52. The increasing order of the reactivity of the four metals is:
    (a) P < Q < R < S   (b) S < R < Q < P
    (c) S < P < Q < R   (d) P < R < Q < S

Case-II:

The figure shown below represents a common type of dialysis called as Haemodialysis. It removes waste products from the blood. Such as excess salts, and urea which are insufficiently removed by the kidney in patients with kidney failure. During the procedure, the patient's blood is cleaned by filtration through a series of semi-permeable membranes before being returned to the blood of the patient. On the basis of this, answer the following questions.

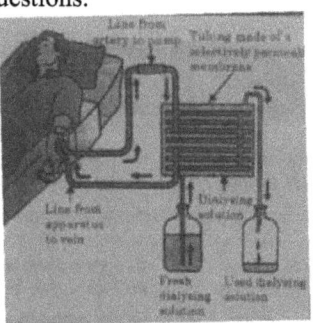

53. The hemodialyzer has semi-permeable lining of tubes which help to :
    (a) To maintain osmotic pressure of blood.
    (b) To filter nitrogenous wastes from the dialyzing solution.
    (c) In passing the waste products in the dialyzing solution.
    (d) To pump purified blood back into the body of the patient.

54. Which one of the following is not a function of Artificial Kidney?
    (a) To remove nitrogenous wastes from the blood.
    (b) To remove excess fluids from the blood.
    (c) To reabsorb essential nutrients from the blood.
    (d) To filter and purify the blood.

55. The 'used dialysing' solution is rich in:
    (a) Urea and excess salts
    (b) Blood cells
    (c) Lymph
    (d) Proteins

56. Which part of the nephron in human kidney, serves the function of reabsorption of certain substances?
    (a) Glomerulus   (b) Bowmans Capsule
    (c) Tubules   (d) Collecting duct

Case-III:

A compound microscope is an instrument which consists of two lenses L_1 called objective, forms a real, inverted and magnified image of the given object. This serves as the object for the second lens L_2; the eye place. The produces the final image, which is inverted with respect to the original object, enlarged and virtual.

57. What types of lenses must be L_1 and L_2?
    (a) Both concave
    (b) Both convex
    (c) L_1 - concave and L_2 - convex
    (d) L_1 - convex and L_2 - concave

58. What is the value and sign of magnification (according to the new Cartesian sign convention) of the image formed by L_1?
    (a) Value = Less than 1 and Sign = Positive
    (b) Value = More than 1 and Sign = Positive
    (c) Value = Less than 1 and Sign = Negative
    (d) Value = More than 1 and Sign = Negative

59. What is the value and sign of (according to new Cartesian sign convention) magnification of the image formed by L_2?
    (a) Value = Less than 1 and Sign = Positive
    (b) Value = More than 1 and Sign = Positive
    (c) Value = Less than 1 and Sign = Negative
    (d) Value = More than 1 and Sign = Negative

60. If power of the eyepiece (L_2) is 5 diopters and it forms an image at a distance of 80 cm from its optical centre, at what distance should the object be?
    (a) 12 cm   (b) 16 cm   (c) 18 cm   (d) 20 cm

Solutions

1. **(c)** When sodium sulphate reacts with barium chloride solution, then insoluble white precipitate of barium sulphate will be formed.

   $$BaCl_2(aq) + Na_2SO_4(aq) \longrightarrow \underset{\text{White PPt.}}{BaSO_4(aq)\downarrow} + 2NaCl(aq)$$

2. **(a)** When highly electropositive metal like Na and K reacts with oxygen, they will form basic oxides i.e. Na_2O and K_2O as basic oxides are soluble in water and form hydroxide while SO_2 and NO_2 are oxides of non-metal which are acidic in nature.

   Bases which are soluble in water are called alkalis. NaOH and KOH, are bases as they generate OH^- ions in water. They are also called as alkalis because they are soluble in water.

3. **(d)** When zinc granules is added in dilute sulphuric acid, then zinc displaces the hydrogen and form zinc sulphate and hydrogen gas as zinc is more reactive than hydrogen. So, an evolved hydrogen gas on burning produces a popping sound.

   $$Zn + H_2SO_4 \longrightarrow ZnSO_4 + H_2$$

   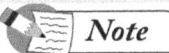
   Generally, metal + dil. acid $\longrightarrow$ salt + $H_2(g)\uparrow$ the reactivity order is Mg > Al > Zn > Fe. copper does not show reaction with dil.acid.

4. **(b)** When sodium reacts with water, it will form sodium hydroxide and hydrogen gas.
   $Na(s) + H_2O(l) \longrightarrow NaOH(aq) + H_2(g)$
   In reactant side; Na and H_2O is multiply by 2 and in product side; NaOH is multiply by 2 to balance the reaction.
   Therefore; the balanced equation is:
   $2Na(s) + 2H_2O(l) \longrightarrow 2NaOH(aq) + H_2(g)$

5. **(c)** (i) In orange, citric acid is present.
   (ii) In sour milk, lactic acid is present.
   (iii) In Ant sting, methanoic acid is present.
   (iv) In Tamarind, tartaric acid is present.

6. **(c)** $C_6H_{12}O_6(aq) + 6O_2(aq) \longrightarrow 6CO_2(aq) + 6H_2O(l)$
   The given reaction is a type of exothermic reaction as energy is released during the reaction.

7. $\overset{+4}{Mn}O_2 + 4H\overset{-1}{Cl} \longrightarrow \overset{+4}{Mn}Cl_2 + 2H_2O + \overset{0}{Cl_2}$

   HCl is oxidised to Cl_2, thus there is increase in oxidation state while MnO_2 is reduced to $MnCl_2$, thus there is decrease in oxidation state. Hence MnO_2 act as an oxidizing agent and HCl act as a reducing agent.

8. **(d)** Bases are bitter and turns red litmus to blue. The pH value for the bases are more than 7 and on addition of few drops of phenolpthalein turns bases into pink in color.

9. **(d)**
   (a) Sodium chloride is a neutral salt of strong acid (HCl) and strong base (NaOH).
   (b) Sodium carbonate is a basic salt of strong base (NaOH) and neak acid (H_2CO_3).
   (c) Sodium Sulphate is a neutral salt of strong base (NaOH) and strong acid (H_2SO_4).
   (d) Sodium Acetate is a basic salt of strong base (NaOH) and weak acid (CH_3COOH).

10. **(c)** The chemical coposition of the reactants changes but total mass of the reactants remains same before and after the chemical reaction.

11. **(d)** Oxygen-rich blood from the lungs comes to the thin-walled upper chamber of the heart on the left, the left atrium. The left atrium relaxes when it is collecting this blood. It then contracts, while the next chamber, the left ventricle, relaxes, so that the blood is transferred to it. When the muscular left ventricle contracts in its turn, the blood is pumped out to the body. De-oxygenated blood comes from the body to the upper chamber on the right, the right atrium, as it relaxes. As the right atrium contracts, the corresponding lower chamber.

12. **(a)** Ethanol (in yeast) and lactic acids (in our muscle cells) are produce in the absence of oxygen during respiration process. While in the presence of oxygen (in mitochondria) glucose will break down ATP (energy, carbon dioxide and water molecules.

13. **(c)** In the case of a single-celled organism, no specific organs for taking in food, exchange of gases or removal of wastes may be needed because the entire surface of the organism is in contact with the environment. Simple diffusion will meet the requirements of all the cells.

14. **(b)** Urea is an excretory product which is generally produced by the breakdown of proteins. In humans, urea is mainly produced in the liver.

15. **(a)** When we breathe in, we lift our ribs and flatten our diaphragm, and the chest cavity becomes larger as a result. Because of this, air is sucked into the lungs and fills the expanded alveoli.
    Inspiration can occur if the pressure within the lungs is less than atmospheric pressure inspiration is initiated by contraction of diaphgram which increases the volume of thoracic chamber.

16. **(b)** Tiny pores (called stomata) present on the surface of the leaves. Massive amounts of gaseous exchange takes place in the leaves through these pores for the purpose of photosynthesis.
17. **(a)** In solar cooker, concave mirror is used as it absorbs all the incident light and reflect it to a single focal point.
18. **(c)** To get magnified image of an object on a screen by a convex lens, object must be either at focus (F) or between F and 2F. When object at F image is at infinity. Hence (c) is the correct option.

 **Note**

Concave mirrors form real images that can be projected outo a screen if the object is farther away than the focal points. If the object is closer than the focal point, the image is fomred up right and large but virtual i.e. cannot be projected onto a screen.

19. **(b)** Concave lens or, diverging lens diverges the incident ray of light.
20. **(b)** Since $\mu_{21} = \dfrac{\sin i}{\sin r}$

    So the bending of light is least for pair of media (A) $\mu = 1.50$ to (B) $\mu = 1.33$

21. **(a)** According to Raleigh's law sccattering $\propto \dfrac{1}{\lambda^4}$ λ_{Red}

    $> \lambda_{Blue}$ so red light is least scattered in the atmosphere.
22. **(b)** As object is placed between pole (P) and focus (F) of a concave mirror so image formed is virtual, erect and magnified. Hence sign positive and value more than 1.
23. **(c)** Angle $\angle 3$ & $\angle 2$ are in same medium so $\angle 3 = \angle 2$ alternate angle.
24. **(c)** The colour of Y is red the colour used to paint the danger signal. When white ray of light passes through a prism it disperses into seven colours VIBGYOR. Red colour deviates or bends the least.
25. **(d)** $CaCO_3(s) \longrightarrow CaO(s) + CO_2(g)$; is a type of thermal decomposition reaction. When calcium carbonate is heated, it decomposes into calcium oxide and carbondioxide.

 **Note**

Reaction (b) and (c) are the examples of photo decom position reactions where decomposition takes place in the presence of light. Reaction in option (a) is the electrolytic process in which decomposition process takes place with electricity.

26. **(c)** The lower the pH value, the higher will be the concentration of hydrogen ions in the solution. The pH value of Gastric juice is less and pH value of vinegar is high. Therefore; the decreasing order of their H^+ ion concentration is $2 > 1 > 4 > 3$.

27. **(d)** The reaction is shown below:

    $K_2CO_3 + 2HCl \longrightarrow 2 KCl + H_2O + CO_2 \uparrow$

    $CO_2 + \underset{\text{Lime water}}{Ca(OH)_2} \longrightarrow \underset{\text{milky ppt.}}{CaCO_3}$

28. **(c)** The structure of $CaCl_2$ is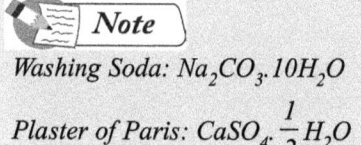

29. **(a)** The reaction in which one element is replaced by another in a compound is known as displacement reaction.

    $Cu(s) + 2\, AgNO_3(aq) \longrightarrow Cu(NO_3)_2\,(aq) + 2Ag\,(s)$

 **Note**

Metals which are more reactive displaces less reactive metal from their salt solution. The order of reactivity is
$Na > Mg > Al > Zn > Fe > Cu > Ag$

30. **(d)** The formula of bleaching powder is $CaOCl_2$ and the formula of baking soda is $NaHCO_3$. Therefore, they do not have the water of crystalisation.

Note

Washing Soda: $Na_2CO_3 . 10H_2O$

Plaster of Paris: $CaSO_4 . \dfrac{1}{2} H_2O$

31. **(a)** Due to non-corrosive nature of sodium hydrogen carbonate, it is used as an ingredient is antacids.
32. **(d)** Burning of natural gas is an exothermic process. When methane gas combines with oxygen, it will produce carbon dioxide and water.

    $CH_4 + 2O_2 \longrightarrow CO_2 + 2H_2O$

33. **(b)** Nitrogen is the most frequently limiting nutrient for crop growth of all the essential nutrients. Nitrogen is the nutrient that typically produces the highest yield response in crop plants, promoting rapid vegetative growth and providing the plant with a healthy green colour.

    Nitrogen is taken up by roots in the inorganic forms of nitrate NO_3^- and ammonium NH_4^+ ions. Once inside the plant, NO_3 is converted to NH_2 and assimilated to form organic compounds.

    Nitrogen addition is not recommended for legume crops such as soybean because they produce their own nitrogen supply. Nitrogen-fixing soil organisms (rhizobium) associated with legume roots capture atmospheric nitrogen and provide it to the plant.
34. **(c)** Light from the sun overhead travelled relatively shorter distance.
35. **(a)** The digestion in stomach is taken care of by the gastric glands present in the wall of the stomach. These release hydrochloric acid, a protein digesting enzyme called pepsin, and mucus. The hydrochloric acid creates an acidic medium which facilitates the action of the enzyme pepsin.

36. **(c)** The following step for this experiment are-
    (i) Take two healthy potted plants which are nearly the same size.
    (ii) Keep them in a dark room for three days.
    (iii) Now place each plant on separate glass plates. Place a watch-glass containing potassium hydroxide by the side of one of the plants. The potassium hydroxide is used to absorb carbon dioxide.
    (iv) Cover both plants with separate bell-jars.
    (v) Use Vaseline to seal the bottom of the jars to the glass plates so that the set-up is air-tight.
    (vi) Keep the plants in sunlight for about two hours.
    (vii) Pluck a leaf from each plant and check for the presence of starch as in the above activity.
    During photosynthesis, plants take in carbon dioxide and converts carbon dioxide, water into oxygen and glucose.

37. **(b)** Both gill and lungs in fish and human respectively, having moist and thin surface for gaseous exchange.

38. **(c)** When person exhale into the test tube , the lime water present into test tube turns milky which indicate the presence of CO_2.

    $Ca(OH)_2 + CO_2 \longrightarrow CaCO_3$
    lime water   calcium carbonate

39. **(c)** As the lens converges the sun rays so lens is convex, so (f) focal length is +(ve). And power of lens
    $$P = \frac{1}{f_{(in\ metre)}} = \frac{1}{\frac{20}{100}} = +5D$$

40. **(d)** Virtual image is formed by a converging or concave mirror only when object is placed between pole and focal point i.e., between 0 cm and 15cm $\left(\because f = \frac{r}{2}\ and\ r = 30\ cm\ given\right)$

41. **(b)** The small intestine of a deer (herbivore) is longer than that of a tiger (carnivore). This is due to the fact that cellulose (a component part of the plant cell wall) takes longer for deer to digest than flesh, which takes less time.

42. **(b)** Phloem is a permanent complex tissue of the plant that helps in the transportation of food. Sieve tubes and companion cells are the two components of phloem tissue that transport food bidirectional.
    Sieve tubes are the cells that conduct food in angiosperms. Companion cells are also present in angiosperms.

43. **(d)** Given : magnification, m = –3 ∴ if u = x then v = 3x cm and f = 30 cm.
    Using lens formula, $\frac{1}{f} = \frac{1}{v} - \frac{1}{u} \Rightarrow \frac{1}{30} = \frac{1}{-3x} - \frac{1}{x}$
    $= \frac{-1-3}{3x}$ or, $\frac{1}{30} = \frac{-4}{3x}$ ∴ $x = \frac{-120}{3} = -40$ cm
    Hence the distance of the object from the lens, u = x = –40 cm.

44. **(b)** As object is at the centre of curvature of the concave mirror so image formed is at the centre of curvature, real, inverted and of the same size as that of object.

    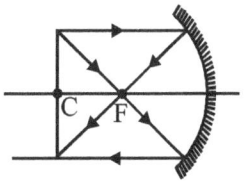

    📝 **Note**
    When object is placed beyond centre of curvature image formed is enlarged and diminished when object is placed between pole and centre of curvature.

45. **(d)** From the diagram,
    $\angle\theta_1 > \angle\theta_2 > \angle\theta_3$
    ∴ $n_1 < n_2 < n_3$ or, $n_3 > n_1$ or n_2

46. **(d)** Speed of light in medium
    $$V_{med} = \frac{Speed\ of\ light\ in\ air}{Speed\ of\ light\ in\ medium}$$
    ∴ $V_A = \frac{3 \times 10^8}{1.5} = 2 \times 10^8$ m/s
    and $V_B = \frac{3 \times 10^8}{1.33} = 2.25 \times 10^8$ m/s

47. **(c)** Here object is placed at a distance of 30 cm i.e., between centre of curvature and infinity so image formed is virtual, erect, diminished between the pole P and focus F behind the mirror.
    $u = -30$ cm, $h_0 = 4$ cm, $f = +10$ cm given
    using mirror formula, $\frac{1}{f} = \frac{1}{v} + \frac{1}{u}$ or $\frac{1}{+10} = \frac{1}{v} + \frac{1}{-30}$
    $\Rightarrow \frac{1}{v} = \frac{1}{30} + \frac{1}{10} = \frac{1+3}{30} = +\frac{4}{30}$ ∴ $v = 7.5$ cm

Now from formula, magnification $M = \dfrac{v}{u} = \dfrac{h_I}{h_0}$

∴ $\dfrac{7.5}{30} = \dfrac{h_I}{4}$ ∴ $h_I = 1$ cm

48. (c) The pH of solution decreases, on addition of acid and the pH value for tap water was around 7.0.

Case I (Qs. 49-52)

49. (b) The metal which reacted violently with cold water needs to be stored in kerosene.

50. (d) Magnesium reacts with hot water and the metal started floating.

51. (a) Metal P combined with oxygen to form an oxide M_2O_3 which reacted with both acids and bases. Hence, act as an amphoteric oxide.

52. (c) The increasing order of reactivity of metal is: S < P < Q < R.

Case II (Qs. 53-56)

53. (c) The haemodialyzer has a semi-permeable lining of tubes which help in passing the waste product into the dialyzing solution.
Dialysis is the process of salute transfer across a semi-permbeable memberane.

54. (c) An artificial kidney does not reabsorb essential nutrient from the blood.

55. (a) The used dialysing solution is rich in waste products from the blood like urea and excess salts.

56. (c) Tubules of the nephron in the human kidney serves the function of reabsorption of certain substances.

Case III (Qs. 57 - 60) : Ray diagram for the formation of image by a compound microscope is shown below :

57. (b) From the diagram, both the lenses L_1 (objective) and L_2 (eyepiece) are convex.

58. (d) From the diagram, the image formed by the objective lens L_1 is magnified and inverted (A' B') so magnification

$M = \dfrac{\text{height of the image}}{\text{height of the object}}$.

Hence M value = more than 1 and sign = negative.

 **Note**

In compound microscope, magnification does not change appreciably if objective and eye-piece are interchanged.

59. (b) The image formed by the eyepiece L_2 is magnified and inverted (A″ B″) of the object A′ B′, so magnification M value = more than 1 and sign = positive.

60. (b) Power of a lens, $P = \dfrac{1}{f(\text{in metre})}$ or $5 = \dfrac{1}{f}$

∴ $f = \dfrac{1}{5} \times 100$

or, $f = 20$ cm and $v = -80$ cm, $u = ?$

using lens formula, $\dfrac{1}{f} = \dfrac{1}{v} - \dfrac{1}{u}$ or, $\dfrac{1}{20} = \dfrac{1}{-80} - \dfrac{1}{u}$

∴ $\dfrac{1}{u} = -\dfrac{1}{20} - \dfrac{1}{80} = \dfrac{-4-1}{80} = -\dfrac{5}{80}$

∴ $u = 16$ cm from the optical centre of the lens L_2.

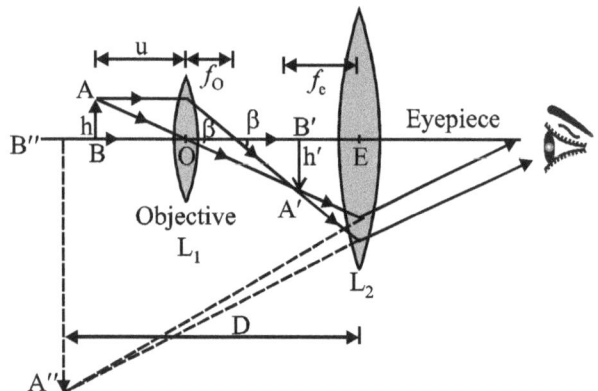

CBSE TOPPER-2020
Answer Sheet

केन्द्रीय माध्यमिक शिक्षा बोर्ड, दिल्ली
सैकण्डरी स्कूल परीक्षा (कक्षा दसवीं)
परीक्षार्थी प्रवेश-पत्र के अनुसार भरें

विषय Subject: SCIENCE

विषय कोड Subject Code: 086

परीक्षा का दिन एवं तिथि
Day & Date of the Examination: WEDNESDAY 4·3·2020

उत्तर देने का माध्यम
Medium of answering the paper: ENGLISH

प्रश्न पत्र के ऊपर लिखे कोड को लिखिये
Write code No. as written on the top of the question paper: **31/3/3**

Set Number: ③

अतिरिक्त उत्तर-पुस्तिका (ओं) की संख्या
No. of supplementary answer-book(s) used: **NIL (0)**

बैंचमार्क विकलांग व्यक्ति
Person with Benchmark Disabilities: Yes / **No**

विकलांगता का कोड
(प्रवेश पत्र के अनुसार)
Code of Disabilities
(as given on Admit Card): —

क्या लेखन - लिपिक उपलब्ध करवाया गया
Whether writer provided: Yes / **No**

यदि दृष्टिहीन है तो सॉफ्टवेयर के नाम एवं सॉफ्टवेयर का नाम
If visually challenged, name of software used: —

*(एक खाने में एक अक्षर लिखें। नाम के प्रत्येक भाग के बीच एक खाना रिक्त छोड़ दें। यदि परीक्षार्थी का नाम 24 अक्षरों से अधिक है, तो केवल नाम के प्रथम 24 अक्षर ही लिखें।)
Each letter be written in one box and one box be left blank between each part of the name. In case Candidate's Name exceeds 24 letters, write first 24 letters.

कार्यालय उपयोग के लिए
Space for office use

SECTION-A

1. a)

2. c)

3. Covalent bonds are formed by the sharing of electrons between two atoms. The electrons shared belong to the valence shell of the atoms.

4. The reason for the observed trend is because atomic size increases down a group since a new shell is added as we move down a group. This increases the distance between the nucleus and the outermost shell of the atom, even though nuclear charge increases.

5. c) 2A

6. a) 2 Ω

7. a) Scattering of light is not enough at such heights

8. d) (A), (B) and (C)

9. c) A has pH greater than 7 and B has pH less than 7

10. b) Formation of crystals by process of crystallization

11. c) lead storage battery manufacturing factories near A and soaps and detergents factories near B.

12. a) This is an ideal setting of the khadin system and A = catchment area; B = saline area & C = shallow dugwell

13. Hydropower can be harnessed by building dams. Hydropower can be harnessed from the potential energy of water at a height or kinetic energy of flowing water. Potential energy of water stored at a height in a reservoir of a dam can be used to rotate a turbine and generate electricity.

b) 1 MW is the power when 10^6 joules of work is done is one second. $1 MW = 10^6 W = \dfrac{10^6 J}{1 s}$

c) Two disadvantages are
- large scale displacement of town inhabitants
- environmental consequences of the weak ecosystem - loss of biodiversity and large scale deforestation.
- Large areas of land have to be sacrificed as they get submerged

d) When water falls from great heights, the blade of the turbine rotates. This mechanical energy is converted to electrical energy by a generator connected to the turbine.

b) 1 MW is the power when 10^6 joules of work is done is one second. $1 MW = 10^6 W = \dfrac{10^6 J}{1 s}$

c) Two disadvantages are
- large scale displacement of town inhabitants
- environmental consequences of the weak ecosystem - loss of biodiversity and large scale deforestation.
- Large areas of land have to be sacrificed as they get submerged.

d) When water falls from great heights, the blade of the turbine rotates. This mechanical energy is converted to electrical energy by a generator connected to the turbine.

14 a) She should eat more fruits and vegetables and reduce her intake of iodised salt.

b) Women face a greater risk of abnormal TSH level during menstruation, while giving birth and after going through menopause.

c) Low TSH level can cause goitre. (swelling of thyroid gland).

d) Iodine is responsible for synthesis of hormone secreted by thyroid gland.

SECTION-B

15 i) Exothermic reaction

$$CaO + H_2O \rightarrow Ca(OH)_2 + heat$$
quick lime   slaked lime

ii) Precipitation reaction (double displacement reaction)

$$Pb(NO_3)_{2(aq)} + KI_{(aq)} \rightarrow PbI_{2(s)} + KNO_{3(aq)}$$
                                    yellow precipitate

16 i) Group Category A (Li, Na, K) forms a Dobereiner's triad. ((34+7)/2 = 23)

ii) Mendeleev placed the elements in different groups as they had different chemical properties: the formula of their oxides and hydrides were different. However, the elements in the same category have same chemical property.

iii) Newland's law of octaves is not applicable to all three. It is applicable only upto calcium. Since Ga and As are found after Ca it is not applicable for group B and C. Every eight element does not show property similar to 1st one in this case.

17 i) $2NaOH_{(aq)} + Zn_{(s)} \longrightarrow Na_2ZnO_2 + H_{2(g)}$
   sodium zincate

ii) $CaCO_{3(s)} + H_2O_{(l)} + CO_{2(g)} \longrightarrow Ca(HCO_3)_{2(aq)}$

iii) $HCl_{(aq)} + H_2O_{(l)} \longrightarrow H_3O^+ + Cl^-$
   hydronium

18 a) Ozone is formed by the action of UV radiations on molecular oxygen. The high energy UV rays split an O_2 molecule into two free oxygen atoms. This free atom combine with molecular oxygen to give ozone. (O_3)

$$O_2 \xrightarrow{UV\ rays} O + O$$

$$O + O_2 \rightarrow O_3$$
$$\text{ozone}$$

Ozone protects all organisms from the harmful ultraviolet radiation from the sun. This radiations is highly damaging to organisms and can cause skin cancer. O_3 prevents UV rays from reaching Earth's surface.

— answer continued below.

~~In 1987, UNEP (United Nations Environment Programme) succeeded in forging an agreement to free CFC production at 1986 levels. These CFC's used to destroy the ozone layer. After this rule manufacturers had to make refrigerators without CFCs.~~

→ In 1980s, the production of chlorofluro carbons (CFCs) increased. CFCs are used in refrigerators and fire extinguishers as coolants.

These CFCs destroy the ozone layer. Since the ozone layer was getting destroyed by the CFCs, amount of ozone in the atmosphere dropped sharply.

19 a) i) Enzyme trypsin helps in the digestion of proteins into amino acids.
ii) Enzyme lipase helps in digestion of fats into fatty acids and glycerol. Both trypsin and lipase are secreted by pancreas and into the small intestine.

b) Function of villi -
- Villi increase the surface area for absorption of digested food.
- Villi are richly supplied with blood vessels which transport the absorbed food to each and every cell in the body, where it is used up for growth, repair and development of the body. It helps energy from food get supplied to cells

20 a) Parent   GG   ×   gg
    Gamete   (G)   (g)

F₁
            Gg × Gg
           green

F₂

	G	g
G	GG green	Gg green
g	Gg green	gg brown

genotypic ratio →
GG : Gg : gg
1 : 2 : 1

phenotypic ratio →
green : brown
3 : 1

i) Colour of stem in F₁ progeny is green.

ii) Percentage of brown stemmed plants = $\frac{1}{4} \times 100$ = 25%

iii) Ratio of GG and Gg = 1 : 2

b) Based on the findings, we can say that green stem colour is dominant trait while brown stem colour is a recessive trait. In F_1 generation no midway traits are seen and all F_1 progeny are green. In F_2 generation we get green stem and brown stem in ratio 3:1. The law of dominance is proved. Every progeny inherits two copies of factors controlling traits. They may be same or different based on parentage.

21 a) i) homologous pairs
  ii) analogous pairs
  iii) homologous pairs
  iv) analogous pairs

b) Organs are homologous if they have the same basic design, structure and components, though they may be modified to best peform different functions. They show common ancestry. Analogous organs may look similar as they peform the same function but their basic structural design is different.

P.T.O

Thus basic structural design is main feature to classify organs as homologous or analogous.

22a) Snell's law of refraction states that the ratio of sine of angle of incidence to sine of angle of refraction is a constant called refraction for a given pair of media and a given colour of light.

This constant is refractive index of second medium with respect to the first.

Refraction through a glass slab

AB - incident ray
CD - emergent ray
$\angle i = \angle e$
→ extended incident ray
→ lateral shift

23 a) i) bifocal of bifocal lenses are used

ii) A bifocal lens consists of a concave lens at the top to help in distant vision and a convex lens at the bottom to help in near vision. A bifocal lens consists of both a concave and convex lens.

b) $P = +3D$

$f = \dfrac{1}{P}$

$= \dfrac{1}{3} m = \dfrac{100}{3} cm = \boxed{33.33 \, cm}$

To correct near vision she needs a lens of focal length 33.33 cm (convex lens)

$P = -3D$

$P = \dfrac{1}{f} \Rightarrow f = \dfrac{1}{P}$

$= \dfrac{1}{-3} = \boxed{-33.33 \, cm}$

To correct distant vision, she needs a lens of focal length $-33.33 \, cm$ (concave lens).

24) i) Magnetic field lines are close together when field is strong. This is seen inside the magnet. However as the distance from the magnet increases, field strength decreases and the field lines begin to spread out. Thus at north pole, the field lines diverge and at south pole they again converge to form parallel lines within the magnet where they move from S to N.

ii) When current is passed through a solenoid, it gains a magnetic field. One end of the solenoid acts as the north pole while the other behaves like the south pole. Thus when freely suspended, it behaves like a freely suspended magnet and points in north-south direction.

iii) A fuse is a protective device which melts when current above a specified values passes through it and hence breaks the circuit protecting it from unduly high current. A fuse is selected based on the current required to flow through the appliance. If a fuse melts it should be replaced with one of same rating. Otherwise, if the rating is higher, more current than required will flow. If the rating is lower, it will melt even when less current flows. Thus since a specific value of current should flow through a circuit, a fuse of same rating should be used.

SECTION-C

25a)

Soaps	Detergents
→ Composition —	
Sodium or potassium salts of long chain carboxylic acids.	Sodium salts of sulphonic acids or ammonium salts with chloride or bromide ends.
→ Action in hard water	
• React with Ca^+ and Mg^+ ions in hard water to form white sticky precipitate called scum.	• The charged particles do not react with Ca^+ and Mg^+ ions in hard water, so no scum is formed.
• less lather formed	• same lather formed as in normal water
• not effective in hard water	• effective even in hard water

b) Ethanol reacts with sodium metal to form sodium ethoxide and hydrogen

$$2 CH_3-CH_2OH + Na \longrightarrow CH_3CH_2ONa + H_2$$
sodium ethoxide

Ethanol behave like an acid as it reacts with a metal to give a salt and hydrogen. Ethanol loses an atom of hydrogen and replaces it with Na. Even some bases show this behaviour.

c) Cyclohexane - C_6H_{12}

[structural diagram of cyclohexane with H atoms]

d) The compound is ethanal.

26 a) Calcium → ·Ca·

~~Oxygen~~

Oxygen → :Ö:

b) Ca ⟶ Ca^{2+} + 2e$^-$
(2,8,8,2)   (2,8,8)

O + 2e$^-$ ⟶ O^{2-}

·Ca· + :Ö: ⟶ Ca^{2+} + [:Ö:]$^{2-}$

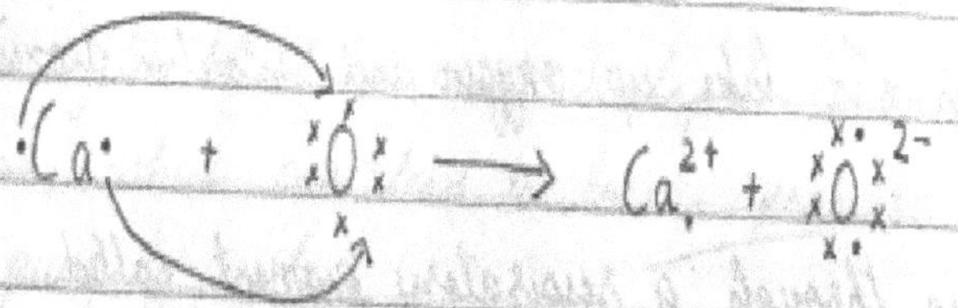

⟶ Ca^{2+}O^{2-}

⟶ CaO

c) The ions present are Ca^{2+} - calcium ion which is a cation
O^{2-} - oxide ion which is an anion

d) CaO is an ionic compound. Its properties are —
- High melting and boiling point.

P.T.O

- Hard solid, brittle - breaks when pressure is applied.
- Soluble in water
- Insoluble in organic solvents like petrol, kerosine
- Conducts electricity is molten and aqueous states.
- Does not conduct electricity in solid state.
- Imparts specific colour to the flame.

27a)
- Blood in the alveolar sac take up oxygen and carbon dioxide is released.
- Blood carries oxygen through a respiratory pigment called haemoglobin which has a high affinity for oxygen.
- Carbon dioxide is transported in dissolved form in our blood as it is more soluble.
- Oxygen rich blood is carried to the left atrium of the heart through the pulmonary vein. The left atrium relaxes as it receives the blood.
- This chamber then contracts while the left ventricle relaxes and the blood is transported to the left ventricle.

- The left ventricle contracts to pump the blood to the various parts of the body through the aorta.
- Valves in heart prevent blood backflow.
- The aorta divides into numerous arteries which carry the blood to different parts. At the tissue, the artery divides into smaller and smaller vessels. The smallest vessel is the capillary which has a one cell thick wall, through which blood transfer of O_2 and glucose take place.

b) If the system of blood vessels develop a leak, it may lead to loss of blood, which can lead to loss in pressure and reduce efficiency of the pumping system.

Thus, to prevent this blood has cells called platelets which circulate around the body. When a leak develops, the platelets help plug the leak by clotting blood at the point of injury.

28 a) ~~Hormonal~~ Chemical methods – oral pills are taken which alter the hormonal balance of the body and ensure egg is not released and fertilisation does not occur. However this has side effects due to change in hormonal balance.

b) Surgical methods – the vas deferens in males and the oviduct fallopian tube in females is blocked by surgical methods. This prevents transfer of sperms in males and ensures egg doesn't reach the uterus in females. In both cases fertilisation cannot occur.

b) Viral – HIV-AIDS and warts
Bacterial – gonorrhoea, and syphilis

c) Advantages of using condom –
- Condoms act as a physical barrier and prevent transfer of sperms. Thus it acts as a contraceptive method and prevents unwanted pregnancy.
- Condoms prevent transmission of STDs (sexually transmitted diseases)

21

~~28a) Be-20m object distance v = -20cm.~~

29 a) Nature of lens is convex. It is used to provide a magnified image of the palm. It is a converging lens. Convex lens is used as it can provide a magnified image in certain positions.

b) The palmist should hold the mirror between 2F and F to obtain a real, magnified image.

c) $f = 10 cm \quad u = -5 cm$

$$\frac{1}{f} = \frac{1}{v} - \frac{1}{u}$$

$$\frac{1}{v} = \frac{1}{f} + \frac{1}{u}$$

$$= \frac{1}{10} + \frac{1}{-5} = \frac{1}{10} - \frac{1}{5} = \frac{1-2}{10} = \frac{-1}{10}$$

$\Rightarrow v = -10 cm$

$\Rightarrow$ Image is formed at the focus on the same side of object (behind object)

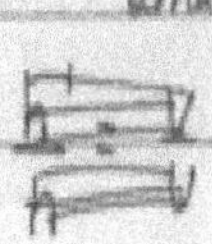

- The image size is enlarged. $M = \frac{v}{u} = \frac{-10}{-5} = 2$
- Image is twice the size of the ~~hand~~ palm (object) $h' = 2h$
- Image is virtual and erect.

30 a) $P = 100\ W$
$V = 200\ V$
$P = \dfrac{V^2}{R}$

$\Rightarrow R = \dfrac{V^2}{P} = \dfrac{200 \times 200\ V}{100\ W}$

Resistance of bulb $= 400\ \Omega$

b) Energy $= (P \times t) \times 3$
Time, $t = 10 \times 30$
$= 300$

$\Rightarrow$ Energy $= Pt \times 3$
$= 100 \times 300 \times 3$
$= 900 \times 100$
$= 90000\ Whr$
$= 90\ kWhr$

c) Total cost $=$ No. of units $\times$ rate
$= 90 \times 6.5 = ₹585$

Sample Paper 1

LATEST PATTERN

BLUE PRINT

S. No.	Chapter Name	Section-A (MCQs & A/R) 1 Mark Q. No.	Section-B (VSAQs) 2 Marks Q. No.	Section-C (SAQs) 3 Marks Q. No.	Section-D (LAQs) 5 Marks Q. No.	Section-E (Case Study) 4 Marks Q. No.	Total Marks
1	Chemical Reactions and Equations	3(Q2,3,17)	1(Q21)	1(Q27)			8
2	Acids, Bases and Salts	3(Q1,4,6)		1(Q28)			6
3	Metals and Non-metals	1(Q5)	1(Q21 OR)			1(Q37)	5
4	Carbon and its Compounds	1(Q7)			1(Q34)		6
5	Life Processes	1(Q8)		1(Q33)		1(Q38)	8
6	Control and Co-ordination	2(Q10,12)	1(Q26)		1(Q35)		7
7	How do Organism Reproduce	1(Q18)	1(Q24)	1(Q29)			6
8	Heredity and Evolution	2(Q11,19)					4
9	Light- Reflection and Refraction			2(Q30,31)		1(Q39)	10
10	Human Eye and Colourful World		1(Q25)				2
11	Electricity	2(Q14,16)					2
12	Magnetic Effects of Electric Current	3(Q13,15,20)		1(Q32)	1(Q36)		11
13	Our Environment	1(Q9)	2(Q22,23)				5
	Total Questions (Total Marks)	20(20)	6(12)	7(21)	3(15)	3(12)	80

* The number given outside the bracket denotes number of questions asked in the sample paper, while the number given inside the bracket denotes marks.

| Sc-2 | SCIENCE-X |

Time Allowed : 3 Hours **Max. Marks : 80**

General Instructions

1. This question paper consists of 39 questions in 5 sections.
2. All questions are compulsory. However, an internal choice is provided in some questions. A student is expected to attempt only one of these questions.
3. **Section A** consists of 20 objective type questions carrying 1 mark each.
4. **Section B** consists of 6 Very Short Answer type questions carrying 02 marks each. Answers to these questions should in the range of 30 to 50 words.
5. **Section C** consists of 7 Short Answer type questions carrying 03 marks each. Answers to these questions should in the range of 50 to 80 words
6. **Section D** consists of 3 Long Answer type questions carrying 05 marks each. Answer to these questions should be in the range of 80 to 120 words.
7. **Section E** consists of 3 source-based/case-based units of assessment of 04 marks each with sub-parts.

SECTION-A

Select and write one most appropriate option out of the four options given for each of the Questions 1 to 20

1. Sodium carbonate is a basic salt because it is a salt of
   (a) strong acid and strong base
   (b) weak acid and weak base
   (c) strong acid and weak base
   (d) weak acid and strong base

2. A balanced chemical equation is in accordance with –
   (a) Avogadro's law
   (b) law of multiple proportion
   (c) law of conservation of mass
   (d) law of gaseous volumes.

3. Chlorine gas reacts with _____ to form bleaching powder.
   (a) dry $Ca(OH)_2$
   (b) dil. solution of $Ca(OH)_2$
   (c) conc. solution of $Ca(OH)_2$
   (d) dry CaO

4. One of the constituents of baking powder is sodium hydrogen carbonate, the other constituent is
   (a) hydrochloric acid
   (b) tartaric acid
   (c) acetic acid
   (d) sulphuric acid

5. Al_2O_3 reacts with
   (a) only water
   (b) only acids
   (c) only alkalis
   (d) both acids and alkalis

6. Which of the following is not a mineral acid?
   (a) Hydrochloric acid
   (b) Citric acid
   (c) Sulphuric acid
   (d) Nitric acid

7. The correct name of the given compound is:

   (a) 2, 3-diethyl heptane
   (b) 5-ethyl-6-methyl octane
   (c) 4-ethyl-3-methyl octane
   (d) 3-methyl-4-ethyl octane

8. The given diagram is marked as A, B, C and D. Label A and C represents

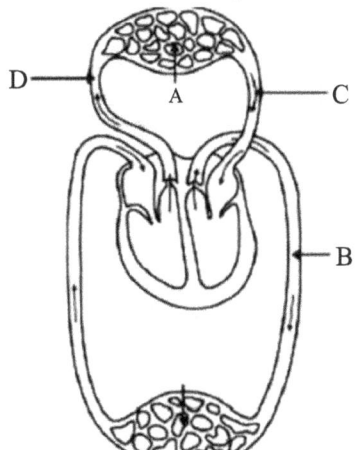

   (a) Lung capillaries and Vena cava from body
   (b) Pulmonary veins from lungs and Aorta to body
   (c) Pulmonary artery to lungs and vena cava from body
   (d) lung capillaries and pulmonary vein from lungs.
9. In the given food chain, suppose the amount of energy at fourth trophic level is 5 kJ, what will be the energy available at the producer level?
   Grass → Grasshopper → Frog → Snake → Hawk
   (a) 5 kJ (b) 50 kJ (c) 500 kJ (d) 5000 kJ
10. Growth of pollen tube towards ovule is an example of
    (a) phototropism (b) geotropism (c) hydrotropism (d) chemotropism
11. A male child will be born if
    (a) father is healthy
    (b) mother is well fed during pregnancy
    (c) genetic composition of child has XY set of chromosomes
    (d) genetic composition of child has XX set of chromosomes.
12. Cytokinins are known to
    (a) inhibit cytoplasmic movement.
    (b) help in retention of chlorophyll.
    (c) influence water movement.
    (d) promote abscission layer formation.
13. Which of the following can produce a magnetic field?
    (a) Electric charges at rest
    (b) Electric charges in motion
    (c) Only by permanent magnets
    (d) Electric charges whether at rest or in motion
14. The resistance of a conducting wire doesn't depend upon:
    (a) Area of cross section
    (b) Length
    (c) Temperature
    (d) Voltage applied
15. Magnetic field lines caused by a solenoid:
    (a) are curves.
    (b) start at north and end at south.
    (c) form closed loops.
    (d) is uniform everywhere.
16. Which of the following statements does not represent Ohm's law?
    (a) Current / Potential difference = Constant
    (b) Potential difference / Current = Constant
    (c) Potential difference = Current × Resistance
    (d) Current = Resistance × Potential difference

Directions: Q.No. 17–20 are **Assertion - Reasoning based questions:** These consist of two statements – Assertion (A) and Reason (R). Answer these questions selecting the appropriate option given below:
(a) Both A and R are true and R is the correct explanation of A
(b) Both A and R are true and R is not the correct explanation of A
(c) A is true but R is false
(d) A is False but R is true

17. **Assertion :** Corrosion of iron is commonly known as rusting.
    Reason : Corrosion of iron occurs in presence of water and air.
18. **Assertion:** Spermatogenesis requires 72-74 days to get completed.
    Reason: Sperms reach the epididymis and stay there for 2-3 days for maturation i.e., to become motile.
19. **Assertion:** The flower colour of sweet pea shows the inheritance of complementary genes.
    Reason: The ratio obtained for complementary gene is 9 : 7.
20. **Assertion:** Magnetic field lines do not intersect each other.
    Reason: There cannot be two direction of magnetic field at a point.

SECTION-B

Q. no. 21 to 26 are Very Short Answer Questions.

21. (a) Write a balanced chemical equation for the reaction of potassium metal with water to give potassium hydroxide and hydrogen gas.
    (b) If in a chemical equation we find an arrow pointing upwards, what does it indicate?

OR

(a) Why do silver ornaments turns blackish after some time ?
(b) Name any two metals which are soft and can be cut with an ordinary knife.

22. (a) We do not clean ponds or lakes, but an aquarium needs to be cleaned regularly. Why?
    (b) Why is ozone layer getting depleted at the higher levels of the atmosphere ? Mention one harmful effect caused by its depletion.
23. What is ozone? How and where is it formed in the atmosphere? Explain how does it affect an ecosystem.
24. In human beings, the statistical probability of getting either a male or a female child is 50%. Give reasons and explain with the help of a diagram.
25. What is meant by dispersion of light? Explain how the ray of white light is dispersed. Which colour deviates more?

OR

Make a diagram to show how hypermetropia is corrected. The near point of a hypermetropic eye is 1m. What is the power of lens required to correct this defect ? Assume that the near point of the normal eye is 25 cm.

26. (a) Name the reproductive and non-reproductive parts of bread mould (Rhizopus).
    (b) List any two advantages of vegetative propagation.

SECTION-C

Q.no. 27 to 33 are Short Answer Questions.

27. (a) What is rancidity ? What is the general name of chemical which are added to fat and oil containing food so as to prevent the development of rancidity?
    (b) Metal X becomes green when left in air, turns black when heated in air. Name the metal and the compounds formed in both the cases?
28. (a) Identify the substances that are oxidised and the substances that are reduced in the following reactions.
    (i) $ZnO(s) + C(s) \longrightarrow Zn(s) + CO(g)$
    (ii) $CuO(s) + H_2(g) \longrightarrow Cu(s) + H_2O(l)$
    (b) Name the oxidising and reducing agent in the following reaction:
    $2H_2S + SO_2 \longrightarrow 2H_2O + 3S\downarrow$

Sample Paper-1

29. (a) Describe the parts of a flower.
    (b) Draw a labelled diagram of the longitudinal section of a flower.
30. An object of height 6 cm is placed perpendicular to the prinipal axis of a concave lens of focal length 5 cm. Use lens formula to determine the position, size and nature of the image if the distance of the object from the lens is 10 cm.
31. If the image formed by a mirror for all positions of the object placed in front of it is always erect and diminshed, what type of mirror is it? Draw a ray diagram to jusity your answer. Where and why do we generally use this type of mirror?
32. On what factors the strength of magnetic field depends around
    (a) a straight current carrying conductor.
    (b) a circular wire carrying current.

OR

Name, state and explain with an example the rule used to determine the direction of force experienced by a current carrying conductor placed in a uniform magnetic field.

33. (a) Draw a diagram depicting human alimentary canal and label gall bladder, liver and pancreas.
    (b) State the roles of liver and pancreas.
    (c) Name the organ which performs the following functions in humans:
        (i) Absorption of digested food
        (ii) Absorption of water

SECTION-D

Q.no. 34 to 36 are Long Answer Questions.

34. Define covalent bond? What do you mean by the term covalency. Give an example of each containing (a) single bond (b) double bond (c) triple bond.

OR

Write down the chemical equations to represent the reaction of ethanoic acid with:
(a) Sodium metal
(b) Sodium carbonate
(c) Sodium hydroxide
(d) Ethanol in the presence of a little conc. H_2SO_4
(e) Heating with NaOH in presence of CaO.

35. (a) Write the names and more one function of each of three growth hormones in plants.
    (b) In the absence of muscle cells, how do plant cells show movement?
36. (i) What is a solenoid?
    (ii) Draw the pattern of magnetic field formed around a current carrying solenoid. Compare this field to that of a bar magnet.
    (iii) Explain an activity to show that a current carrying conductor experiences a force when placed in a magnetic field.

SECTION-E

Q.no. 37 to 39 are case - based/data -based questions with 2 to 3 short sub - parts. Internal choice is provided in one of these sub-parts.

37. Read the following case/passage and answer the questions.

Non-metals are the elements which are generally poor conductors of heat and electricity except for graphite which conducts electricity. Most properties of non-metals are the opposite of metals. They are neither malleable nor ductile. Non-metals form negatively charged ions by gaining electrons on reaction with metals. Non-metals form oxides which are either acidic or neutral. Non-metals have a wide variety of uses. Non-metals are used in the manufacture of rubber, for tires, in gunpowder, fireworks and other material in fertilizers, as disinfectant.

(a) (i) Name the element which shows conducting property like metals.
    (ii) Which insulating material is used for the coating of electrical wires?
(b) Give reason for non-metals not used as reducing agent.

OR

(b) Among P_2O_5, Al_2O_3, Fe_2O_3 which one is acidic oxide and why?

38. Read the following case/passage and answer the questions.

The main excretory system in humans is the urinary system. The skin also acts as an organ of excretion by removing water and small amounts of urea and salts. They remove urea, toxins, medications and excess ions and farm urine. The kidneys also balance water and salts as well as acids and bases. Nephron is called as functional unit of kidney. It is the structure that actually produces urine in the process of removing waste and excess substances from the blood.

(i) What is the approximate length and thickness of kidneys?

(ii) Which structure allows the entry of blood vessels, lymph vessels and nerves to enter kidney?

(iii) Write the correct order of processes that occur in urine formation?

(iv) What is the order of toxicity among ammonia, urea and uric aicd (from lower to higher)?

39. Read the following case/passage and answer the questions.

The bending of the light ray from its path in passing from one medium to the other medium is called refraction of light. If the refracted ray bends towards the normal relative to the incident ray (Passing obliquely), then the second medium is said to be denser than the first medium. But if the refracted ray bends away from the normal, then the second medium is said to be rarer than the first medium. If a ray of light passing normally i.e., at right angles from one medium to another optical medium then it does not bend or deviate from its path. Refraction of light takes place due to change in the speed of light as it enters from one medium to another medium.

(a) You are given water, mustard oil, glycerine and kerosene. In which of these media, a ray of light incident obliquely at same angle would bend the most?

(b) For the same angle of incidence; the angle of refraction in three different media A, B and C are 150°; 25° and 35° respectively. In which medium velocity of light will be minimum?

(c) Explain : A stick partly immersed in water appears to be bent at the surface of water.

OR

(c) Light enters from air to glass having refractive index 1.50. What is the speed of light in the glass ? The speed of light in vaccum is 3×10^8 m / sec.

2 Sample Paper

LATEST PATTERN

BLUE PRINT

S. No.	Chapter Name	Section-A (MCQs & A/R) 1 Mark Q. No.	Section-B (VSAQs) 2 Marks Q. No.	Section-C (SAQs) 3 Marks Q. No.	Section-D (LAQs) 5 Marks Q. No.	Section-E (Case Study) 4 Marks Q. No.	Total Marks
1	Chemical Reactions and Equations	2(Q1,5)	1(Q21)			1(Q37)	8
2	Acids, Bases and Salts	3(Q2,7,17)		1(Q27)			6
3	Metals and Non-metals	2(Q3,6)		1(Q28)			5
4	Carbon and its Compounds	1(Q4)	1(Q 21 OR)		1(Q34)		6
5	Life Processes	3(Q9,11,20)	1(Q24)	1(Q33)			8
6	Control and Co-ordination	2(Q10,19)	1(Q23)	1(Q30)			7
7	How do Organism Reproduce		1(Q25)		1(Q36)		7
8	Heredity and Evolution	1(Q12)	1(Q26)				3
9	Light- Reflection and Refraction			2(Q29,31)			6
10	Human Eye and Colourful World		1(Q22)			1(Q38)	6
11	Electricity	3(Q14,15,18)			1(Q35)		8
12	Magnetic Effects of Electric Current	2(Q13,16)		1(Q32)			5
13	Our Environment	1(Q8)				1(Q39)	5
	Total Questions (Total Marks)	20(20)	6(12)	7(21)	3(15)	3(12)	80

* The number given outside the bracket denotes number of questions asked in the sample paper, while the number given inside the bracket denotes marks.

Sc-8 **SCIENCE-X**

Time Allowed : 3 Hours **Max. Marks : 80**

General Instructions

1. This question paper consists of 39 questions in 5 sections.
2. All questions are compulsory. However, an internal choice is provided in some questions. A student is expected to attempt only one of these questions.
3. **Section A** consists of 20 objective type questions carrying 1 mark each.
4. **Section B** consists of 6 Very Short Answer type questions carrying 02 marks each. Answers to these questions should in the range of 30 to 50 words.
5. **Section C** consists of 7 Short Answer type questions carrying 03 marks each. Answers to these questions should in the range of 50 to 80 words
6. **Section D** consists of 3 Long Answer type questions carrying 05 marks each. Answer to these questions should be in the range of 80 to 120 words.
7. **Section E** consists of 3 source-based/case-based units of assessment of 04 marks each with sub-parts.

SECTION-A

Select and write one most appropriate option out of the four options given for each of the Questions 1 to 20

1. White silver chloride in sunlight turns to –
   (a) grey (b) yellow (c) remain white (d) red
2. Which one of the following can be used as an acid-base indicator by a visually impared student?
   (a) litmus (b) Turmeric (c) Vanilla essence (d) Petunia leaves
3. Which of the following is not an allotropic form of carbon?
   (a) Diamond (b) Graphite (c) Coal gas (d) None of these
4. Organic compounds will always contain –
   (a) carbon (b) hydrogen (c) nitrogen (d) sulphur
5. Which of the following is not a physical change?
   (a) Boiling of water to give water vapour.
   (b) Melting of ice to give water.
   (c) Dissolution of salt in water.
   (d) Combustion of Liquefied Petroleum Gas (LPG).
6. Which of the following non-metals are not present in aqua regia?
   (a) N (b) Cl (c) P (d) All of these are present
7. Which of the following substances will not give carbon dioxide on treatment with dilute acid?
   (a) Marble (b) Limestone (c) Baking soda (d) Lime
8. The chemical notation of ozone is
   (a) CFCs (b) O_2O (c) O_3 (d) Both (b) & (c)
9. Which of the following statement is not true for stomatal apparatus?

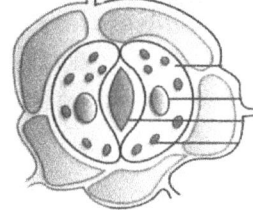

   (a) Inner walls of guard cells are thick
   (b) Guard walls invariably possess chloroplast and mitochondria
   (c) Guard cells are always surrounded of subsidiary cells
   (d) Stomata are involved in gaseous exchange

10. From the given figure identify the part of human brain controlling most of the involuntary actions:

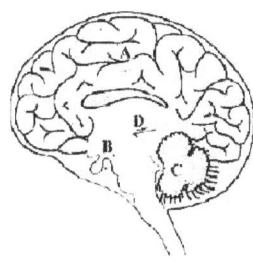

    (a) A & B (b) B & C (c) C & D (d) D & A

11. In the given diagram some organs are labelled as A,B,C and D respectively. Choose the correct sequence.

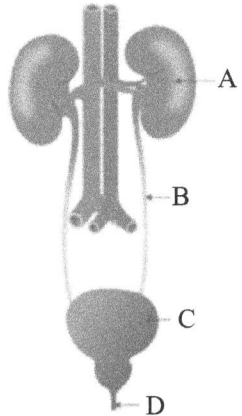

    (a) A: Kidney, B: Urinary bladder, C: Urethra, D: Ureter
    (b) A: Kidney, B: Ureter, C: Urinary bladder, D: Urethra
    (c) A: Kidney, B: Urethra, C: Collecting duet, D: Anus
    (d) A: Kidney, B: Seminiferous tubules, C: Uterus, D: Ureter

12. In one of Mendel's experiments a plant heterozygous for tallness (f1) was self fertilized, resulting in 748 tall plants and 252 dwarf plants
    What is the most likely expected ratios?
    (a) 1 : 1 (b) 2 : 1 (c) 3 : 1 (d) 9 : 3 : 3 : 1

13. Which of the following statements is incorrect regarding magnetic field lines?
    (a) The direction of magnetic field at a point is taken to be the direction in which the north pole of a magnetic compass needle points.
    (b) Magnetic field lines are closed curves
    (c) If magnetic field lines are parallel and equidistant, they represent zero field strength
    (d) Relative strength of magnetic field is shown by the degree of closeness of the field lines

14. The maximum resistance which can be made using four resistors each of resistance $\frac{1}{2} \Omega$ is
    (a) 2 Ω (b) 1 Ω (c) 2.5 Ω (d) S Ω

15. The charge of 150 coulomb flows through a wire in one minute. What is the electric current flowing through it?
    (a) 2.5 A (b) 3.5 A (c) 4.5 A (d) 5.5 A

16. Which of the following correctly describes the magnetic field near a long straight wire?
    (a) The field consists of straight lines perpendicular to the wire.
    (b) The field consists of straight lines parallel to the wire.
    (c) The field consists of radial lines originating from the wire.
    (d) The field consists of concentric circles centred on the wire.

Directions: Q.No. 17–20 are **Assertion - Reasoning based questions:** These consist of two statements – Assertion (A) and Reason (R). Answer these questions selecting the appropriate option given below:
(a) Both A and R are true and R is the correct explanation of A
(b) Both A and R are true and R is not the correct explanation of A
(c) A is true but R is false
(d) A is False but R is true

17. **Assertion :** Aqueous solution of ammonium nitrate turns blue litmus red.
    Reason : Ammonium nitrate is salt of strong acid and strong base.
18. **Assertion:** Bulbs are usually filled with chemically active gases.
    Reason: Nitrogen and argon gases are filled in order to prolong the life of the filament.
19. **Assertion:** Transmission of the nerve impulse across a synapse is accomplished by neurotransmitters.
    Reason: Transmission across a synapse usually requires neurotransmitters because there is small space i.e., synaptic cleft, that separates one neuron from another.
20. **Assertion:** Blood of insects is colourless.
    Reason: The blood of insect does not play any role in transport of oxygen.

SECTION-B
Q. no. 21 to 26 are Very Short Answer Questions.

21. Why are unsaturated hydrocarbons more reactive than saturated hydrocarbons?
    OR
    State one difference between:
    (i) Combination and decomposition reaction.
    (ii) Displacement and double displacement reaction.
22. How will you use two identical prisms so that a narrow beam of white light incident on one prism emerges out of the second prism as white ligth? Draw the diagram.
    OR
    What is a rainbow? Draw a labelled diagram to show the formation of a rainbow.
23. Give an example of a plant hormone that (i) promotes growth (ii) inhibits growth
24. Name the component of blood which transport:
    (i) Food, carbon dioxide and nitrogenous wastes   (ii) Oxygen.
25. In the following figure showing a germinating gram seed, name the parts labelled as A, B and C :

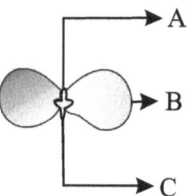

Why is part 'B' considered to be important during germination?
26. Name the part of *Bryophyllum* where the buds are produced for vegetative propagation.

SECTION-C
Q.no. 27 to 33 are Short Answer Questions.

27. Write the name of acid and base that formed the following salt.
    (a) KCl   (b) $Al_2(SO_4)_3$ (c) K_2SO_4
28. (a) How can you obtain pure metal from metals of high reactivity?
    (b) Magnesium when reacts with hot water starts floating. Explain.
29. Mention the types of mirrors used as (i) rear view mirrors (ii) shaving mirors. List two reasons to jutify your answers in each case.
30. (a) An old man is advised by his doctor to take less sugar in his diet. Name the disease from which the man is suffering . Mention the hormone due to imbalance of which he is suffering from this hormone? Which gland secretes this hormone?
    (b) Name the endocrine gland which secretes growth hormone. What will be the effect of the following on a person:
        (i) Deficiency of growth hormone.
        (ii) Excess secretion of growth hormone.
31. What is meant by power of a lens? What does its sign (+ ve or – ve) indicate? State its S.I. unit. How is this unit related to focal length of a lens?

32. (a) Name the poles P, Q, R and S of the magnets in the following figures 'a' and 'b':

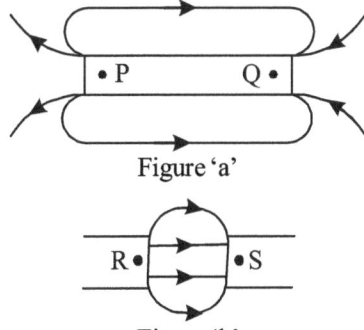

Figure 'a'

Figure 'b'

(b) State the inference drawn about the direction of the magnetic field lines on the basis of these diagrams.

OR

When is the force experienced by a current - carrying straight conductor placed in a uniform magnetic field.
(i) Maximum;   (ii) Minimum?

33. State the difference between transport of materials in xylem and phloem.

OR

Explain how water and minerals are transported in plants?

SECTION-D

Q.no. 34 to 36 are Long Answer Questions.

34. The molecules of alkene family are represented by a general formula C_nH_{2n}. Now answer the following :
(a) What do 'n' and '$2n$' signify?
(b) What is the molecular formula of alkene when n = 6?
(c) What is the molecular formula of the alkene if there are six H atoms in it?
(d) What is the molecular formula and structural formula of the first member of the alkene family?
(e) Write the molecular formulae of lower and higher homologues of an alkene which contains four carbon atoms.

OR

Give two differences between soap and synthetic detergents? Give the name of the by product of soap industry? How is it formed?

35. What does an electric circuit mean? Name a device that helps to maintain a potential difference across a conductor in a circuit. When do we say that the potential difference across a conductor is 1 volt? Calculate the amount of work done in shifting a charge of 2 coulombs from a point A to B having potentials 110 V and 25 V respectively.

36. Differentiate between the following :
(i) Pollen tube and style.
(ii) Fission in *Amobea* and *Plasmodium*
(iii) Fragmentation and regeneration
(iv) Bud of *Hydra* and bud of *Bryophyllum*
(v) Vegetative propagation and spore formation

SECTION-E

Q.no. 37 to 39 are case - based/data -based questions with 2 to 3 short sub - parts. Internal choice is provided in one of these sub-parts.

37. Read the following case/passage and answer the questions.

The reaction between MnO_2 with HCl is depicted in the following diagram. It was observed that a gas with bleaching abilities was released.

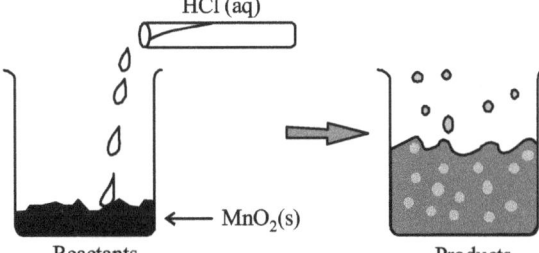

(a) Mention the name of the reaction takimng place in the above experiment with chemical reaction.
(b) What is the special use of the gas produced in the reaction? Write the chemical reaction involved in the usage.

OR

MnO_2 and HCl both are getting reduced – justify this statement.

38. Read the following case/passage and answer the questions.

The phenomenon of decomposition of the white light into its seven component colours when passing through a prism or through a transparent object delimited by non parallel surfaces is called dispersion of light. A beam of light containing all the visible spectrum of the light is white, because the sum of all the colors generates the white color. The light is decomposed in all the component colours, Violet, Indigo, Blue, Green, Yellow, Orange and Red, called as VIBGYOR. The band of the coloured components of a light beam is called its spectrum. The phenomenon can be explained by thinking that light of different colours (different wavelengths) has different velocities while travelling in a medium $v_m = f\lambda_m$.
Hence, the change in velocity of light observed when the light passes from the air to the glass, depends on the wavelength.

(a) A prism ABC (with BC as base) is placed in different orientations. A narrow beam of white light is incident on the prism as shown in figure. In which of the following cases, after dispersion, the third colour from the top corresponds to the colour of the sky?

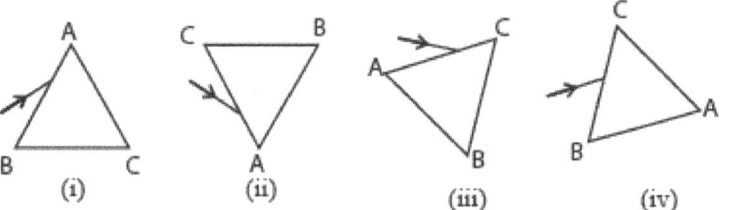

(b) When white light is allowed to pass through a glass prism, which colour deviates the least?
(c) When white light is allowed to pass through a glass prism, which colour deviates the most?

OR

Why does the sun appear white at noon?

39. Read the following case/passage and answer the questions.

Nature provided us well-balanced environment in which there was a perfect harmony among the living organism in regard to food chain and the ecosystem was so well regulated that every organism was enjoying its full quota of a biotic factors with the advancement of mental ability, man become most dominant form of life or Earth to fulfill the requirement of ever increasing human population, man began to exploit natural resources through deforestation unplanned, profit oriented, capitalism and technological advancement. This led to the degradation of environment and appearance of different problems eg-solid waste, disposal, ozone depletion and other pollution related problems.

(i) The ozone layer absorbs what range of wavelength of the sun's radiation?
(ii) Now-a-days, which type of cups are being generally used in trains for serving tea/coffee/ soup etc. on daily basis?
(iii) Carefully observe the diagram(s) given below-

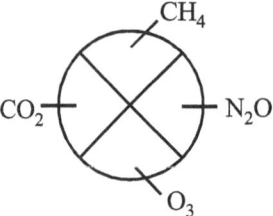

% concentration of which greenhouse gas is maximum?
(iv) Mention a prime health risk associated with greater UV radiation through the atmosphere due to the depletion of the ozone layer?

3 Sample Paper

LATEST PATTERN

BLUE PRINT

S. No.	Chapter Name	Section-A (MCQs & A/R) 1 Mark Q. No.	Section-B (VSAQs) 2 Marks Q. No.	Section-C (SAQs) 3 Marks Q. No.	Section-D (LAQs) 5 Marks Q. No.	Section-E (Case Study) 4 Marks Q. No.	Total Marks
1	Chemical Reactions and Equations	3(Q1,6,7)		1(Q27)			6
2	Acids, Bases and Salts	1(Q2)	1(Q21)		1(Q34)		8
3	Metals and Non-metals	2(Q3,5)	1(Q OR 21)			1(Q37)	6
4	Carbon and its Compounds	2(Q4,17)		1(Q28)			5
5	Life Processes	2(Q8,11)		1(Q31)		1(Q38)	9
6	Control and Co-ordination	1(Q10)	1(Q24)	1(Q32)			6
7	How do Organism Reproduce	2(Q12,19)	2(Q25,23)				6
8	Heredity and Evolution	2(Q9,20)	1(Q26)				4
9	Light- Reflection and Refraction	2(Q13,18)			1(Q36)	1(Q39)	11
10	Human Eye and Colourful World	1(Q15)					1
11	Electricity	1(Q14)	1(Q22)	1(Q30)			6
12	Magnetic Effects of Electric Current	1(Q16)		2(Q29,33)			7
13	Our Environment				1(Q35)		5
	Total Questions (Total Marks)	**20(20)**	**6(12)**	**7(21)**	**3(15)**	**3(12)**	**80**

* The number given outside the bracket denotes number of questions asked in the sample paper, while the number given inside the bracket denotes marks.

Time Allowed : 3 Hours **Max. Marks : 80**

General Instructions

1. This question paper consists of 39 questions in 5 sections.
2. All questions are compulsory. However, an internal choice is provided in some questions. A student is expected to attempt only one of these questions.
3. **Section A** consists of 20 objective type questions carrying 1 mark each.
4. **Section B** consists of 6 Very Short Answer type questions carrying 02 marks each. Answers to these questions should in the range of 30 to 50 words.
5. **Section C** consists of 7 Short Answer type questions carrying 03 marks each. Answers to these questions should in the range of 50 to 80 words
6. **Section D** consists of 3 Long Answer type questions carrying 05 marks each. Answer to these questions should be in the range of 80 to 120 words.
7. **Section E** consists of 3 source-based/case-based units of assessment of 04 marks each with sub-parts.

SECTION-A

Select and write one most appropriate option out of the four options given for each of the Questions 1 to 20

1. Which of the following can be decomposed by the action of light?
   (a) NaCl   (b) KCl   (c) AgCl   (d) CuCl

2. A sample of soil is mixed with water and allowed to settle. The clear supernatant solution turns the pH paper yellowish-orange. Which of the following would change the colour of this pH paper to greenish-blue?
   (a) Lemon juice   (b) Vinegar   (c) Common salt   (d) An antacid

3. Pure gold is –
   (a) 24 carats   (b) 22 carats   (c) 20 carats   (d) 18 carats

4. Pentane has the molecular formula C_5H_{12}. It has
   (a) 5 covalent bonds   (b) 12 covalent bonds   (c) 16 covalent bonds   (d) 17 covalent bonds

5. Among Mg, Cu, Fe, Zn the metal that does not produce hydrogen gas in reaction with hydrochloric acid is
   (a) Cu   (b) Zn   (c) Mg   (d) Fe

6. Take about 1.0g $CaCO_3$ in a test tube. Heat it over a flame, a colourless gas comes out. The reaction is called a
   (a) decomposition reaction   (b) displacement reaction
   (c) double decomposition reaction   (d) double displacement reaction

7. A substance A reacts with another substance B to produce the product C and a gas D. If a mixture of the gas D and ammonia is passed through an aqueous solution of C, baking soda is formed. The substances A and B are
   (a) HCl and NaOH   (b) HCl and Na_2CO_3 (c) Na and HCl   (d) Na_2CO_3 and H_2O

8. Which of the following statements are correct in reference to the role of A (shown in the given diagram) during a breathing cycle in human beings?

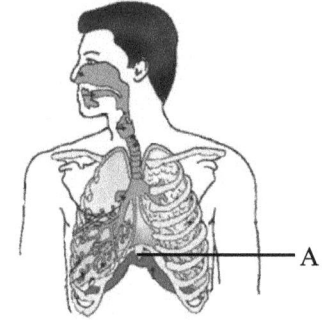

   (i) It helps to decrease the residual volume of air in lungs.
   (ii) It flattens as we inhale.
   (iii) It gets raised as we inhale.
   (iv) It helps the chest cavity to become larger.
   (a) (ii) and (iv)   (b) (iii) and (iv)   (c) (i) and (ii)   (d) (i), (ii) and (iv)

9. A pea plant with round green (RRyy) pea seed is crossed another pea plant with wrinkled yellow (rrYY) seeds. What would be the nature of seed in the first generation (F_1 generation)?
   (a) Round green (b) Wrinkled green (c) Wrinkled yellow (d) Round yellow
10. Sequence of events which occured in a reflex action are
   (a) Receptor - motor neuron - CNS - sensory neuron - effector muscle
   (b) Effector muscle - CNS - sensory nerve - sensory organ
   (c) CNS - sensory neuron - motor neuron - effector muscle
   (d) Receptor organ - sensory neuron - CNS - motor neuron - effector muscle
11. A student was asked to write a stepwise procedure to demonstrate that carbon dioxide is necessary for photosynthesis. He wrote the following steps. The wrongly worded step is –

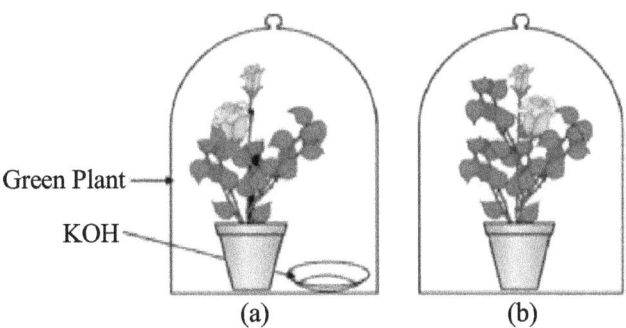

   (a) Both potted plants are kept in dark room for at least three days.
   (b) Bottom of the bell jars is sealed to make them air tight.
   (c) Both potted plants are kept in sunlight after the starch test.
   (d) A leaf from both the plants is taken to test the presence of starch.
12. From the following drawing of flowers identify the flower which will self pollinate?

13. If the refractive indices for water and diamond relative to air are 1.33 and 2.4 respectively, then the refractive index of diamond relative to water is –
   (a) 5.5 (b) 1.80 (c) 3.19 (d) None of these
14. Resistance of conductor is doubled keeping the potential difference across it constant. The rate of generation of heat will
   (a) become one fourth (b) be halved (c) be doubled (d) become four times
15. The least distance of distinct vision for a young adult with normal vision is about
   (a) 25 m (b) 2.5 cm (c) 25 cm (d) 2.5 m
16. The force experienced by a curetn-carrying conductor placed in a magnetic field is the largest when the angle between the conductor and the magnetic field is:
   (a) 45° (b) 60° (c) 90° (d) 180°

Directions: Q.No. 17–20 are Assertion - Reasoning based questions: These consist of two statements – Assertion (A) and Reason (R). Answer these questions selecting the appropriate option given below:
(a) Both A and R are true and R is the correct explanation of A
(b) Both A and R are true and R is not the correct explanation of A
(c) A is true but R is false
(d) A is False but R is true

17. **Assertion:** Carbon monoxide is extremely poisonous in nature.
    Reason: Carbon monoxide is formed by complete combustion of carbon.
18. **Assertion:** Convex mirror is used as a driver mirror.
    Reason: Images formed by convex mirror are diminished in size.
19. **Assertion:** In very rare cases, a surrogate mother may have to be used to bring up in vitro fertilised ovum to maturity.
    Reason: Success rate of test tube baby is more than 90%
20. **Assertion:** The principal of segregation given by Mendel is the principle of purity of gametes
    Reason: Gametes are pure for a character and do not mix up.

SECTION-B

Q. no. 21 to 26 are Very Short Answer Questions.

21. pH of two samples of cold drinks A and B are 2 and 5. Which is more unhealthy?

    OR

    $CuSO_4 + Fe \longrightarrow FeSO_4 + Cu$
    $FeSO_4 + Zn \longrightarrow ZnSO_4 + Fe.$
    On the basis of above reactions, indicate which is most reactive and which is least reactive?

22. (i) What is meant by the statement: The potential difference between two points is 1 volt?
    (ii) What do the symbols given represent in a circuit? Write one function of each.

    (a)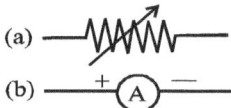

    (b) ──+─(A)─── ──

    OR

    The resistance of a wire of 0.01 cm radius is 10Ω. If the resistivity of the material of the wire is 50×10^{-8} ohm meter, find the length of the wire.

23. (a) What are the phases of menstrual cycle ?
    (b) What is difference between menarche and menopause?

24. What is phototropism? Describe an activity to demonstrate phototropism.

    OR

    (a) Write an activity to show phototropism and geotropism?
    (b) What type of movement is shown by mimosa plant leaves when touched with a finger?

25. Name the parts A, B and C shown in the following diagram and state one function of each.

    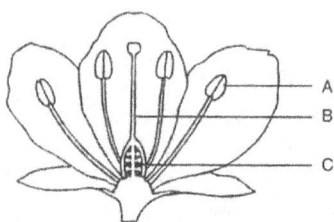

26. In one of his experiments with pea plants, Mendel observed that when a pure tall pea plant is crossed with a pure dwarf pea plant. In the first generation, F_1 only tall plants appear.
    (i) What happens to the traits of the dwarf plants in this case ?
    (ii) When the F_1 generation plants were self-fertilised, he observed that in the plants of second generation, F_2 both tall plants and dwarf plants were present. Why it happened? Explain briefly.

SECTION-C

Q.no. 27 to 33 are Short Answer Questions.

27. When you mix solution of lead (II) nitrate and potassium iodide,
    (i) What is the colour of the precipitate formed? Name the compound involved.
    (ii) Write balanced chemical equation for the reaction.
    (iii) Is this a double displacement reaction ?

28. Why is fuel oil considered a better fuel than coal in industries? Give any three reasons.

    OR

    Explain allotropy in carbon?

29. Explain whether an alpha particle will experience any force in a magnetic field if:
    (i) it is placed in the field at rest.
    (ii) it moves in the magnetic field parallel to field lines.
    (iii) it moves in the magnetic field perpendicular to field lines.

30. Give reason for the following:
    (i) Why are copper and aluminium wires used as connecting wires?
    (ii) Why is tungsten used for filament of electric lamps?
    (iii) Why is lead-tin alloy used for fuse wires?

31. (i) Mention the site of exchange of material between the blood and surrounding cells.
    (ii) Draw a schematic representation of transport and exchange of oxygen and carbon dioxide.

32. (a) Draw a neat diagram of human brain and label on it the following parts:
   (i) Mid brain   (ii) Pituitary gland   (iii) Cerebellum   (iv) Cerebrum
   (b) Which is the main thinking part of brain?

33. (i) What is meant by a magnetic field? Mention two paramenters that are necessary to describe it completely.
   (ii) If field lines of a magnetic field are crossed at a point, what does it indicate?

OR

What is an electromagnet? How can we determine north and south pole of an electromagnet with the help of magnetised iron bar

SECTION-D

Q.no. 34 to 36 are Long Answer Questions.

34. Give one example in each of the following case:
   (a) A base which is not an alkali.
   (b) A hydrogen containing compound which is not an acid.
   (c) A hydroxide which is highly soluble in water.
   (d) An oxide which is a base.
   (e) A weak mineral acid.

OR

Write balanced equation to satisfy each statement.
   (a) Acid + Active metal $\longrightarrow$ Salt + Hydrogen
   (b) Acid + Base $\longrightarrow$ Salt + Water
   (c) Acid + Carbonate / Bicarbonate $\longrightarrow$ Salt + Water + Carbon dioxide
   (d) Acid + Metal oxide $\longrightarrow$ Salt + Water
   (e) Base + Metal $\longrightarrow$ Salt + Hydrogen

35. What activities do you perform that are good for the biosphere? What activities do you perform that harm the biosphere?

36. To construct ray diagrams, two rays of light are generally so chosen that it is easy to determine their directions after reflection from a mirror. Choose two such rays and state the path/ direction of these rays after reflection from a concave mirror. Use these two rays to find the position and nature of the image of an object placed at a distance of 8 cm from concave mirror of focal length 12 cm.

SECTION-E

Q.no. 37 to 39 are case - based/data -based questions with 2 to 3 short sub - parts. Internal choice is provided in one of these sub-parts.

37. Read the following case/passage and answer the questions.

Metals are electropositive elements. They can easily lose electrons to form ions. Metals show distinguished physical as well as chemical properties. Generally most of the metals are ductile and malleable with exception such as mercury. These properties make them valuable for commercial as well as domestic uses. Reaction of a metal with water is one of important chemical property. Metals like sodium and potassium reacts with cold water while magnesium reacts with hot water. Metals like aluminium, zinc do not react with hot/cold water but they easily react with steam. When a metal react with hot/cold water the products are metal hydroxide and hydrogen, and when it react with steam, the product are metal oxide and hydrogen. Some metals like sodium, potassium react violently with water.

   (a) Write the chemical reaction of Na Al and Zn with water.
   (b) What is ductility?

OR

   (b) Al, Cu, Ag, Au – which one is the most ductile metal?

38. Read the following case/passage and answer the questions.

The heart is a tough operating mechanism which moves blood around the body through a very advanced system called arteries and capillaries, the blood is then carried back to the heard by means of veins. Blood pressure is the thrust of this blood in the body pushing up against the inside wall of the arteries as the heart is pumping.

   (i) What is the normal Blood pressure range?
   (ii) What happens when the decrease in blood volume is greater that 10%?

(iii) Identify the person having normal blood pressure from the graph.

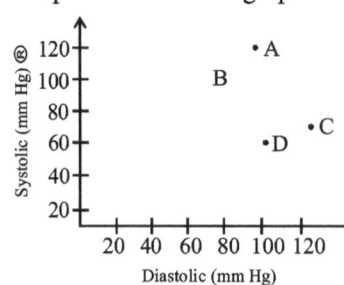

(iv) Why blood pressure changes from aorta to capillaries?

39. Read the following case/passage and answer the questions.
A relationship among the object distance (u), the image distance (v) and the focal length (f) of a mirror is called the mirror formula.

The formula is given by $\dfrac{1}{f} = \dfrac{1}{u} + \dfrac{1}{v}$

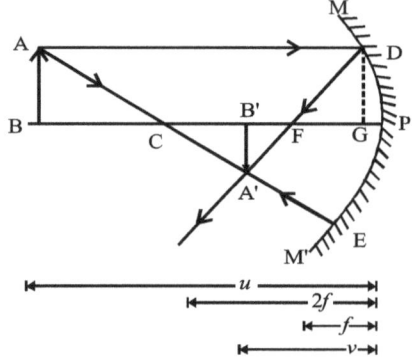

(a) What is the relation between focal length and radius of curvature?
(b) What are the possible positions of an object in front of concave mirror to get enlarged image.
(c) According to sign conventions for mirrors what sign is given to image distance?
OR
Magnification of a mirror is always less than 1, which mirror is this?

4 Sample Paper
LATEST PATTERN

BLUE PRINT

S. No.	Chapter Name	Section-A (MCQs & A/R) 1 Mark Q. No.	Section-B (VSAQs) 2 Marks Q. No.	Section-C (SAQs) 3 Marks Q. No.	Section-D (LAQs) 5 Marks Q. No.	Section-E (Case Study) 4 Marks Q. No.	Total Marks
1	Chemical Reactions and Equations	2(Q3,7)	1(Q OR 21)	1(Q27)			5
2	Acids, Bases and Salts	3(Q2,6,17)		1(Q28)			6
3	Metals and Non-metals	1(Q1)	1(Q21)		1(Q34)		8
4	Carbon and its Compounds	2(Q4,5)				1(Q37)	6
5	Life Processes	2(Q8,19)	1(Q26)	1(Q33)			7
6	Control and Co-ordination	2(Q9,12)	1(Q22)			1(Q38)	8
7	How do Organism Reproduce	2(Q10,20)	1(Q23)				4
8	Heredity and Evolution	1(Q11)			1(Q36)		6
9	Light- Reflection and Refraction	2(Q13,14)	1(Q25)		1(Q35)		9
10	Human Eye and Colourful World			1(Q30)			3
11	Electricity	2(Q16,18)		1(Q31)		1(Q39)	9
12	Magnetic Effects of Electric Current	1(Q15)		1(Q29)			4
13	Our Environment		1(Q24)	1(Q32)			5
	Total Questions (Total Marks)	20(20)	6(12)	7(21)	3(15)	3(12)	80

* The number given outside the bracket denotes number of questions asked in the sample paper, while the number given inside the bracket denotes marks.

Time Allowed : 3 Hours **Max. Marks : 80**

General Instructions

1. This question paper consists of 39 questions in 5 sections.
2. All questions are compulsory. However, an internal choice is provided in some questions. A student is expected to attempt only one of these questions.
3. **Section A** consists of 20 objective type questions carrying 1 mark each.
4. **Section B** consists of 6 Very Short Answer type questions carrying 02 marks each. Answers to these questions should in the range of 30 to 50 words.
5. **Section C** consists of 7 Short Answer type questions carrying 03 marks each. Answers to these questions should in the range of 50 to 80 words
6. **Section D** consists of 3 Long Answer type questions carrying 05 marks each. Answer to these questions should be in the range of 80 to 120 words.
7. **Section E** consists of 3 source-based/case-based units of assessment of 04 marks each with sub-parts.

SECTION-A

Select and write one most appropriate option out of the four options given for each of the Questions 1 to 20

1. Aluminium does not oxidise readily in air because –
   (a) it is high in the electrochemical series.
   (b) it is low in the electrochemical series.
   (c) the metal does not combine with oxygen.
   (d) the metal is covered with a layer of oxide which does not rub off.
2. Which of the following acid does not react with metals?
   (a) sulphuric acid   (b) phosphoric acid   (c) carbonic acid   (d) nitric acid
3. In which of the following the identity of initial substance remains unchanged?
   (a) Curdling of milk   (b) Formation of crystals by process of crystallisation
   (c) Fermentation of grapes   (d) Digestion of food
4. Which compound represents the vinegar?
   (a) HCOOH   (b) CH_3CHO (c) HCHO   (d) CH_3COOH
5. Which one of the following statement is incorrect about graphite and diamond ?
   (a) Graphite is smooth and slippery.
   (b) Diamond is good conductor of heat.
   (c) Graphite is a good conductor of electricity.
   (d) Physical and chemical properties of graphite and diamond are same.
6. If a sample of water containing detergents is provided to you, which of the following methods will you adopt to neutralize it?
   (a) Treating the water with baking soda   (b) Treating the water with vinegar
   (c) Treating the water with caustic soda   (d) Treating the water with washing soda
7. In a balance equation $H_2SO_4 + xHI \rightarrow H_2S + yI_2 + zH_2O$, the values of x, y, z are–
   (a) $x=3, y=5, z=2$ (b) $x=4, y=8, z=5$ (c) $x=8, y=4, z=4$ (d) $x=5, y=3, z=4$
8. Select the correct schematic representation of blood circulation in human from the followings :

(a) 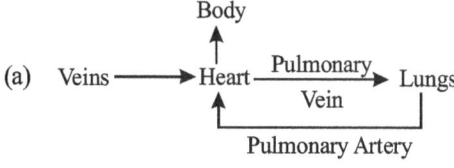   (b)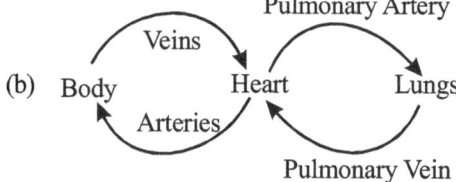

(c) 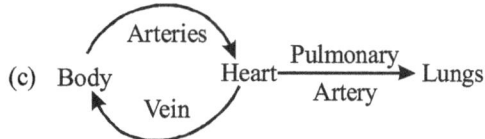   (d)

9. A high concentration of synthetic auxins is generally used for
   (a) weed control.
   (b) enhancing root initiation.
   (c) controlling of cell enlargement.
   (d) preventing the growth of the lateral buds.
10. The correct route that sperm follows when it releases from the testis of a mammal:
    (a) Vas deferens → Epididymis → Urethra
    (b) Urethra → Epididymis → Vas deferens
    (c) Epididymis → Urethra → Vas deferens
    (d) Epididymis → Vas deferens → Urethra
11. Assuring that both parent plants in the diagram below are homozygous, why would all of the F1 generation have yellow phenotype?

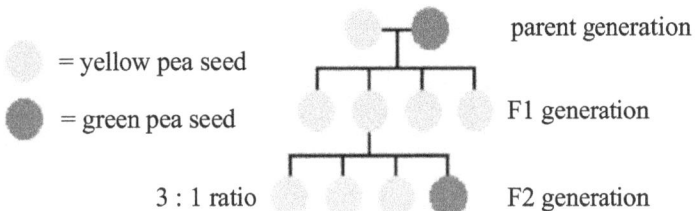

    (a) because the F1 genotypes are homozygous
    (b) because yellow is dominant over green
    (c) because both parents passed on yellow alleles.
    (d) None of the above
12. Which of the following is an example of reflex action?
    (a) To shoot the bird after aiming
    (b) Watering of the mouth of seeing the good edibles
    (c) To obey the order
    (d) To read story
13. An object is placed 40 cm from a concave mirror of focal length 20 cm. The image formed is
    (a) real, inverted and same in size
    (b) real, inverted and smaller
    (c) virtual, erect and larger
    (d) virtual, erect and smaller
14. What is the power of a concave lens whose focal length is – 75.0 cm?
    (a) 1.33 D
    (b) – 13.3 D
    (c) 13.3 D
    (d) – 1.33 D
15. Which of the following property of a proton canot change while it moves freely in a magnetic field?
    (a) mass
    (b) speed
    (c) velocity
    (d) momentum
16. The heating element of an electric heater should be made with a material, which should have
    (a) high specific resistance and high melting point
    (b) high specific resistance and low melting point
    (c) low specific resistance and low melting point
    (d) low specific resistance and high melting point

Directions: Q.No. 17–20 are Assertion - Reasoning based questions: These consist of two statements – Assertion (A) and Reason (R). Answer these questions selecting the appropriate option given below:
(a) Both A and R are true and R is the correct explanation of A
(b) Both A and R are true and R is not the correct explanation of A
(c) A is true but R is false
(d) A is False but R is true

17. **Assertion :** All alkalis are bases but all bases are not alkali.
    Reason : Water soluble bases are alkali.
18. **Assertion:** Electric fuse wire is made of an alloy of law melting point.
    Reason: Resistivity of an alloy is less than the resistivity of a pure metal.
19. **Assertion:** Hydrochloric acid helps in the digestion of food in the stomach.
    Reason: Hydrochloric acid creates an acidic medium to activate protein digesting enzymes.
20. **Assertion:** Petals help during the process of pollination.
    Reason: They attract insects.

SECTION-B

Q. no. 21 to 26 are Very Short Answer Questions.

21. $3MnO_2 + 4Al \longrightarrow 3Mn + 2Al_2O_3$.
    State which is more reactive, Mn or Al, and why?

    OR

    What are the differences between corrosion and combustion?
22. How is the movement of leaves of the sensitive plant different from the movement of a shoot towards light?
23. Name the part A, B and C shown in the diagram and write function [any one].

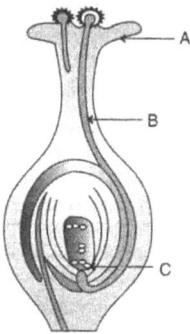

24. In the following food chain, 100 J of energy is available to the lion. How much energy was available to the producer?
    Plant → Deer → Lion
25. State the laws of refraction of light. Explain the term 'absolute refractive index of a medium' and write an expression to relate it with the speed of ligt in vacuum.

    OR

    What is meant by power of a lens? Write its SI unit. A student uses a lens of focal length 40 cm and another of –20 cm. Write the nature and power of each lens.
26. Where does aerobic respiration occur in a cell? Draw the flow chart showing breaking down of glucose by various pathways.

SECTION-C

Q.no. 27 to 33 are Short Answer Questions.

27. How many of the following is/are example of both oxidation and reduction reactions and why?
    (i) $CaCO_3(s) \xrightarrow{\Delta} CaO(s) + CO_2(g)$
    (ii) $Na_2SO_4(aq) + BaCl_2(aq) \xrightarrow{\Delta} BaSO_4(s) + 2NaCl(aq)$
    (iii) $CuO(s) + H_2(g) \longrightarrow Cu(s) + H_2O(l)$
    (iv) $4Na(s) + O_2(g) \longrightarrow 2Na_2O(s)$

28. Why do HCl, HNO$_3$ etc. show acidic character in aqueous solutions while solutions of compounds like alcohol and glucose do not show acidic character?
29. What is overloading and short circuiting? what is the function of earth wire?
30. (a) With the help of labelled ray diagram show the path followed by a narrow beam of monochromatic light when it passes through a glass prism.
    (b) What would happen if this beam is replaced by a narrow beam of white light?
31. Draw symbol of:
    (i) Rheostat,   (ii) Voltmeter,   (iii) Electric bulb

    OR

    Study the following electric circuit (i) the current flowing in the circuit and (ii) the potential difference across 10Ω resistor

    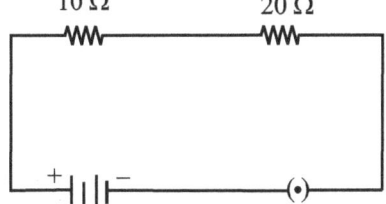

32. You have been selected to talk on "ozone layer and its protection" in the school assembly on 'Environment Day'.
    (i) Why should ozone layer be protected to save the environment?
    (ii) List any two ways that you would stress in your talk to bring in awareness amongst your fellow friends that would also help in protection of ozone layer as well as the environment.
33. (a) How does the transport of material in xylem and phloem occur?
    (b) What is translocation?

SECTION-D

Q.no. 34 to 36 are Long Answer Questions.

34. What are the advantages and disadvantages of using carbon as a reducing agent in the metallurgy?

    OR

    In what forms are metal found in nature? With the help of examples explain how metals react with oxygen and dilute acids. Also write chemical equations for the reaction.
35. The image of candle flame placed at a distance of 40 cm from a spherical lens is formed on a screen placed on the other side of the lens at a distance of 40 cm from the lens. Identify the types of lens and write its focal length. What will be the nature of the image formed if the canle flame is shifted 25 cm towards the lens? Draw ray diagram to justify.
36. How do Mendel's experiments show that.
    (i) traits may be dominant or recessive
    (ii) inheritance of two traits is independent of each other

SECTION-E

Q.no. 37 to 39 are case - based/data -based questions with 2 to 3 short sub - parts. Internal choice is provided in one of these sub-parts.

37. Read the following case/passage and answer the questions.

    A carbon atom attached to one, two, three and four other carbon atoms is called primary, secondary, tertiary and quaternary carbon respectively. Now consider following compound and answer the following questions.

    $$\overset{F}{CH_3}-\overset{E}{CH_2}-\overset{D}{CH_2}-\overset{\overset{\displaystyle CH_3}{|}}{\underset{\underset{\displaystyle CH_3}{|}}{\overset{C}{C}}}-\overset{B}{\underset{\underset{\displaystyle CH_3}{|}}{CH}}-\overset{A}{CH_3}$$

    (a) What is the IUPAC name of the compound.
    (b) What is valency of carbon atom? Draw the electron dot structure of methane.
    (c) How many carbon stoms are primary, secondary, tertiary and quarternary carbon.

    OR

    (i) What is the formula and electron dot structure of butane?
    (ii) What do you understand by functional group?

38. Read the following case/passage and answer the questions.
   While conducting experiments to study the effect of various stimuli on the plants, it was observed that the roots of a plant X grow and bend towards two stimuli A and B but bend away from a third stimulus C. The stem of the plant X, however, bends away and from stimuli A and B but bends towards the stimulus C. The stimulus B is known to act on the roots due to too much weight of the earth. Keeping these points in mind, answer the following questions.
   (i) What could stimulus A be?
   (ii) Name the stimulus B.
   (iii) What could stimulus C be?
   (iv) The branches of a fallen tree in a forest grow straight up in response to two stimuli. What could be these two stimuli out of A, B and C? Also name these two stimuli.

39. Read the following case/passage and answer the questions.
   When the electric current is passed through a conductor then conductor gets heated, this effect is known as the heating effect of current. As current flows through a conductor, the free electrons lose energy which is converted into heat. When an electric charge Q moves against a potential difference V, the amount of work done (W) is given by $W = Q \times V$

   According to Ohm's law, $R = \dfrac{V}{I}$

   or potential difference, $V = I \times R$
   Now, substituting the values
   $W = I \times t \times I \times R$
   $H = I^2 \times R \times t$
   (a) A heater coil is cut into two equal parts and only one part is used in the heater. Find the heat generated.
   (b) What happens to the heat produced when current is doubled?
   (c) Name two devices which work on heating effect of electric current.

   OR

   (c) An electric iron of resistance 20 Ω takes a current of 5A. Calculate the heat developed in 30 sec.

5 Sample Paper
LATEST PATTERN

BLUE PRINT

S. No.	Chapter Name	Section-A (MCQs & A/R) 1 Mark Q. No.	Section-B (VSAQs) 2 Marks Q. No.	Section-C (SAQs) 3 Marks Q. No.	Section-D (LAQs) 5 Marks Q. No.	Section-E (Case Study) 4 Marks Q. No.	Total Marks
1	Chemical Reactions and Equations	3(Q2,7,17)			1(Q34)		8
2	Acids, Bases and Salts	1(Q4)	1(Q21)			1(Q37)	7
3	Metals and Non-metals	1(Q3)	1(Q21 OR)	1(Q27)			4
4	Carbon and its Compounds	3(Q1,5,6)		1(Q28)			6
5	Life Processes	1(Q9)	1(Q22)			1(Q39)	7
6	Control and Co-ordination	1(Q10)	1(Q23)	1(Q29)			6
7	How do Organism Reproduce	1(Q11)	1(Q26)		1(Q35)		8
8	Heredity and Evolution	2(Q12,19)	1(Q24)				4
9	Light- Reflection and Refraction	3(Q13,15,18)		2(Q31,32)			9
10	Human Eye and Colourful World	1(Q14)	1(Q25)				3
11	Electricity	1(Q16)				1(Q38)	5
12	Magnetic Effects of Electric Current			1(Q33)	1(Q36)		8
13	Our Environment	2(Q8,20)		1(Q30)			5
	* Total Questions (Total Marks)	20(20)	6(12)	7(21)	3(15)	3(12)	80

* The number given outside the bracket denotes number of questions asked in the sample paper, while the number given inside the bracket denotes marks.

Time Allowed : 3 Hours
Max. Marks : 80

General Instructions

1. This question paper consists of 39 questions in 5 sections.
2. All questions are compulsory. However, an internal choice is provided in some questions. A student is expected to attempt only one of these questions.
3. **Section A** consists of 20 objective type questions carrying 1 mark each.
4. **Section B** consists of 6 Very Short questions carrying 02 marks each. Answers to these questions should in the range of 30 to 50 words.
5. **Section C** consists of 7 Short Answer type questions carrying 03 marks each. Answers to these questions should in the range of 50 to 80 words
6. **Section D** consists of 3 Long Answer type questions carrying 05 marks each. Answer to these questions should be in the range of 80 to 120 words.
7. **Section E** consists of 3 source-based/case-based units of assessment of 04 marks each with sub-parts.

SECTION-A

Select and write one most appropriate option out of the four options given for each of the Questions 1 to 20

1. The functional group represent alcohol is –
    (a) –OH (b) –CHO (c) –COOH (d) >C=O
2. The following reaction is an example of a
    $4NH_3(g) + 5O_2(g) \longrightarrow 4NO(g) + 6H_2O(g)$
    1. displacement reaction
    2. combination reaction
    3. redox reaction
    4. neutralisation reaction
    (a) 1 and 4 (b) 2 and 3 (c) 1 and 3 (d) 3 and 4
3. Which of the following are not ionic compounds?
    (i) KCl (ii) HCl (iii) CCl_4 (iv) NaCl
    (a) (i) and (ii) (b) (ii) and (iii) (c) (iii) and (iv) (d) (i) and (iii)
4. Which of the following acid does not react with metals?
    (a) sulphuric acid (b) phosphoric acid
    (c) carbonic acid (d) nitric acid
5. Methane, ethane and propane are said to form a homologous series because all are –
    (a) hydrocarbons
    (b) saturated compounds
    (c) aliphatic compounds
    (d) differ from each other by a CH_2 group
6. Which of the following options is false about a soap?
    (a) The soap solution in water is neutral and can be used to wash all kinds of fabrics.
    (b) Soap forms lather only in soft water.
    (c) Soap is a metallic salt of higher fatty acids.
    (d) Soap cannot be used in slightly acidic medium.
7. Which of the following are exothermic processes?
    1. Reaction of water with quick lime
    2. Dilution of an acid
    3. Evaporation of water
    4. Sublimation of camphor (crystals)
    (a) 1 and 2 (b) 2 and 3 (c) 1 and 4 (d) 3 and 4
8. In the given food chain, suppose the amount of energy at fourth trophic level is 5 kJ, what will be the energy available at the producer level?
    Grass → Grasshopper → Frog → Snake → Hawk
    (a) 5 kJ (b) 50 kJ (c) 500 kJ (d) 5000 kJ

9. Photosynthesis in an aquatic plant was measured by counting the number of O_2 bubbles coming out of the cut end of the plant. What will happen to O_2 production if you use a pipe to blow air from your mouth into water in the beaker?

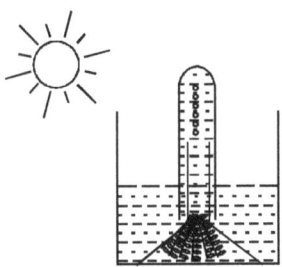

   (a) Air from mouth contains O_2 which is being added to the plant. Hence increase in O_2 production.
   (b) Air from mouth contains CO_2 which is utilized in photosynthesis. Hence, increase in O_2 production.
   (c) Bacteria from mouth will infect plant. Hence reduction in O_2 production.
   (d) Water is already in contact with air. Hence air from mouth will have no effect.

10. Electrical impulse travels in a neuron from
    (a) Dendrite → axon → axonal end → cell body
    (b) Cell body → dendrite → axon → axonal end
    (c) Dendrite → cell body → axon → axonal end
    (d) Axonal end → axon → cell body → dendrite

11. The development of offspring from any part of body is called
    (a) Asexual reproduction
    (b) Sexual reproduction
    (c) Vegetative reproduction
    (d) All the above

12. Which of the following is a dominant character according to Mendel?
    (a) Dwarf plant and yellow fruit
    (b) Terminal fruit and wrinkled seed
    (c) White testa and yellow pericarp
    (d) Green coloured pod and rounded seed

13. An object is placed 20.0 cm in front of a concave mirror whose focal length is 25.0 cm. What is the magnification of the object?
    (a) +5.0
    (b) −5.0
    (c) +0.20
    (d) −0.20

14. The reason for using red light in traffic signals to stop vehicles.
    (a) Red light has shorter wavelength
    (b) Red light has longer wavelength
    (c) Red light is very bright and attractive
    (d) Red light has highest angle of refraction

15. Where should an object be placed in front of a convex lens to get a real image of the size of the object?
    (a) At the principal focus of the lens
    (b) At twice the focal length
    (c) At infinity
    (d) Between the optical centre of the lens and its principal focus.

16. A cylindrical conductor of length l and uniform area of cross-section A has resistance R. Another conductor of length $2l$ and resistance R of the same material has area of cross-section.
    (a) $A/2$
    (b) $3A/2$
    (c) $2A$
    (d) $3A$

Directions: Q.No. 17–20 are Assertion - Reasoning based questions: These consist of two statements – Assertion (A) and Reason (R). Answer these questions selecting the appropriate option given below:
(a) Both A and R are true and R is the correct explanation of A
(b) Both A and R are true and R is not the correct explanation of A
(c) A is true but R is false
(d) A is False but R is true

17. **Assertion :** Decomposition of vegetable matter into compost is an endothermic reaction.
    Reason : Heat is required in an endothermic reaction.

18. **Assertion:** A point object is placed at a distance of 26 cm from a convex mirror of focal length 26 cm. The image will not form at infinity.
    Reason: For above given system, the equation $\frac{1}{u}+\frac{1}{v}=\frac{1}{f}$ gives $v = \infty$.

19. **Assertion:** The principal of segregation given by Mendel is the principle of purity of gametes.
    Reason: Gametes are pure for a character and do not mix up.
20. **Assertion:** Lichens are bio-indicators of air pollution.
    Reason: They do not grow in Delhi.

SECTION-B

Q. no. 21 to 26 are Very Short Answer Questions.

21. pH of a solution changes from 4 to 3 what changes in hydrogen ion concentration do you expect?

OR

Metals replace hydrogen from acid, whereas non-metals do not. Why?

22. The inner lining of the small intestine has numerous finger like projections. What are they called? List their functions.
23. Name the hormone which regulates carbohydrates, protein and fat metabolism in our body. Which gland secretes this hormone? Why is it important for us to have iodised salt in out diet?
24. Give Mendel's First Law of Heredity.
25. A person suffering from long sightedness cannot see objects before 1.5 m distinctly. Suggest a lens with proper focal length and power for his remedy. Assume the near point of the normal eye to be 25 cm.

OR

Make a diagram to show how hypermetropia is corrected

26. Mention the two functions of human testes.

SECTION-C

Q.no. 27 to 33 are Short Answer Questions.

27. A non-metal A is an important constituent of our food and forms two oxides B and C. Oxide B is toxic whereas C causes global warming. Identify A, B and C.
28. Write the IUPAC names of the following:

    (i) $CH_3 - \underset{\underset{OH}{|}}{CH} - COOH$

    (ii) $CH_3COOCH_2CH_3$

    (iii) $CH_3CH_2 - \underset{\underset{OH}{|}}{CH} - CH_2OH$

29. Give one example of following plants:
    (a) Which is (i) positively phototropic and (ii) negatively geotropic.
    (b) Which is positively hydrotropic as well as positively geotropic?
    (c) Which synthesises auxin?
30. You have been selected to talk on " ozone layer and its protection" in the school assembly on 'Environment Day'.
    (i) Why should ozone layer be protected to save the environment?
    (ii) List any two ways that you would stress in your talk to bring in awareness amongst your fellow friends that would also help in protection of ozone layer as well as the environment.
31. A student wants to project the image of a candle flame on a screen 48 cm in front of a mirror by keeping the flame at a distance of 12 cm from its pole.
    (i) Suggest the type of mirror he should use.
    (ii) Find the linear magnification of the image produced.
    (iii) How far is the image from its object?
    (iv) Draw ray diagram to show the image formation in this case.
32. An object of height 4.0 cm is placed at a distance of 30 cm from the optical centre 'O' of a convex lens of focal length 20 cm. Draw a ray diagram to find the position and size of the image formed. Mark optical centre 'O' and principal focus 'F' on the diagram. Also find the approximate ratio of size of the image to the size of the object.

33. Derive the relation for equivalent resitance when three resistances are connected in parallel.

OR

(i) Explain three applications of heating effect of electricity.

(ii) A shop is fitted with five 40W fans and four 100W bulbs. Find the cost of using the fans for 10 hrs a day and the bulbs for 6 hrs each day for 25 days at 30p per unit of electrical energy.

SECTION-D

Q.no. 34 to 36 are Long Answer Questions.

34. What happens when a solution of Na_2CO_3 is mixed with a solution of $CaCl_2$? Support your answer with the help of total ionic and net ionic equation.

OR

Balance the following equations.

(a) $CaCO_3 \xrightarrow{\Delta} CaO + CO_2$
(b) $Na + O_2 \longrightarrow Na_2O$
(c) $H_2O_2 \longrightarrow H_2O + O_2$
(d) $Al + H_3PO_4 \longrightarrow AlPO_4 + H_2$
(e) $Ca(OH)_2 + HCl \longrightarrow CaCl_2 + H_2O$
(f) $Mg + N_2 \longrightarrow Mg_3N_2$
(g) $C_2H_6 + O_2 \longrightarrow CO_2 + H_2O$
(h) $Mg_3N_2 + H_2O \longrightarrow Mg(OH)_2 + NH_3$
(i) $H_2S + O_2 \longrightarrow S + H_2O$
(j) $BF_3 + NaH \longrightarrow B_2H_6 + NaF$

35. (i) Identify the process depicted in the picture given below:

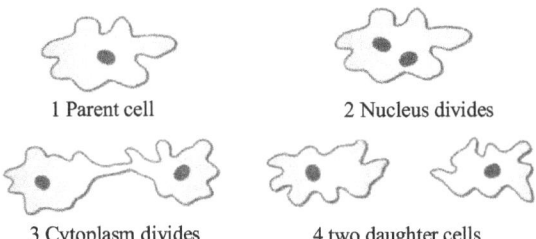

1 Parent cell   2 Nucleus divides

3 Cytoplasm divides   4 two daughter cells

(a) Name the organism that divide by the above process.
(b) Compare the above process with multiple fission.
(c) State the type of reproduction in the above process and define it.

(ii) Differentiate between fission in *Amoeba* and *Leishmania*.

36. A student was asked to perform an experiment to study the force on a current carrying conductor in a magnetic field. He took a small aluminum rod AB, a strong horse shoe magnet, some connecting wires, a battery and a switch and connected them as shown. He observed that on passing current, the rod gets displaced. On reversing the direction of current, the direction of displacement also gets reversed. On the basis of your understanding of this phenomenon, answer the following questions :

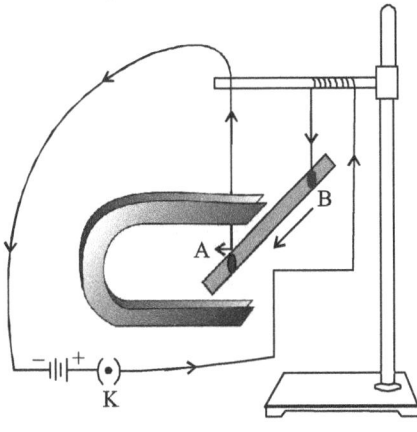

(a) Why does the rod get displaced on passing current through it ?
(b) State the rule that determines the direction of the force on the conductor AB.
(c) (i) In the above experimented set up, when current is passed through the rod, it gets displaced towards the left. What will happen to the displacement if the polarity of the magnet and the direction of current both are reversed ?
   (ii) Name any two devices that use current carrying conductors and magnetic field.

OR

Draw the pattern of magnetic field lines produced around a current carrying straight conductor held vertically on a horizontal cardboard. Indicate the direction of the field lines as well as the direction of current flowing through the conductor.

SECTION-E

Q.no. 37 to 39 are case - based/data -based questions with 2 to 3 short sub - parts. Internal choice is provided in one of these sub-parts.

37. Read the following case/passage and answer the questions.

The strength of a base depends on the concentration of the hydroxyl ions present in a solution. Greater the number of hydroxyl ion present, greater is the strength of base. However, some bases do not dissociate to any appreciable extent in water, e.g. NH_4OH. Some bases dissolve in water to form alkali. Examples of such bases are sodium hydroxide and potassium hydroxide. The acidity of bases is the number of hydroxyl ions that the basic molecule can produce in the aqueous solution.

(a) What are the characterstic features of bases? Mention at leas two
(b) Explain the strength of basicity

OR

Give examples of two diacidic bases. What is the conjugate acid of $\overset{\ominus}{N}H_2$?

38. Read the following case/passage and answer the questions.

We define the electric current, or simply the current, to be the net amount of charges or electrons passing per unit time across any section through a conductor. If the charges are positive, the current is assumed to flow in the direction of charges and if the charges are negative, the current is in a direction opposite to the charges.

If ΔQ is the amount of charge that passes through a particular area in a time interval Δt, the average current, I_{av}, is equal to the ratio of the charge to the time interval.

i.e., $I_{av} = \dfrac{\Delta Q}{\Delta t}$

(a) What does an electric circuit means?
(b) Define the unit of current.
(c) Calculate the number of electrons constituting one coulomb of charge.

OR

(c) What is meant by saying that the potential difference between two points is 1 V?

39. Read the following case/passage and answer the questions.

Heterotrophic nutrition is a type of nutrition in which organisms obtain that food from other sources. Such type of the organisms that depend upon outside sources for their food are called as heterotrophs.

Heterotrophic nutrition is classified as saprophytic, holozoic and parasitic nutrition.

(i) Give an example of parasite.
(ii) Define heterotrophic made of nutrition.
(iii) Mention any organism which exhibit saprotrophic mode of nutrition.
(iv) Which type of organisms are capable of converting carbon dioxide into sugar?

6 Sample Paper
LATEST PATTERN

BLUE PRINT

S. No.	Chapter Name	Section-A (MCQs & A/R) 1 Mark Q. No.	Section-B (VSAQs) 2 Marks Q. No.	Section-C (SAQs) 3 Marks Q. No.	Section-D (LAQs) 5 Marks Q. No.	Section-E (Case Study) 4 Marks Q. No.	Total Marks
1	Chemical Reactions and Equations	1(Q4)		1(Q27)		1(Q37)	8
2	Acids, Bases and Salts	3(Q3,6,17)	1(Q21)				5
3	Metals and Non-metals	1(Q1)			1(Q34)		6
4	Carbon and its Compounds	3(Q2,5,7)	1(Q21 OR)	1(Q28)			6
5	Life Processes	2(Q8,13)	1(Q22)			1(Q38)	8
6	Control and Co-ordination	1(Q19)	1(Q25)				3
7	How do Organism Reproduce	2(Q16,20)	1(Q26)	1(Q31)			7
8	Heredity and Evolution	2(Q14,15)	1(Q24)	1(Q33)			7
9	Light- Reflection and Refraction	2(Q10,12)		1(Q32)			5
10	Human Eye and Colourful World			1(Q29)		1(Q39)	7
11	Electricity	3(Q9,11,18)	1(Q23)	1(Q30)			8
12	Magnetic Effects of Electric Current				1(Q35)		5
13	Our Environment				1(Q36)		5
	* Total Questions (Total Marks)	20(20)	6(12)	7(21)	3(15)	3(12)	80

* The number given outside the bracket denotes number of questions asked in the sample paper, while the number given inside the bracket denotes marks.

Sc-32 **SCIENCE-X**

Time Allowed : 3 Hours   Max. Marks : 80

General Instructions

1. This question paper consists of 39 questions in 5 sections.
2. All questions are compulsory. However, an internal choice is provided in some questions. A student is expected to attempt only one of these questions.
3. **Section A** consists of 20 objective type questions carrying 1 mark each.
4. **Section B** consists of 6 Very Short Answer type questions carrying 02 marks each. Answers to these questions should in the range of 30 to 50 words.
5. **Section C** consists of 7 Short Answer type questions carrying 03 marks each. Answers to these questions should in the range of 50 to 80 words
6. **Section D** consists of 3 Long Answer type questions carrying 05 marks each. Answer to these questions should be in the range of 80 to 120 words.
7. **Section E** consists of 3 source-based/case-based units of assessment of 04 marks each with sub-parts.

SECTION-A

Select and write one most appropriate option out of the four options given for each of the Questions 1 to 20

1. The ability of metals to be drawn into thin wire is known as
    (a) ductility (b) malleability (c) sonorousity (d) conductivity
2. Which of the following does not belong to the same homologous series?
    (a) CH_4 (b) C_2H_6 (c) C_3H_8 (d) C_4H_8
3. Which of the following statement is true for acids?
    (a) Bitter and change red litmus to blue
    (b) Sour and change red litmus to blue
    (c) Sour and change blue litmus to red
    (d) Bitter and change blue litmus to red
4. Ferrous sulphate does not produce on heating
    (a) ferric oxide (b) sulphur dioxide
    (c) oxygen (d) water
5. Glacial acetic acid is –
    (a) 100% acetic acid free of water (b) solidified acetic acid
    (c) gaseous acetic acid (d) frozen acetic acid
6. The pH of the gastric juices released during digestion is
    (a) less than 7 (b) more than 7 (c) equal to 7 (d) equal to 0
7. When methane is burnt in an excess of air, the products of combustion are –
    (a) C and H_2O (b) CO and H_2O (c) CO_2 and H_2 (d) CO_2 and H_2O
8. Which one of the following conditions is true for the state of stomata of a green leaf shown in the given diagram?

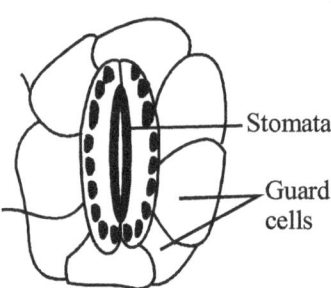

(a) Large amount of water flows into the guard cells.
(b) Gaseous exchange is occurring in large amount.
(c) Large amount of water flows out from the guard cells.
(d) Large amount of sugar collects in the guard cells.

9. A 24V potential difference is applied across a parallel combination of four 6 ohm resistor. The current in each resistor is
    (a) 1 A
    (b) 4 A
    (c) 16 A
    (d) 36 A
10. Which of the following lenses would you prefer to use while reading small letters found in a dictionary?
    (a) A convex lens of focal length 50 cm
    (b) A concave lens of focal length 50 cm
    (c) A convex lens of focal length 5 cm
    (d) A concave lens of focal length 5 cm
11. The filament of an electric bulb is of tungsten because
    (a) Its resistance is negligible
    (b) It is cheaper
    (c) Its melting point is high
    (d) Filament is easily made
12. Focal length of a lens is 25 cm. In dioptre, power of lens will be
    (a) 0.04
    (b) 0.4
    (c) 4
    (d) 2.5
13. Identify the two components of Phloem tissue that help in transportation of food in plants
    (a) Phloem parenchyma & sieve tubes
    (b) Sieve tubes & companion cells
    (c) Phloem parenchyma & companion cells
    (d) Phloem fibres and sieve tubes
14. A complete set of chromosomes inherited as a unit from one parent, is known as
    (a) Karyotype
    (b) Gene pool
    (c) Genome
    (d) Genotype
15. Mendel's law of segregation is based on separation of alleles during
    (a) gametes formation
    (b) seed formation
    (c) pollination
    (d) embryonic development
16. Puberty in males comes between or is at.
    (a) 10 - 14 years
    (b) 12 - 15 years
    (c) 13 - 16 years
    (d) 14 years

Directions: Q.No. 17–20 are Assertion - Reasoning based questions: These consist of two statements – Assertion (A) and Reason (R). Answer these questions selecting the appropriate option given below:
(a) Both A and R are true and R is the correct explanation of A
(b) Both A and R are true and R is not the correct explanation of A
(c) A is true but R is false
(d) A is False but R is true

17. **Assertion :** H_3PO_4 and H_2SO_4 are known as polybasic acids.
    Reason : They have two or more than two protons per molecule of the acid.
18. **Assertion:** Resistance of a copper wire of length 1 metre and area of cross-section 1 mm^2 is same as the resistance of an aluminium wire of length 1 metre and area of cross-section of 1 mm^2.
    Reason: Resistance of a metallic conductor depends on the nature of the material of the conductor.
19. **Assertion:** Suppression of growth of axillary buds is called apical dominance.
    Reason: It is due to effect of downward movement of auxin from apical region towards the lower side.
20. **Assertion:** The cardiac muscular walls of ventricle are thicker than auricles.
    Reason: This help to prevent the backflow of the blood into chamber.

SECTION-B

Q. no. 21 to 26 are Very Short Answer Questions.

21. Name the products formed from chlor-alkali process.

OR

Write the molecular formula of first two members of homologous series having functional group - Cl.

22. What is the importance of transpiration?
23. Define electric current. Name the particles that constitute electric current flowing through the metallic wires.

OR

Show four different ways in which three resistors of 'r' ohm each may be connected in a circuit. In which case is the equivalent resistance of the combination:
   (i) Maximum
   (ii) Minimum
24. Differentiate between phototropism and geotropism?
25. Give an example of a plant hormone that (i) promotes growth (ii) inhibits growth
26. Name the reproductive parts of an angiosperm. Where are these parts located? Explain the structure of its male reproductive part.

OR

What is puberty? Mention any two changes that are common to both boys and girls in early teenage years.

SECTION-C

Q.no. 27 to 33 are Short Answer Questions.

27. Define the term decomposition reaction. Give one example each of thermal decomposition and electrolytic decomposition.
28. Give the molecular formula of one homologues of each of the following:
   (a) C_6H_{14}
   (b) C_3H_6
   (c) C_4H_8
29. (a) With the help of labelled ray diagram show the path followed by a narrow beam of monochromatic light when it passes through a glass prism.
    (b) What would happen if this beam is replaced by a narrow beam of white light?
30. V–I graph for a conductor is as shown in figure.

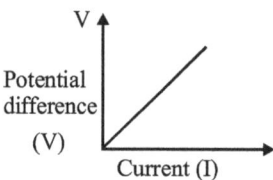

   (i) What do you infer from this graph?
   (ii) State the law expressed here.
   (iii) Name the physical quantity represented by the slope of this graph and state its SI unit.

OR

In the given circuit, calculate:

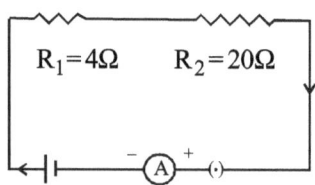

   (i) the total resistance of the circuit
   (ii) the current through the circuit, and
   (iii) the potential difference across R_1 and R_2
31. Explain the process of regeneration in planaria. How is this process different from reproduction?

32. Draw the following diagram, in which a ray of light is incident on a concave/convex mirror, on your answer sheet. Show the path of this ray, after reflection, in each case.

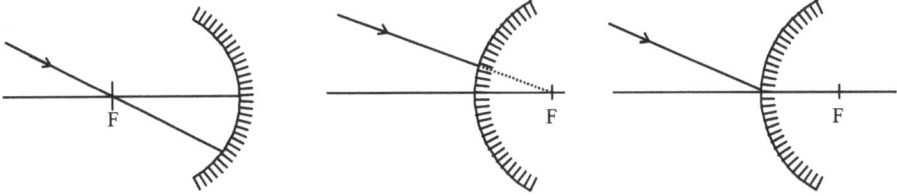

33. A green stemmed tomato plant denoted by (GG) is crossed with a tomato plant with purple stem denoted by (gg).
    (i) What colour of the stem would you expect in their F1 progeny?
    (ii) In what ratio would you find the green and purple coloured stem in plants of F2 progeny?
    (iii) What conclusion can be drawn for the above observations?

SECTION-D

Q.no. 34 to 36 are Long Answer Questions.

34. (a) Give reasons for the following:
    (i) Metals are regarded as electropositive elements.
    (ii) Articles made of aluminium do not corrode even though aluminium is an active metal.
    (b) On placing a piece of zinc metal in a solution of mercuric chloride it acquires a shining silvery surface but when it is placed in a solution of magnesium sulphate no change is observed. Give reason.

OR

(a) When a metal X is treated with cold water, it gives a basic salt Y with molecular formula XOH (molecular mass = 40) and liberates a gas Z which easily catches fire. Identify X, Y and Z and also write the reaction involved.
(b) Which two metals do not corrode easily? Give an example in each case to support that:
    (i) Corrosion of some metals is an advantage.
    (ii) Corrosion of some metals is a serious problem.

35. (i) What is meant by the terms alternating current and direct current?
    (ii) Name a source of alternating current and a source of direct current.
    (iii) Mention the frequency of AC supply in India.
    (iv) State two important advantages of alternating current over direct current.

36. What is the meaning of the effect of energy in an ecosystem? Explain with example how energy is lost at the various energy levels.

SECTION-E

Q.no. 37 to 39 are case - based/data -based questions with 2 to 3 short sub - parts. Internal choice is provided in one of these sub-parts.

37. Read the following case/passage and answer the questions.

Chemistry in Automobiles:

For an internal combustion engine to move a vehicle down the road, it must convert the energy stored in the fuel into mechanical energy to drive the wheels. In your car, the distributor and battery provide this starting energy by creating an electrical "spark", which helps in combustion of fuels like gasoline. Below is the reaction depicting complete combustion of gasoline in full supply of air:

$2C_8H_{18}(l) + 25O_2(g) \longrightarrow 16\ 'X' + Y$

(a) What are 'X' and 'Y'? What types of chemical reaction occuring during the combustion of fuel?
(b) What is the reason of inactivity of nitrogen in combustion reaction although it is the most abundant gas in the atmosphere?

OR

(b) What happens when combustion of fuel happens in limited air supply?

38. Read the following case/passage and answer the questions.

The heart is a tough operating mechanism which moves blood around the body through a very advanced system called arteries and capillaries, the blood is then carried back to the heard by means of veins. Blood pressure is the thrust of this blood in the body pushing up against the inside wall of the arteries as the heart is pumping.

(i) What is responsible for generating blood pressure?
(ii) What is the normal Blood pressure range?
(iii) What happens when the decrease in blood volume is greater that 10%?
(iv) Draw the graphs that best describe the blood pressure (Bp) change when blood moves from aorta to capillaries?

39. Read the following case/passage and answer the questions.

When a ray of light enters the eye, it is refracted at the cornea. This refraction produces a real inverted and diminished image of distant objects on the retina. When the object is kept at different distances then, we may expect the image to be formed at different distances from the lens. It means, it may not form on the retina always. When eye loses its ability to adjust its focal length, person is unable to view nearby or far away objects.

(a) A person having a myopic eye uses a concave lens of focal length 50 cm. What is the power of the lens ?
(b) A person having the nearest distance of distinct vision of 32 cm uses a reading lens of 8 cm focal length. What is the magnification of his reading lens ?
(c) What is the far point and near point of the human eye with normal vision ?

OR

(c) The far point of a myopic person is 80 cm in front of the eye. What is the nature and power of the lens required to correct the problem ?

7. Sample Paper

LATEST PATTERN

BLUE PRINT

S. No.	Chapter Name	Section-A (MCQs & A/R) 1 Mark Q. No.	Section-B (VSAQs) 2 Marks Q. No.	Section-C (SAQs) 3 Marks Q. No.	Section-D (LAQs) 5 Marks Q. No.	Section-E (Case Study) 4 Marks Q. No.	Total Marks
1	Chemical Reactions and Equations	1(Q17)	1(Q21)		1(Q34)		8
2	Acids, Bases and Salts	2(Q1,2)	1(Q21 OR)			1(Q37)	6
3	Metals and Non-metals	3(Q3,4,5)		1(Q27)			6
4	Carbon and its Compounds	2(Q6,7)		1(Q28)			5
5	Life Processes	2(Q8,13)		1(Q30)			5
6	Control and Co-ordination	2(Q14,19)	1(Q22)		1(Q36)		9
7	How do Organism Reproduce	1(Q15)	1(Q23)				3
8	Heredity and Evolution	2(Q16,20)	1(Q26)			1(Q38)	8
9	Light- Reflection and Refraction			1(Q32)			3
10	Human Eye and Colourful World	2(Q9,11)	1(Q24)		1(Q35)		9
11	Electricity	2(Q10,12)				1(Q39)	6
12	Magnetic Effects of Electric Current	1(Q18)		2(Q29, 31)			7
13	Our Environment		1(Q25)	1(Q33)			5
	Total Questions (Total Marks)	20(20)	6(12)	7(21)	3(15)	3(12)	80

* The number given outside the bracket denotes number of questions asked in the sample paper, while the number given inside the bracket denotes marks.

Time Allowed : 3 Hours
Max. Marks : 80

General Instructions

1. This question paper consists of 39 questions in 5 sections.
2. All questions are compulsory. However, an internal choice is provided in some questions. A student is expected to attempt only one of these questions.
3. **Section A** consists of 20 objective type questions carrying 1 mark each.
4. **Section B** consists of 6 Very Short Answer type questions carrying 02 marks each. Answers to these questions should in the range of 30 to 50 words.
5. **Section C** consists of 7 Short Answer type questions carrying 03 marks each. Answers to these questions should in the range of 50 to 80 words
6. **Section D** consists of 3 Long Answer type questions carrying 05 marks each. Answer to these questions should be in the range of 80 to 120 words.
7. **Section E** consists of 3 source-based/case-based units of assessment of 04 marks each with sub-parts.

SECTION-A

Select and write one most appropriate option out of the four options given for each of the Questions 1 to 20

1. Which salt can be classified as an acid salt?
   (a) Na_2SO_4 (b) BiOCl (c) Pb(OH)Cl (d) Na_2HPO_4
2. Plaster of Paris hardens by –
   (a) giving of CO_2 (b) changing into $CaCO_3$ (c) combining with water (d) giving out water
3. Generally, non-metals are not conductors of electricity. Which of the following is a good conductor of electricity?
   (a) Diamond (b) Graphite (c) Sulphur (d) Fullerene
4. The electronic configurations of three elements X, Y and Z are X- 2, 8; Y - 2, 8, 7 and Z - 2, 8, 2. Which of the following is correct?
   (a) X is a metal
   (b) Y is a metal
   (c) Z is a non-metal
   (d) Y is a non-metal and Z is a metal
5. The correct order of increasing chemical reactivity is –
   (a) Zn < Fe < Mg < K
   (b) Fe < Mg < Zn < K
   (c) Fe < Mg < K < Zn
   (d) Fe < Zn < Mg < K
6. What does isomerism explain?
   (a) A difference in molecular formulae.
   (b) A difference in molecular weights.
   (c) A difference in chemical properties and structural formulae.
   (d) A difference in molecular composition.
7. Which of the following options is false about a soap?
   (a) The soap solution in water is neutral and can be used to wash all kinds of fabrics.
   (b) Soap forms lather only in soft water.
   (c) Soap is a metallic salt of higher fatty acids.
   (d) Soap cannot be used in slightly acidic medium.
8. The correct order of processes that occur in urine formation is
   (a) glomerular filtration → secretion → reabsorption
   (b) secretion → glomerular filtration → reabsorption
   (c) glomerular filtration → reabsorption → secretion
   (d) secretion → reabsorption → glomerular filtration
9. Which of the following statements is **not true** for scattering of light?
   (a) Colour of the scattered light depends on the size of particles of the atmosphere.
   (b) Red light is least scattered in the atmosphere.
   (c) Scattering of light takes place as various colours of white light travel with different speed in air.
   (d) The fine particles in the atmospheric air scatter the blue light more strongly than red. So the scattered blue light enters our eyes.
10. The length of a wire is doubled and the radius is doubled. By what factor does the resistance change
    (a) 4 times as large (b) twice as large (c) unchanged (d) half as large

Sample Paper-7

11. A person got his eyes tested. The optician's prescription for the spectacles reads:
    Left eye : – 3.00 D   Right eye : – 3.50 D
    The person is having a defect of vision called :
    (a) presbyopia   (b) myopia   (c) astigmatism   (d) hypermetropia
12. Device used to measure electric current is:
    (a) Ammeter   (b) Voltmeter   (c) Galvanometer   (d) Generator
13. Consider the following statements in connection with the functions of the blood vessels marked A and B in the diagram of a human heart as shown.

    (i) Blood vessel A – It carries carbon dioxide rich blood to the lungs.
    (ii) Blood vessel B – It carries oxygen rich blood from the lungs.
    (iii) Blood vessel B – Left atrium relaxes as it receives blood from this blood vessel.
    (iv) Blood vessel A – Right atrium has thick muscular wall as it has to pump blood to this blood vessel.
    This correct statements are
    (a) (i) and (ii) only   (b) (ii) and (iii) only   (c) (ii), (iii) and (iv)   (d) (i), (ii) and (iii)
14. Artificial ripening of fruits is carried out by
    (a) Auxin   (b) Gibberellin   (c) Abscisic acid   (d) Ethylene
15. Which out of the following processes does not lead to the formation of clones
    (a) Fertilisation   (b) Fasion   (c) Tissue culture   (d) Fragmentation
16. If a homozygous red-flowered plant is crossed with a homozygous white-flowered plant, the offspring would be
    (a) Half red-flowered   (b) Half white-flowered   (c) All red-flowered   (d) Half pink-flowered

Directions: Q.No. 17–20 are Assertion - Reasoning based questions: These consist of two statements – Assertion (A) and Reason (R). Answer these questions selecting the appropriate option given below:
(a) Both A and R are true and R is the correct explanation of A
(b) Both A and R are true and R is not the correct explanation of A
(c) A is true but R is false
(d) A is False but R is true

17. **Assertion:** A reducing agent is a substance which can either accept electron.
    Reason: A substance which helps in oxidation is known as reducing agent.
18. **Assertion:** A soft iron far placed inside a solenoid carrying current is magnetised.
    Reason: Magnetic field inside a long solenoid carrying current is non-uniform.
19. **Assertion:** A person has lost most of its intelligence memory and judgement.
    Reason: A person has operated a tumour located in the cerebrum.
20. **Assertion:** Mendel successfully postulated laws of heredity.
    Reason: Mendel recorded and analysed results of breeding experiments quantitatively

SECTION-B

Q. no. 21 to 26 are Very Short Answer Questions.

21. What is the combination reaction ? Give one example of a combination reaction which is also exothermic.
    OR
    Fresh milk has pH of 6. How do you think pH will change as it turns into curd? Explain your answer.
22. Where does cerebro-spinal fluid occur in our body ? Mention any two of its functions.
23. Name the primary sex organs in males and females ?
24. Define angle of deviation. Why do different components of white light split up into spectrum when it passes through a triangular glass prism.
    OR
    Why does the sky appear dark instead of blue to an astronaut ?
25. Give reason why a food chain cannot have more than four trophic levels.
26. Do genetic combination of mothers play a significant role in determining the sex of a new born ?

SECTION-C

Q.no. 27 to 33 are Short Answer Questions.

27. Define Aqua-regia. State two important properties of it.
28. How was petroleum formed?
29. It is necessary to connect an earth wire to electric appliances having metallic covers. Why? How will you identify earth wire in household circuit?
30. What is the role of valves in the human heart?

OR

What is the function of bicuspid and tricuspid valve?

31. A straight conductor passes vertically through a cardboard sprinkled with iron filings. Show the setting of the iron filings when a weak current is passed in the downward direction. What changes occur if,
    (i) the strength of the current is increased.
    (ii) the single conductor is replaced by several parallel conductors with current flowing in the same. direction.
32. A ray of light travelling in air enters obliquely into water. Does the light ray bend towards the normal or away from the normal? Why?

OR

The diagram given below shows an object O and its image I.

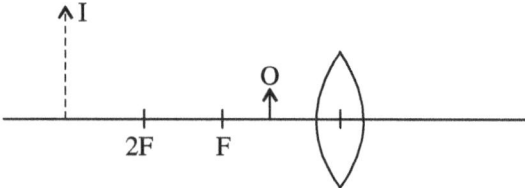

Without actually drawing the ray diagram, state the following :
  (i) Type of lens (Converging/Diverging)
  (ii) Name two optical instruments where such an image is obtained.
  (iii) List three characteristics of the image formed if this lens is replaced by a concave mirror of focal length 'f' and an object is placed at a distance 'f/2' in front of the mirror.

33. In the following food chain, only 2J of energy was available to the peacocks. How much energy would have been present in Grass? Justify your answer.

GRASS → GRASS HOPPER → FROG → SNAKE → PEACOCK

SECTION-D

Q.no. 34 to 36 are Long Answer Questions.

34. Write down balanced chemical reactions for given statements.
    (a) When iron (III) oxide is heated with aluminium powder, then aluminium oxide and iron metal are formed.
    (b) When silver nitrate solution is added to sodium chloride solution, a white precipitate of silver chloride and sodium nitrate solution are formed.
    (c) When chlorine gas react with potassium iodide solution, potassium chloride and iodine are formed.
    (d) When copper oxide is heated with magnesium powder magnesium oxide and copper are formed.
    (e) When a copper strip is placed in a solution of silver nitrate, then copper nitrate solution and silver metal are formed.

OR

(a) $Si_2H_6 + H_2O \longrightarrow Si(OH)_4 + H_2$
(b) $C_2H_6 + Cl_2 \longrightarrow C_2H_5Cl + HCl$
(c) $B_4H_{10} + O_2 \longrightarrow B_2O_3 + H_2O$
(d) $H_2 + N_2 \longrightarrow NH_3$
(e) $CS_2 + O_2 \longrightarrow CO_2 + SO_2$
(f) $N_2O_5 \longrightarrow N_2O_4 + O_2$
(g) $KNO_3 \longrightarrow KNO_2 + O_2$
(h) $NH_4NO_3 \longrightarrow N_2O + H_2O$
(i) $NH_4NO_2 \longrightarrow N_2 + H_2O$
(j) $NaHCO_3 \longrightarrow Na_2CO_3 + H_2O + CO_2$

35. (a) A person is suffering from both myopia and hypermetropia.
    (i) What kind of lenses can correct this defect?
    (ii) How are these lenses prepared?
    (b) A person needs a lens of power +3D for correcting his near vision and –3D for correcting his distant vision. Calculate the focal lengths of the lenses required to correct these defects.

36. (a) What are 'hormones'?
(b) List four characteristics of hormones.
(c) Name the hormone required for the following:
   (i) Functioning of mammary glands.
   (ii) Regulation of calcium and phosphate in blood.
   (iii) Lowering of blood glucose.
   (iv) Development of moustache and beard in human male.

SECTION-E

Q.no. 37 to 39 are case - based/data -based questions with 2 to 3 short sub - parts. Internal choice is provided in one of these sub-parts.

37. Read the following case/passage and answer the questions.

Baking Soda is also defined as Sodium Bicarbonate. The Medieval Egyptians first quarried Natron, a natural deposit which mainly consists of Na_2CO_3. They used it as soap. In the year 1971, $NaHCO_3$ was first manufactured by a ***French chemist named Nicolas Leblanc***. It was in the year 1846, John Dwight and Austin Church started a manufacturing unit to produce baking soda using sodium carbonate and carbon dioxide. Solvay process is used for the production of sodium bicarbonate and sodium carbonate industrially. This process is used mainly because it is inexpensive and less number of raw materials are used to produce necessary chemicals. Sodium bicarbonate is widely used in kitchen and in the various household work mainly because of its versatility, usefulness and its cheap price.

(a) What are the raw materials used in the preparation of sodium bicarbonate?
(b) During indigestion, the stomach produces too much acid which can cause pain and irritation. In such cases what are the compounds can be used as antacids?

OR

(b) What are the components of backing powder? Mention the use of sodium bicarbonate.

38. Read the following case/passage and answer the questions.

The way in which traits are passed from one generation to the next and sometimes skip generations was first explained by gregor Mendel. By experimenting with pea plant breeding, Mendel developed three principles of inheritance that described the transmission of genetic trait, before anyone know genes existed. Mendel's insight greatly expanded the understanding of genetic inheritance and led to the development of new experimental methods.

(i) Assuring that both parent plants in the diagram below are homozygous, why would all of the F1 generation have yellow phenotype?

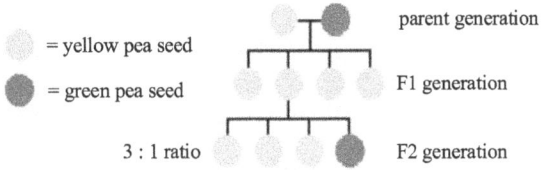

(ii) How did Mendel's studies in genetics differ from earlier studies of breeding and inheritance?
(iii) In a plant, red fruit (R) is dominant over yellow fruit (r) and tallness (T) is dominant over shortness (t). If a plant with RR Tt genotype is crossed with a plant that is rrtt.
(iv) Select the correct match

Cross	Progeny
A. RRYY × RRYY (Round yellow)	Round, yellow only (Round yellow)
B. RrYy × RrYy (Round, yellow)	Round yellow and (Round, yellow) round green only
C. rryy × rryy (wrinkled, green) (wrinkled, green)	Wrinkled, yellow only
D. RRYY × rryy (Round, yellow)	Round green only (Wrinkled, green)

39. Read the following case/passage and answer the questions.

In many practical applications to have desired value of resistance two or more resistances are required to be combined. This can be done in two ways : in series and in parallel. Sometimes resistances are to be combined in such a way that some resistances be in series and some in parallel. Such a combination is called mixed grouping. If, in an electrical circuit, two or more resistances connected between two points are replaced by a single resistance such that there is no change in the current of the circuit and in the potential difference between those two points, then the single resistance is called the 'equivalent resistance'. When the resistance of a circuit is to be increased, they are combined in series and when heavy current is to be passed, they are combined in parallel so as to decrease the total resistance.

(a) Two resistances of X ohm and Y ohm are connected. In which case the resultant resistance will be
  (i) more than X and Y   (ii) less than X and Y?
(b) Why we connect a large number of electric bulbs for decorating buildings as during festivals such as Diwali or marriage function in series circuit not in parallel circuit?
(c) What are the advantages of connecting electrical devices in parallel with the battery instead of connecting them in series ?

OR

How can three resistors of resistances 2 Ω, 3 Ω and 6 Ω be connected to give a total resistance of
  (i) 4 Ω,   (ii) 1 Ω

Sample Paper 8

LATEST PATTERN

BLUE PRINT

S. No.	Chapter Name	Section-A (MCQs & A/R) 1 Mark Q. No.	Section-B (VSAQs) 2 Marks Q. No.	Section-C (SAQs) 3 Marks Q. No.	Section-D (LAQs) 5 Marks Q. No.	Section-E (Case Study) 4 Marks Q. No.	Total Marks
1	Chemical Reactions and Equations	3(Q1,6,7)	1(Q21 OR)	1(Q27)			6
2	Acids, Bases and Salts	1(Q2)			1(Q34)		6
3	Metals and Non-metals	2(Q3,17)	1(Q21)			1(Q37)	8
4	Carbon and its Compounds	2(Q4,5)		1(Q28)			5
5	Life Processes	1(Q20)	1(Q22)			1(Q38)	7
6	Control and Co-ordination	1(Q16)	1(Q25)	1(Q33)			6
7	How do Organism Reproduce	2(Q13,18)			1(Q36)		7
8	Heredity and Evolution	1(Q14)	2(Q23,26)				5
9	Light- Reflection and Refraction			1(Q29)		1(Q39)	7
10	Human Eye and Colourful World	3(Q8,10,19)	1(Q24)				5
11	Electricity	1(Q11)		2(Q30,32)			7
12	Magnetic Effects of Electric Current	1(Q15)			1(Q35)		6
13	Our Environment	2(9,12)		1(Q31)			5
	Total Questions (Total Marks)	20(20)	6(12)	7(21)	3(15)	3(12)	80

* The number given outside the bracket denotes number of questions asked in the sample paper, while the number given inside the bracket denotes marks.

SCIENCE-X

Time Allowed : 3 Hours
Max. Marks : 80

General Instructions

1. This question paper consists of 39 questions in 5 sections.
2. All questions are compulsory. However, an internal choice is provided in some questions. A student is expected to attempt only one of these questions.
3. **Section A** consists of 20 objective type questions carrying 1 mark each.
4. **Section B** consists of 6 Very Short Answer type questions carrying 02 marks each. Answers to these questions should in the range of 30 to 50 words.
5. **Section C** consists of 7 Short Answer type questions carrying 03 marks each. Answers to these questions should in the range of 50 to 80 words
6. **Section D** consists of 3 Long Answer type questions carrying 05 marks each. Answer to these questions should be in the range of 80 to 120 words.
7. **Section E** consists of 3 source-based/case-based units of assessment of 04 marks each with sub-parts.

SECTION-A

Select and write one most appropriate option out of the four options given for each of the Questions 1 to 20

1. Which of the following statements is incorrect?
   (a) A chemical equation tells us about the substances involved in a reaction.
   (b) A chemical equation informs us about the symbols and formula of substances involved in a reaction.
   (c) A chemical equation tells us about the atom or molecules of the reactants and products involved in a reaction.
   (d) A chemical equation does not represents energy changes during a reaction.

2. Common salt besides being used in kitchen can also be used as the raw material for making
   (i) washing soda
   (ii) bleaching powder
   (iii) baking soda
   (iv) slaked lime
   (a) (i) and (ii)
   (b) (i), (ii) and (iv)
   (c) (i), (ii) and (iii)
   (d) (i), (iii) and (iv)

3. An element A is soft and can be cut with a knife. This is very reactive to air and cannot be kept open in air. It reacts vigorously with water. Identify the element from the following
   (a) Mg
   (b) Na
   (c) P
   (d) Ca

4. Which of the following are isomers?
   (a) Butane and isobutene
   (b) Ethane and ethene
   (c) Propane and propyne
   (d) Butane and isobutane

5. Which of the following statements is not correct?
   (a) Graphite is much less dense than diamond
   (b) Graphite is black and soft
   (c) Graphite has low melting point
   (d) Graphite feels smooth and slippery

6. A student added dilute HCl to a test tube containing zinc granules and made following observations which one is correct?
   (a) The zinc surface became dull and black.
   (b) A gas evolved which burns with a pop sound.
   (c) The solution remained colourless.
   (d) The solution becomes green in colour.

7. Electrolysis of water is a decomposition reaction. The mole ratio of hydrogen and oxygen gases liberated during electrolysis of water is
   (a) 1 : 1
   (b) 2 : 1
   (c) 4 : 1
   (d) 1 : 2

8. In the diagram given below, X and Y are the end colours of the spectrum of white light. The colour of 'Y' represents the

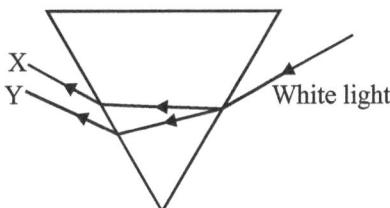

   (a) Colour of sky as seen from earth during the day.
   (b) Colour of the sky as seen from the moon.
   (c) Colour used to paint the danger signals.
   (d) Colour of sun at the time of noon.
9. Which of the following is an result of biological magnification:
   (a) Top level predators may be harmed by toxic chemicals in environment.
   (b) Increase in carbon dioxide
   (c) The green-house effect will be most significance at the poles
   (d) Energy is lost at each trophic level of a food chain
10. The sky appears dark to passengers flying at very high altitudes mainly because :
    (a) Scatterings of light is not enough at such heights.
    (b) There is no atmosphere at great heights.
    (c) The size of molecules is smaller than the wavelength of visible light.
    (d) The light gets scattered towards the earth.
11. What should be the characteristic of fuse wire?
    (a) High melting point, high specific resistance
    (b) Low melting point, low specific resistance
    (c) High melting point, low specific resistance
    (d) Low melting point, high specific resistance
12. UV rays cause cancer but in stratosphere the same UV rays are helping us, how?
    (a) They divert harmful UV rays back to sun.
    (b) They convert oxygen in stratosphere into ozone.
    (c) UV rays are not present in stratosphere.
    (d) UV rays reach the earth surface then bounce back carrying ozone to stratosphere.
13. What is not common among these between sperm and ova?
    (a) Both have nucleus
    (b) Both are produced in germ cells
    (c) Both have 21 chromosomes
    (d) Both have mitochondria
14. Sex determination in humans is due to the presence of:
    (a) Presence of X-chromosome in female
    (b) Presence of only Y-chromosome in male
    (c) Formation of two types of eggs by female
    (d) Formation of two types of spems by male
15. At the time of short circuit, the current in the circuit
    (a) reduces substantially.
    (b) does not change.
    (c) increases heavily.
    (d) very continuously.
16. Parasympathetic nervous system increases the activity of:
    (a) Gut, iris and urinary bladder
    (b) Heart, adrenal and sweat gland
    (c) Heart, pancreas and lachrymal gland
    (d) Lachrymal gland and sweat gland

Directions: Q.No. 17–20 are **Assertion - Reasoning based questions:** These consist of two statements – Assertion (A) and Reason (R). Answer these questions selecting the appropriate option given below:
(a) Both A and R are true and R is the correct explanation of A
(b) Both A and R are true and R is not the correct explanation of A
(c) A is true but R is false
(d) A is False but R is true

17. **Assertion:** Electric wires are made up of copper.
    Reason: Non-metals are bad conductor of electricity.
18. **Assertion:** Male urethra is also called urinogenital duct.
    Reason: The male urethra carrier urine and sperms.
19. **Assertion:** When a ray of light passes through a prism, it bends towards the thicker part of the prism.
    Reason: An incident ray strikes a prism, undergoes refraction and comes out as an emergent ray.
20. **Assertion:** Glomerulus acts as a dialysis bag.
    Reason: Bowman's capsule is found in heart.

SECTION-B
Q. no. 21 to 26 are Very Short Answer Questions.

21. What is metallic lustre?

OR

What is the role of oxidation to reduction reaction in living creatures?

22. Name the main organs of the human digestive system in the order they participate in the process of digestion. Describe how digestion of carbohydrates take place in our body.

OR

(a) Where does digestion of fat take place in our body?
(b) How is small intestine designed to absorb digested food?

23. How do Mendel's experiments show that traits may be dominant or recessive ?
24. A man who wears glasses of power 3 dioptre must hold a newspaper at least 25 cm away to see the print clearly. How far away would the newspaper have to be if he took off the glasses and still wanted clear vision?

OR

How can we determine the focal length and power of the concave lens required to correct a myopic eye?

25. Define neuron. Name the parts of neuron where:
    (i) Information is acquired.
    (ii) Impulse must be converted into chemical signal for onwards transmission.
26. If a trait A exists in 10% of a population of an asexually reproducing species and a trait B exists in 60% of the same population, which trait is likely to have arisen earlier ?

SECTION-C
Q.no. 27 to 33 are Short Answer Questions.

27. Give one example of each with their chemical and molecular formulae:
    (a) Carbonate salt   (b) Chloride salt
    (c) Copper salt   (d) Sodium salt
    (e) Nitrate salt   (f) Sulphate salt
28. (a) Ethane, Ethene, Ethanoic acid, Ethyne, Ethanol
    From the list of compound given above, name:
    (i) The compound with – OH as a part of its structure.
    (ii) The compound with – COOH as a part of its structure.
    (iii) Homologues and Homologous series with general formula C_nH_{2n}.

(b) Write the IUPAC names of the following:
  (i) $CH_3 - \underset{\underset{CH_3}{|}}{CH} - COOH$
  (ii) $CH_3COOCH_2CH_3$
  (iii) $CH_3CH_2 - \underset{\underset{OH}{|}}{CH} - CH_2OH$

29. If the image formed by a lens for all position of an object placed in front of it is always erect and diminished, what is the nature of this lens? Draw a ray diagram to justify your answer. It the numerical value of the power of this lens of 10 D, what is its focal length in the Cartesian system?

30. (i) Establish the relation between kilowatt-hour and joules.
    (ii) A 2000 W of electric geyser is used every day for 1 hour. How many units of electrical energy will it consume in 30 days?

31. What is the reason that a food chain consists of only 3-5 steps?

32. State the factors on which resistance of a conductor depends.

OR

A torch bulb is rated 5V and 500 mA. Calculate its (i) power, (ii) resistance, (iii) energy consumed when it is lighted for 4 hours.

33. (a) Write the names and more one function of each of three growth hormones in plants.
    (b) In the absence of muscle cells, how do plant cells show movement?

SECTION-D

Q.no. 34 to 36 are Long Answer Questions.

34. (a) A metal carbonate X on reacting with an acid gives a gas which when passed through a solution Y gives the carbonate back. On the other hand, a gas G that is obtained at anode during electrolysis of brine is passed on dry Y, it gives a compound Z, used for disinfecting drinking water. Identity X, Y, G and Z.
    (b) Write the chemical formula of plaster of paris.

OR

(a) What will be the action of the following substances on litmus paper?
Dry HCl gas, moistened NH_3 gas, lemon juice, carbonated soft drink, curd, soap solution.
(b) A milkman adds a very small amount of baking soda to fresh milk.
   (i) Why does he shift the pH of the fresh milk from 6 to slightly alkaline?
   (ii) Why does this milk take a long time to set as curd?

35. What are magnetic field lines? List three characteristics of these lines. Describe in brief an activity to study the magnetic field lines due to a current flowing in a circular coil.

36. (i) Name the organ that produces sperms as well a secretes a hormone in human males. Name the hormone it secretes and write its functions.
    (ii) Name the parts of the human female reproductive system where fertilisation occurs.
    (ii) Explain how the developing embryo gets nourishment inside the mother's body.

SECTION-E

Q.no. 37 to 39 are case - based/data -based questions with 2 to 3 short sub - parts. Internal choice is provided in one of these sub-parts.

37. Read the following case/passage and answer the questions.
    The huge annual loss due to corrosion is a national waste and should be minimized.
    Following are some methods which are helpful to prevent corrosion
    (i) Coating the iron surface with paint or oil or grease prevents moist oxygen from coming in contact with the metal and thus effectively prevents rusting of iron.
    (ii) Galvanisation : Iron is blasted with fine sand to make the surface rough dipped in molten zinc and then cooled. A thin layer of zinc forms on the iron surface. Since zinc is more reactive than iron, it acts as a sacrificial metal and is preferentially oxidised thus preventing oxidation of iron.
    (iii) Electroplating with tin, nickel or chromium also prevents rusting.
    (iv) Alloying (mixing iron in its molten state with other metals) prevents rusting. Stainless steel is an alloy of iron with Cr or Ni.
    (a) What is corrosion ?
    (b) How do we present corrosion ?

OR

(b) (i) How do we protect the bottom of ship made of iron ?

(ii) What is the most durable metal plating on iron to protect against corrosion ?

38. Read the following case/passage and answer the questions.

A star-shaped figure was cut in the black paper strip used for covering the leaf of a destarched plant used for demonstrating that light is necessary for photosynthesis. At the end of the experiment when the leaf was tested for starch with iodine, the star shaped figure on the leaf was found to be blue-black in colour.

(i) When iodine was added to a particular vegetable, which has been crushed into a paste, blue-black colour was obtained. What it indicates ?

(ii) Write the combination of relevant materials required for setting up an experiment to show that light is necessary for photosynthesis?

(iii) In order to destarch the leaves for an experiment to show that sunlight is necessary for photosynthesis, the _____.

(iv) In the experiment to prove that light is necessary for photosynthesis, which substance is required?

39. Read the following case/passage and answer the questions.

The bending of the light ray from its path in passing from one medium to the other medium is called refraction of light. If the refracted ray bends towards the normal relative to the incident ray (Passing obliquely), then the second medium is said to be denser than the first medium. But if the refracted ray bends away from the normal, then the second medium is said to be rarer than the first medium. If a ray of light passing normally i.e., at right angles from one medium to another optical medium then it does not bend or deviate from its path. Refraction of light takes place due to change in the speed of light as it enters from one medium to another medium.

(a) Refractive indices of benzene and kerosene oil are 1.5 and 1.4 respectively. Which is optically denser?

(b) What do you understand by optically denser and optically rarer medium?

(c) Explain laws of refraction of light.

OR

(c) Light enters from air to glass having refractive index 1.50. What is the speed of light in the glass ? The speed of light in vaccum is 3×10^8 m / sec.

Sample Paper 9
LATEST PATTERN

BLUE PRINT

S. No.	Chapter Name	Section-A (MCQs & A/R) 1 Mark Q. No.	Section-B (VSAQs) 2 Marks Q. No.	Section-C (SAQs) 3 Marks Q. No.	Section-D (LAQs) 5 Marks Q. No.	Section-E (Case Study) 4 Marks Q. No.	Total Marks
1	Chemical Reactions and Equations	2(Q2,3)		1(Q33)			5
2	Acids, Bases and Salts	2(Q1,17)	1(Q21)	1(Q28)			5
3	Metals and Non-metals	1(Q5)	1(Q21 OR)		1(Q36)		8
4	Carbon and its Compounds	3(Q4,6,7)				1(Q38)	7
5	Life Processes	2(Q12,20)	1(Q22)		1(Q34)		9
6	Control and Co-ordination	1(Q13)				1(Q37)	7
7	How do Organism Reproduce	2(Q14,16)		1(Q30)			5
8	Heredity and Evolution	2(Q15,19)	1(Q25)				4
9	Light- Reflection and Refraction	1(Q10)		1(Q31)		1(Q39)	8
10	Human Eye and Colourful World	1(Q8)		1(Q29)			4
11	Electricity	1(Q9)	1(Q24)		1(Q35)		8
12	Magnetic Effects of Electric Current	2(Q11,18)		1(Q27)			5
13	Our Environment		1(Q23)	1(Q32)			5
	Total Questions (Total Marks)	20(20)	6(12)	7(21)	3(15)	3(12)	80

* The number given outside the bracket denotes number of questions asked in the sample paper, while the number given inside the bracket denotes marks.

Time Allowed : 3 Hours **Max. Marks : 80**

General Instructions

1. This question paper consists of 39 questions in 5 sections.
2. All questions are compulsory. However, an internal choice is provided in some questions. A student is expected to attempt only one of these questions.
3. **Section A** consists of 20 objective type questions carrying 1 mark each.
4. **Section B** consists of 6 Very Short Answer type questions carrying 02 marks each. Answers to these questions should in the range of 30 to 50 words.
5. **Section C** consists of 7 Short Answer type questions carrying 03 marks each. Answers to these questions should in the range of 50 to 80 words
6. **Section D** consists of 3 Long Answer type questions carrying 05 marks each. Answer to these questions should be in the range of 80 to 120 words.
7. **Section E** consists of 3 source-based/case-based units of assessment of 04 marks each with sub-parts.

SECTION-A

Select and write one most appropriate option out of the four options given for each of the Questions 1 to 20

1. During the preparation of hydrogen chloride gas on a humid day, the gas is usually passed through the guard tube containing calcium chloride. The role of calcium chloride taken in the guard tube is to
   (a) absorb the evolved gas
   (b) moisten the gas
   (c) absorb moisture from the gas
   (d) absorb Cl^- ions from the evolved gas

2. Lead nitrate on decomposition gives-
   (a) lead oxide   (b) nitrogen dioxide   (c) oxygen   (d) All of these

3. Which one of the following processes involve chemical reactions?
   (a) Storing of oxygen gas under pressure in a gas cylinder
   (b) Liquefaction of air
   (c) Keeping petrol in a China dish in the open
   (d) Heating copper wire in the presence of air at high temperature.

4. Observe the following pairs of organic compounds :
   (i) C_4H_9OH and $C_5H_{11}OH$
   (ii) $C_7H_{15}OH$ and $C_5H_{11}OH$
   (iii) $C_6H_{13}OH$ and C_3H_7OH
   Which of these pair is a homologous series according to increasing order of carbon atom?
   (a) (iii) only   (b) (ii) only   (c) (i) only   (d) All of these

5. The composition of aqua-regia is
   (a) Dil.HCl : Conc. HNO_3
       3 : 1
   (b) Conc.HCl : Dil. HNO_3
       3 : 1
   (c) Conc.HCl : Conc.HNO_3
       3 : 1
   (d) Dil.HCl : Dil.HNO_3
       3 : 1

6. Carbon exists in the atmosphere in the form of :
   (a) carbon monoxide only.
   (b) carbon monoxide in traces, and carbon dioxide.
   (c) carbon dioxide only.
   (d) coal

7. 'Drinking alcohol' is very harmful and it ruins the health. 'Drinking alcohol' stands for –
   (a) drinking methyl alcohol
   (b) drinking ethyl alcohol
   (c) drinking propyl alcohol
   (d) drinking isopropyl alcohol

8. A student sitting on the last bench in the class cannot read the writing on the blackboard clearly but he can read the book lying on his desk clearly. Which of the following statement is correct about the student?
   (a) The near point of his eyes has receded away.
   (b) The near point of his eyes has come closer to him.
   (c) The far point of his eyes has receded away.
   (d) The far point of his eyes has come closer to him.
9. 20 coulomb charge is flowing in 0.5 second from a point in an electric circuit then value of electric current in amperes will be
   (a) 10   (b) 40   (c) 0.005   (d) 0.05
10. If the speed of light in medium 1 and medium 2 are 2.5×10^8 ms^{-1} and 2×10^8 ms^{-1}, respectively, then the refractive index of medium 1 with respect to medium 2 is _____.
    (a) $\dfrac{3}{2.5}$ (b) $\dfrac{2}{2.5}$ (c) $\dfrac{2.5}{3}$ (d) $\dfrac{2.5}{2}$
11. The strength of magnetic field inside a long current carrying straight solenoid is
    (a) more at the ends than at the centre   (b) minimum in the middle
    (c) same at all points   (d) found to increase from one end to the other
12. The normal systolic and diastolic pressure is about
    (a) 120 mmHg and 80 mmHg   (b) 80 mmHg and 90 mmHg
    (c) 90 mmHg and 120 mmHg   (d) 120 mmHg and 90 mmHg
13. What is the correct direction of flow of electrical impulses?
    (a)    (b)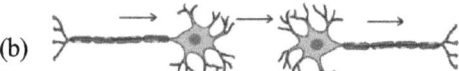
    (c) 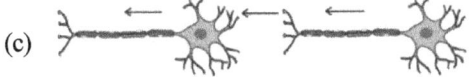   (d)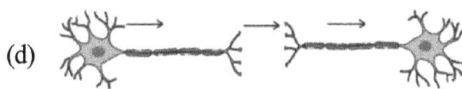
14. Offspring formed by asexual method of reproduction have greater similarity among themselves because
    (i) asexual reproduction involves only one parent
    (ii) asexual reproduction does not involve gametes
    (iii) asexual reproduction occurs before sexual reproduction
    (iv) asexual reproduction occurs after sexual reproduction
    (a) (i) and (ii)   (b) (i) and (iii)   (c) (ii) and (iv)   (d) (iii) and (iv)
15. State which law is shown in the given figure

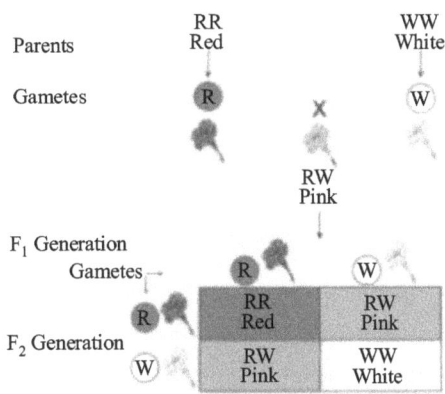

    (a) Law of dominance   (b) Crossing over
    (c) Law of independent assortment   (d) None of these

16. Refer to given below diagram and choose the correct option

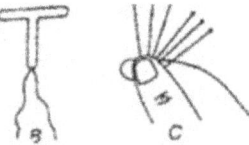

(a) A - copper T - Bimplants
(b) A - Jubectomy, B - implants
(c) A - Vaseclomy, B - Tubestomy
(d) A - copper T, B - Tempons

Directions: Q.No. 17–20 are Assertion - Reasoning based questions: These consist of two statements – Assertion (A) and Reason (R). Answer these questions selecting the appropriate option given below:
(a) Both A and R are true and R is the correct explanation of A
(b) Both A and R are true and R is not the correct explanation of A
(c) A is true but R is false
(d) A is False but R is true

17. **Assertion :** After white washing the walls, a shine white finish on walls is obtained after two to three days.
    Reason : Calcium Oxide reacts with Carbon dioxide to form Calcium Hydrogen Carbonate which gives shiny white finish.
18. **Assertion :** Force experienced by moving charge will be maximum if direction of velocity of charge is perpendicular to applied magnetic field.
    Reason : Force on moving charge is independent of direction of applied magnetic field.
19. **Assertion:** The flower colour of sweet pea shows the inheritance of complementary genes.
    Reason: The ratio obtained for complementary gene is 9 : 7.
20. **Assertion:** Fishes use gills, whereas reptiles, birds and mammals respire through lungs.
    Reason: Amphibians like frogs can respire through their moist skin also.

SECTION-B
Q. no. 21 to 26 are Very Short Answer Questions.

21. Name the gas which is liberated when an acid reacts with a metal. Illustrate with an example. How will you test the presence of this gas?

OR

State reason for the following :
(i) Non-metals cannot displace hydrogen from the acids.
(ii) Hydrogen is not a metal, yet it is placed in the activity series of metals.
22. Why is sino-atrial node also called pace maker ?
23. Accumulation of harmful chemicals in our bodies can be avoided. Explain how this can be achieved?
24. Show how would you join three resistors, each of resistance 9 Ω so that the equivalent resistance of the combination is (i) 13.5 Ω, (ii) 6 Ω?

OR

(a) Write Joule's law of heating.
(b) Two lamps, one rated 100 W; 220 V, and the other 60 W; 220 V, are connected in parallel to electric mains supply. Find the current drawn by two bulbs from the line, if the supply voltage is 220V.
25. Mendel blended his knowledge of Science and mathematics to keep the count of the individuals exhibiting a particular trait in each generation. He observed a number of contrasting visible characters controlled in pea plants in a field. He conducted many experiments to arrive at the laws of inheritance.
    (a) If only one pair of contrasting characters like tall and short plants is taken, plants obtained in F1 generation are not of medium height. Why ?
    (b) Name the recessive traits in above case.
    (c) Mention the type of the new combinations of plants obtained in F_2 progeny along with their ratio, if F_1 progeny was allowed to self pollinate.
26. What are plant hormones? Give two different types of plant hormones and state their function briefly.

SECTION-C

Q.no. 27 to 33 are Short Answer Questions.

27. What is a solenoid? Draw the pattern of magnetic field lines of (i) a current carrying solenoid and (ii) a bar magnet. List two distinguishing features between the two fields.

OR

When does an electric short circuit occur?

28. Differentiate between:
    (a) Strong acid and Weak acid.
    (b) Strong acid and Concentrated acid.

29. State the cause of dispersion of white light by a glass prism. How did Newton, using two identical glass prisms, show that white light is made of seven colours? Draw a ray diagram to show the path of a narrow beam of white light, thought a combination of two identical prisms arranged together in inverted position with respect to each other, when it is allowed to fall obliquely on one of the face of the first prism of the combination.

30. What happens when:
    (i) Accidentaly, *Planaria* gets cut into many pieces?
    (ii) *Bryophyllum* leaf falls on the wet soil?
    (iii) On maturation sporangia of *Rhizopus* bursts?

31. A spherical mirror produces an image of magnification – 1on a screen placed at a distance of 50 cm from the mirror.
    (i) Write the type of mirror.
    (ii) Find the distance of the image from the object.
    (iii) What is the focal length of the mirror?
    (iv) Draw the ray diagram to show the image formation in this case.

32. What is ozone? How and where is it formed in the atmosphere?

33. Give chemical equation to show the changes that occur when green coloured ferrous sulphate crystals are heated.

SECTION-D

Q.no. 34 to 36 are Long Answer Questions.

34. (a) Draw a diagram of excretory system in human beings and label the following parts. Aorta, kidney, urinary bladder and urethra.
    (b) How is urine produced and eliminated?

35. (i) With the help of circuit diagram derive the formula for the equivalent resistance for three resistance connected in series?
    (ii) Three resistors are connected as shown in the following figure. Through the resistor 5 ohm a current of 1 A is flowing.

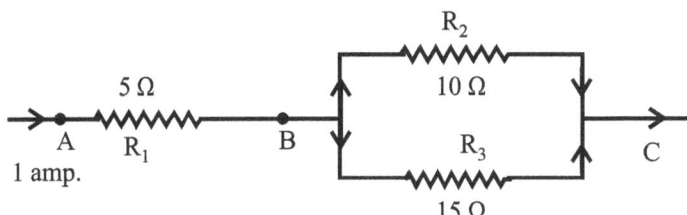

    (a) What is the total resistance?
    (b) What is the potential difference across AB and BC?
    (c) What is the current through other two resistors?

36. What is an alloy? Name the constituents of (a) brass (b) bronze (c) solder. Give one use of each.

OR

(a) Which metals does not stick to glass?
(b) Which metal is commonly used in thermit welding?
(c) What is the nature of zinc oxide?
(d) Will the CO (carbon monoxide) change the colour of blue litmus solution?
(e) What is the nature of phosphorus oxide?

SECTION-E

Q.no. 37 to 39 are case-based/data-based questions with 2 to 3 short sub-parts. Internal choice is provided in one of these sub-parts.

37. Read the following case/passage and answer the questions.

    While conducting experiments to study the effect of various stimuli on the plants, it was observed that the roots of a plant X grow and bend towards two stimuli A and B but bend away from a third stimulus C. The stem of the plant X, however, bends away and from stimuli A and B but bends towards the stimulus C. The stimulus B is known to act on the roots due to too much weight of the earth. Keeping these points in mind, answer the following questions.

    (i) What could stimulus A be?
    (ii) Name the stimulus B.
    (iii) What could stimulus C be?
    (iv) The branches of a fallen tree in a forest grow straight up in response to two stimuli. What could be these two stimuli out of A, B and C? Also name these two stimuli.

    OR

    (i) How does a plant react to stimuli?
    (ii) Why the roots of a plant bend towards stimuli A?

38. Read the following case/passage and answer the questions.

    Reactions in which an atom or a group of atoms is replaced by some other atom or another group of atoms without causing any change in the structure of the remaining part of the molecule, are called substitution reactions.

    All organic compounds containing double or triple bonds give addition reactions, i.e., alkenes, alkynes and aromatic hydrocarbons give addition reactions.

    Reactions in which the compounds react with oxygen and form carbon dioxide and water is known as combustion reaction. This process occurs with release of great amount of heat.

    (a) Define substitution reaction with example.
    (b) Identify the types of reactions:
    (i) $CH_2 = CH_2 + H_2 \rightarrow CH_3 - CH_3$
    (ii) $C_2H_6 + O_2 \rightarrow 2CO_2 + 3H_2O$

    OR

    (b) (i) Combustion reactions are exothermic-comment.
    (ii) Why is the conversion of ethanol to ethanoic acid an oxidation reaction?

39. Read the following case/passage and answer the questions.

    A thin spherical lens with refractive index greater than that of surrounding behaves as a convergent or convex lens i.e. converges parallel rays. Its central (i.e. paraxial) portion is thicker than marginal one. If a number of lenses are placed in close contact with each other, then the power of the combination of lenses is equal to the algebraic sum of the powers of individual lenses.

    (a) What is the importance of optical centre of lens?
    (b) If focal length of a convex lens is 20 cm. Find it's power.
    (c) Power of lens is 4 diopter. Find 'f' in cm and name the lens.

    OR

    (i) Find the power of a concave lens of focal length 2 m.
    (ii) Define 1 dioptre of power of a lens.

10 Sample Paper
LATEST PATTERN

BLUE PRINT

S. No.	Chapter Name	Section-A (MCQs & A/R) 1 Mark Q. No.	Section-B (VSAQs) 2 Marks Q. No.	Section-C (SAQs) 3 Marks Q. No.	Section-D (LAQs) 5 Marks Q. No.	Section-E (Case Study) 4 Marks Q. No.	Total Marks
1	Chemical Reactions and Equations	3(Q1,4,5)	1(Q26)	1(Q28)			8
2	Acids, Bases and Salts	1(Q2)			1(Q36)		6
3	Metals and Non-metals	2(Q3,6)		1(Q33)			5
4	Carbon and its Compounds	2(Q7,20 (A/R))				1(Q38)	6
5	Life Processes	1(Q18)	1(Q21)			1(Q37)	7
6	Control and Co-ordination	1(Q9)	1(Q22)		1(Q35)		8
7	How do Organism Reproduce	1(Q15)	1(Q23)	1(Q32)			6
8	Heredity and Evolution	2(Q12,16)	1(Q24)				4
9	Light- Reflection and Refraction	2(Q 10, 11)	1(Q25)				4
10	Human Eye and Colourful World	2(Q 8,19)		2(Q27,30)			8
11	Electricity				1(Q34)	1(Q39)	9
12	Magnetic Effects of Electric Current	1(Q13)		1(Q29)			4
13	Our Environment	2(Q17,14)		1(Q31)			5
	* Total Questions (Total Marks)	20(20)	6(12)	7(21)	3(15)	3(12)	80

* The number given outside the bracket denotes number of questions asked in the sample paper, while the number given inside the bracket denotes marks.

Sc-56 **SCIENCE-X**

Time Allowed : 3 Hours Max. Marks : 80

General Instructions

1. This question paper consists of 39 questions in 5 sections.
2. All questions are compulsory. However, an internal choice is provided in some questions. A student is expected to attempt only one of these questions.
3. **Section A** consists of 20 objective type questions carrying 1 mark each.
4. **Section B** consists of 6 Very Short Answer type questions carrying 02 marks each. Answers to these questions should in the range of 30 to 50 words.
5. **Section C** consists of 7 Short Answer type questions carrying 03 marks each. Answers to these questions should in the range of 50 to 80 words
6. **Section D** consists of 3 Long Answer type questions carrying 05 marks each. Answer to these questions should be in the range of 80 to 120 words.
7. **Section E** consists of 3 source-based/case-based units of assessment of 04 marks each with sub-parts.

SECTION-A

Select and write one most appropriate option out of the four options given for each of the Questions 1 to 20

1. In the equation, $NaOH + HNO_3 \rightarrow NaNO_3 + H_2O$ nitric acid is acting as –
   (a) an oxidising agent
   (b) an acid
   (c) a nitrating agent
   (d) a dehydrating agent

2. An aqueous solution 'A' turns phenolphthalein solution pink. On addition of an aqueous solution 'B' to 'A', the pink colour disappears. The following statement is true for solution 'A' and 'B'.
   (a) A is strongly basic and B is a weak base.
   (b) A is strongly acidic and B is a weak acid.
   (c) A has pH greater than 7 and B has pH less than 7.
   (d) A has pH less than 7 and B has pH greater than 7.

3. Food cans are coated with tin and not with zinc because
   (a) zinc is costlier than tin
   (b) zinc has higher melting point than tin
   (c) zinc in more reactive than tin
   (d) zinc is less reactive than tin

4. When CO_2 is passed through lime water, it turns milky. The milkiness in due to formation of –

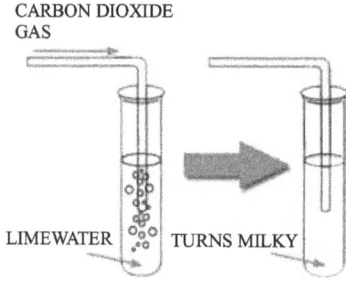

   (a) $CaCO_3$
   (b) $Ca(OH)_2$
   (c) H_2O
   (d) CO_2

5. Identify the endothermic process from the following
   (a) Addition of conc. HCl to water
   (b) $CH_4(g) + 2O_2(g) \longrightarrow CO_2(g) + 2H_2O(l)$
   (c) $H_2O(l) \longrightarrow H_2O(g)$
   (d) $CaO(s) + H_2O(l) \longrightarrow Ca(OH)_2(aq)$

6. An element can react with oxygen to give a compound with high melting point. This compound is also water soluble. The element is likely to be
   (a) Calcium
   (b) Carbon
   (c) Silicon
   (d) Iron

7. Pentane has the molecular formula C_5H_{12}. It has
   (a) 5 covalent bonds
   (b) 12 covalent bonds
   (c) 16 covalent bonds
   (d) 17 covalent bonds

8. The danger signals installed at the top of tall buildings are red in colour. These can be easily seen from a distance because among all other colours, the red light
   (a) is scattered the most by smoke or fog
   (b) is scattered the least by smoke or fog
   (c) is absorbed the most by smoke or fog
   (d) moves fastest in air
9. Which is the correct sequence of the components of a reflex arc?
   (a) Receptors → Muscles → Sensory neuron → Motor neuron → Spinal cord
   (b) Receptors → Motor neuron → Spinal cord → Sensory neuron → Muscle
   (c) Receptors → Spinal cord → Sensory neuron → Motor neuron → Muscle
   (d) Receptors → Sensory neuron → Spinal cord → Motor neuron → Muscle
10. The path of a ray of light coming from air passing through a rectangular glass slab traced by four students shown as A, B, C and D in the figure. Which one of them is correct?

    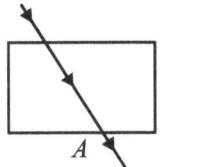 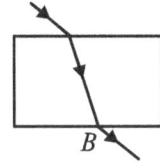 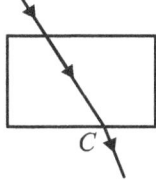 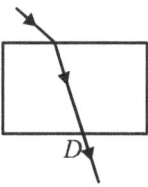

    (a) A (b) B (c) C (d) D
11. A convex mirror is used
    (a) by a dentist
    (b) for shaving
    (c) as a rear view mirror in vehicles
    (d) as a light reflector for obtaining a parallel beam of light.
12. In the experiment conducted by Mendel, RRyy (round green) and rrYY (wrinkled, yellow) seeds of pea plant were used. In the F_2 generation 240 progeny were produced, out of which 15 progeny had specific characteristics. What were the characteristics?
    (a) round and green
    (b) round and yellow
    (c) wrinkle and yellow
    (d) wrinkle and green
13. The magnetic field inside a long straight solenoid-carrying current
    (a) is zero.
    (b) decrease as we move towards its end.
    (c) increases as we move towards its end.
    (d) is the same at all points.
14. The following diagram shows a simple version of energy flow through food web.

    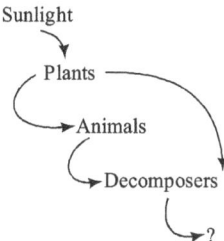

    What happens to energy having the decomposers?
    (a) It is used by the decomposers itself.
    (b) It is reflected from the surface of earth.
    (c) It is lost as heat
    (d) It is used in natural biocomposting

15. The given figure shows the male reproductive system. Some structures are marked as 1, 2, 3 and 4. Identify the structure whose removal will came the sperm to be reacted with acidic urine in the urethra.

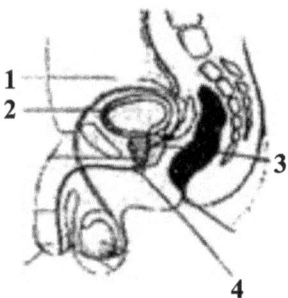

    (a) 1   (b) 2   (c) 3   (d) 4

16. If two parents have the genotypes AA × aa, the probability of having an aa genotype in the F_1 generation is –
    (a) 25 percent
    (b) 50 percent
    (c) 75 percent
    (d) None of the above

Q.No. 17–20 are Assertion - Reasoning based questions: These consist of two statements – Assertion (A) and Reason (R). Answer these questions selecting the appropriate option given below:
(a) Both A and R are true and R is the correct explanation of A
(b) Both A and R are true and R is not the correct explanation of A
(c) A is true but R is false
(d) A is False but R is true

17. **Assertion:** In a greenhouse the glass panel lets the light in but does not allow heat to escape.
    Reason: The greenhouse effect is naturally occuring phenomenon that is responsible for heating of Earth's surface and atmosphere.
18. **Assertion:** Blood of insects is colourless.
    Reason: The blood of insect does not play any role in transport of oxygen.
19. **Assertion:** Clouds are generally white.
    Reason: Larger particles like dust and water drops scatter light of all colours, almost equally and all the colours reach our eyes equally.
20. **Assertion :** The correct IUPAC name for the compound

$$H_3C - \overset{\overset{\displaystyle CH_3}{|}}{CH} - CH_2 - \overset{\overset{\displaystyle CH_3}{|}}{CH} - CH_2 - CH_3$$

is 2, 4 dimethyl hexane not 3, 5 dimethyl hexane

Reason: When the parent chain has two or more substitutents, numbering must be done in such a way that the sum of the locants on the parent chain is the lowest possible.

SECTION-B

Q. no. 21 to 26 are Very Short Answer Questions.

21. What is the importance of transpiration?

OR

What is the role of valves in the human heart?

22. Write the main functions of the following:
    (i) Sensory neuron
    (ii) Cranium
    (iii) Vertebal column
    (iv) Motor neuron.
23. What is STDs (sexually transmitted diseases)? Give some example ?
24. How do Mendel's experiments show that.
    (i) traits may be dominant or recessive?
    (ii) inheritance of two traits is independent of each other?
25. Name the type of mirror used in the following situations:
    (i) Headlights of a car
    (ii) Solar furnace
    Support your answer with reasons.

OR

Mention the kind of lens that can form:
(i) Real, inverted and magnified image
(ii) Virtual, erect and magnified image
(iii) Real, inverted and diminished image
(iv) Virtual, erect and diminished image.

26. Write the chemical involved in the following chemical reactions :
    (i) White washing
    (ii) Black and white photography

OR

Give one difference between covalent and ionic compound. Illustrate your answer with a suitable example?

SECTION-C

Q.no. 27 to 33 are Short Answer Questions.

27. What is meant by scattering of light? The sky appears blue. Explain this phenomena with reason.
28. Mention with reason the colour changes observed when :
    (i) silver chloride is exposed to sunlight.
    (ii) copper powder is strongly heated in the presence of oxygen.
    (iii) a piece of zinc is dropped in copper sulphate solution.
29. Give reasons for the following :
    (i) There is either a convergence or a divergence of magnetic field lines near the ends of a current carrying straight solenoid.
    (ii) The current carrying solenoid when suspended freely rests along a particular direction.
    (iii) The burnt out fuse should be replaced by another fuse of identical rating.

OR

An electric oven of 2 kW power rating is operated in a domestic circuit (220 V) that has a current rating of 5 A. What result do you expect ? Explain.

30. A prism causes dispersion of white light while a rectangular glass block does not. Explain.
31. Explain the fertilization process in human beings in detail?
32. "Energy flow in food chains is always unidirectional". Justify this statement. Explain how the pesticides enter a food chain and subsequently get into our body.
33. A metal 'X' combines with a non-metal 'Y' by the transfer of electrons to form a compound Z.
    (i) State the type of bond in compound Z.
    (ii) What can you say about the melting point and boiling point of compound Z?
    (iii) Will this compound dissolve in kerosene or petrol?
    (iv) Will this compound be a good conductor of electricity?

SECTION-D

Q.no. 34 to 36 are Long Answer Questions.

34. (i) Derive a formula for the equivalent resistance for three resistances connected in parallel?
    (ii) Find the equivalent resistance and total current in the circuit, if the point P and R are connected to a 6V battery.

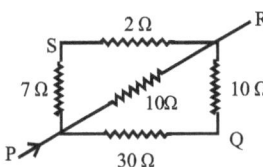

35. (i) Define reflex arc. Draw a flowchart showing the sequence of event which occur during sneezing .
    (ii) List four plant hormones. Write one function of each.
36. (a) Name the properties of baking powder responsible for the following uses:
    (i) Baking industry
    (ii) As an antacid
    (iii) As soda-acid fire extinguisher
    (b) Acid when react with metals release hydrogen gas but there is one acid which when reacts with metals does not release hydrogen except for two metals. Prove this statement.

OR

(a) What do you mean by the family of salts?
(b) Why do HCl, HNO_3, etc., show acidic characters in aqueous solutions while solutions of compounds like alcohol and glucose do not show acidic character?
(c) A weak acid is added to a concentrated solution of hydrochloric acid. Does the solution become more or less acidic?

SECTION-E

Q.no. 37 to 39 are case - based/data -based questions with 2 to 3 short sub - parts. Internal choice is provided in one of these sub-parts.

37. Read the following case/passage and answer the questions.

   Heterotrophic nutrition is a type of nutrition in which organisms obtain that food from other sources. Such type of the organisms that depend upon outside sources for their food are called as heterotrophs.

   Heterotrophic nutrition is classified as saprophytic, holozoic and parasitic nutrition.

   (i) Give two example of parasite.
   (ii) What do you understand by heterotropic nutrition?
   (iii) Give an example of saprotroph.
   (iv) Which mode of nutrition can fix carbon dioxide into sugar?

38. Read the following case/passage and answer the questions.

   The given diagram represent an experiment in which a test tube contains 1 mL of ethanol (absolute alcohol) and 1 mL glacial acetic acid along with a few drops of concentrated H_2SO_4. Observe the diagram and answer the following questions.

   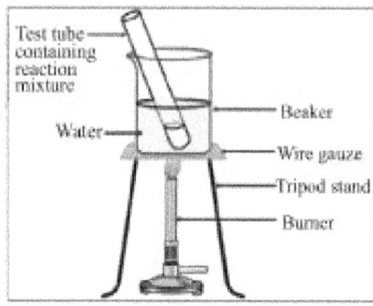

   (a) Name the type of reaction taking place in this experiment.
   (b) Write the chemical equation. Give two uses of the resulting product.
   (c) Why reverse of this reaction is known as saponification reaction?

   OR

   How do detergents/soaps act on cleaning the cloth?

39. Read the following case/passage and answer the questions.

   The heat generated when current passes through a resistive material is used in many common devices. The material through which the current passes is surrounded by an insulating substance in order to prevent the current from flowing through the cook to the earth when he or she touches the pan. Hair dryer, in which a fan blows air past heating coils. In this case the warm air can be used to dry hair, but on a broader scale this same principle is used to dry clothes and to heat buildings. Other practical application includes heater, toaster, electric kettle etc.

   (a) Why are coils of electric toasters and electric irons made of an alloy rather than a pure metal?
   (b) Why does the cord of an electric heater not glow while the heating element does?
   (c) What determines the rate at which energy is delivered by a current?

   OR

   (c) How much current will an electric heater draw from 220 V, if the resistance of the heater is 40Ω?

SOLUTIONS

SAMPLE PAPER-1

1. **(d)** The salt of a weak acid (carbonic acid, H_2CO_3) and a strong base (sodium hydroxide, NaOH) is sodium carbonate (Na_2CO_3).

   $$\underset{\text{Sodium hydroxide}}{2NaOH} + \underset{\text{Carbonic acid}}{H_2CO_3} \longrightarrow \underset{\substack{\text{Sodium Carbonate}\\\text{(Salt)}}}{Na_2CO_3} + \underset{\text{Water}}{2H_2O}$$

2. **(c)**
3. **(a)** dry $Ca(OH)_2$
4. **(b)** Baking powder is a mixture of baking soda $NaHCO_3$, (sodium hydrogen carbonate) and a mild edible acid like tartaric acid.
5. **(d)** Al_2O_3 is an amphoteric oxide, so it can react with both acids and alkalis, e.g.
6. **(b)** Citric acid is an example of organic acid or edible acid while HCl, H_2SO_4 and HNO_3 are mineral acids.
7. **(c)** The name of the compound is 4-ethyl-3-methyl octane.
8. **(d)**
9. **(d)** Only 10% of the energy entering a particular trophic level of organisms is available for transfer to the next higher trophic level according to 10% law. In this food chain, at the 4th trophic level, only 5 kJ energy is available to the snake. Thus, the energy available at the producer level will be 5000 kJ.
10. **(d)** Growth of pollen tube towards ovule is an example of chemotropism.
11. **(c)** Because 'XX' chromosomes comes from mother and 'XY' chromosomes comes from father it means 'XY' chromosomes is responsible for male child.
12. **(b)**
13. **(b)** Magnetic field (B) is produced by moving charge.
14. **(d)** The resistance of a conducting wire doesn't depend upon applied voltage.
15. **(c)** Magnetic fields lines caused by solenoid forms close loop.
16. **(d)** Ohm's law states that the potential difference (voltage) across an ideal conductor is proportional to the current through it.
    V = IR
17. **(b)** Corrosion occurs due to oxidation of iron.
18. **(c)** Assertion is correct but Reason is incorrect.
    Sperm reach the epididymis and stay there for 8-17 days for maturation.
19. **(a)** Both Assertion and Reason are correct and the Reason is a correct explanation of Assertion.
    9 purple and 7 white flowers are obtained in sweet pea (Lathyrus odoratus).
20. **(a)**

21. (a) $2K(s) + 2H_2O(l) \longrightarrow 2KOH(aq) + H_2(g)$ (1 mark)
    (b) Gaseous state (1 mark)

    OR

    (a) Silver ornaments gradually turn black due to the formation of a thin silver sulphite layer on their surface by the action of hydrogen sulphide gas present in air. (1 mark)
    (b) (i) Sodium (ii) Potassium (½ + ½ = 1 mark)

22. (a) Ponds and Lakes are natural ecosystems as they contain decomposers which act as a cleaning agents, whereas an aquarium is an artificial ecosystem, which do not contain decomposers that clean it. Hence It need to be clean periodically.
    (b) Ozone Layer getting depleted at the higher levels of the atmosphere due to effect of chlorofluorocarbons (CFCs).
    Its harmful effect is skin cancer. (1 + 1 marks)

23. Ozone is molecule which contains three atoms of oxygen (O_3). It is highly poisonous gas present on the upper layer of the atmosphere. (1 mark)
    Formation of ozone – The UV radiations split some molecular oxygen (O_2) apart into free oxygen atoms (O + O). These atoms then combine with molecular oxygen to form ozone. (1 mark)

    OR

    $$O_2 \xrightarrow{UV} O + O$$
    $$O + O_2 \longrightarrow \underset{(\text{Ozone})}{O_3}$$ (2 marks)

24. A child inheriting an X chromosome from the father would be a girl (XX) while a child inheriting a Y chromosome from the father would be a boy (XY). Chromosome is the sex of the child & determined by what inherited from father, therefore the probability of having either male or female child is 50%. (1 mark)

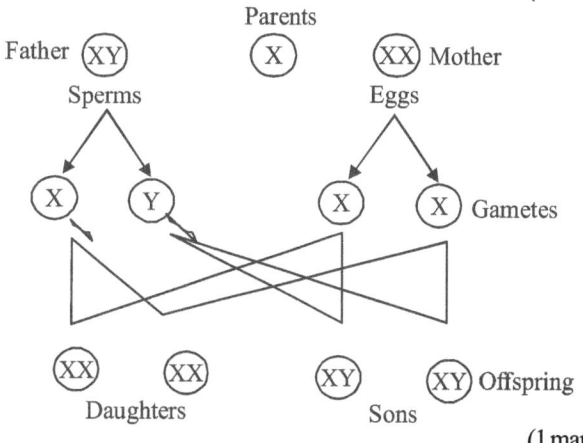

(1 mark)

25. When white light splits into its seven constituent colours (VIBGYOR) on passing through a prism, is known as dispersion of light.

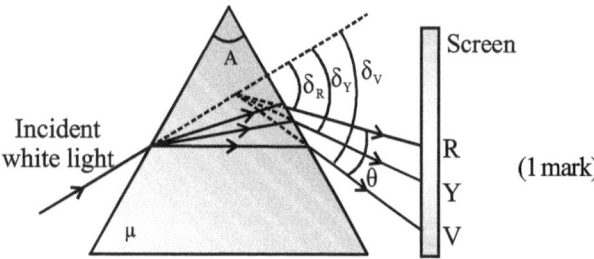

(1 mark)

Refractive index of glass is different for different components of white light. As different colours of light pass through a prism, they bend through different angles with respect to the incident ray.
The red light bends the least while the violet bends the most. Thus, the rays of different colours emerge along different paths and get dispersed. (1 mark)

OR

Hypermetropia is corrected by using convex lens of suitable focal length.
v = –1 m = –100 cm
u = –25 cm
According to lens formula,
$$\frac{1}{v} - \frac{1}{u} = \frac{1}{f}$$ (½ mark)
Near point of a Hypermetropic eye
$$\frac{1}{f} = -\frac{1}{100} - \frac{1}{-25} = -\frac{1}{100} + \frac{1}{25}$$
$$\frac{1}{f} = \frac{-1+4}{100} = \frac{3}{100}$$ (½ mark)
Hypermetropic eye
$$f = \frac{100}{3} cm$$
Power, $P = \frac{1}{f} = \frac{3 \times 100}{100} = 3D$ (½ mark)

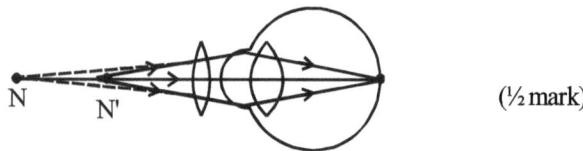

(½ mark)

Correction for Hypermetropic eye

26. (a) Reproductive part of bread mould is sporangium. While non-reproductive part of bread mould is hyphae.
    (b) Advantages of vegetative propagation are:
        (i) Produces identical quality as the parent.

(ii) Plants do not have seed viablities, hence can be reproduce. (1 + 1 marks)

27. (a) The oil and fat containing food when left exposed to air reacts with oxygen and gets oxidised forming a toxic chemical called rancid, this process is called rancidity. The general name of the chemicals that are added to prevent this oxidation are called as antioxidants. For example, Nitrogen gas is anti-oxidant. (1½ marks)
    (b) Metal X is copper. Green compound is due to formation of copper carbonate and black colour compound is due to the formation of copper oxide. (1½ marks)

28. (a)
    (i) $$ZnO + C \longrightarrow Zn + CO$$
    Reduction (removal of oxygen) — above
    Oxidation (addition of oxygen) — below
    Therefore the substance
    Oxidised = C,   Reduced = Zn (1 mark)

    (ii) $$CuO + H_2 \longrightarrow Cu + H_2O$$
    Reduction (removal of oxygen) — above
    Oxidation (addition of oxygen) — below
    Therefore the substance: (1 mark)
    Oxidised = H_2,   Reduced = CuO

    (b) H_2S is the reducing agent while SO_2 is the oxidising agent. (1 mark)

29. (a) A flower is a seed-bearing part of a plant, consisting of reproductive organs (stamens and carpels) that are typically surrounded by a brightly coloured corolla (petals) and a green calyx (sepals). A typical flower consists of following parts:
    (i) **Sepals:** It is the outer whorl of the flower. It is usually green in colour but in some flower it may be coloured to attract insects.
    (ii) **Petals:** It is the second whorl of flower and consists of coloured petals.
    (iii) **Stamen:** It is male reproductive part of a flower. Each stamen consists of a stalk called filament and a flattened top called the anther.
    (iv) **Carpel:** Carpels have a swollen ovary at the base, an alongated middle style and a terminal stigma. The ovary contains ovules. Each ovule possess an egg which is female gamete. (4 × ½ = 2 marks)

(b)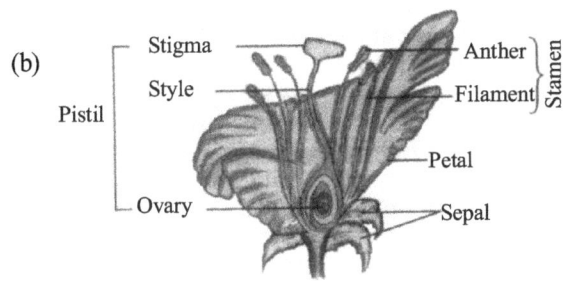

(1 mark)

30. A concave lens always forms a virtual and erect image on the same side of the object.
Image on the same side of the object.
Image distance, $v = ?$
Focal length, $f = -5$ cm
Object distance $u = -10$ cm

$$\frac{1}{f} = \frac{1}{v} - \frac{1}{u}$$

$$\frac{1}{v} = \frac{1}{f} + \frac{1}{u} = \frac{1}{-5} + \frac{1}{-10}$$

$$= \frac{-1-2}{10} = \frac{-3}{10}$$

(1½ marks)

$v = -3.3$ cm

$$\frac{\text{Size of the image}}{\text{Size of the object}} = + \frac{v}{u}$$

$$\frac{h}{6} = \frac{3.3}{10}$$

$$h_1 = \frac{6 \times 3.3}{10} = \frac{19.8}{10} = 1.98 \text{ cm.}$$

(1½ marks)

Size of the image is 1.98 cm.

31. Convex mirror (1 mark)

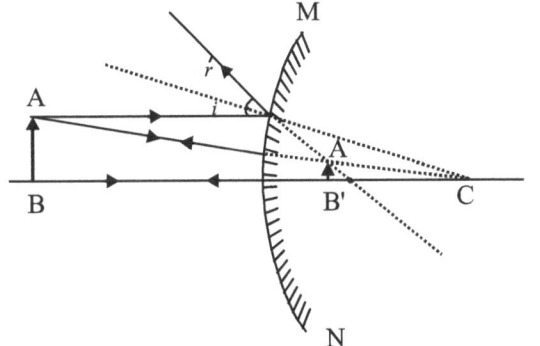

Use: As rear view mirror in vehicles and also in malls, hotels, airports for security reasons because it forms an erect image, and wider field of view. (1 mark)

The type of a mirror is convex mirror.

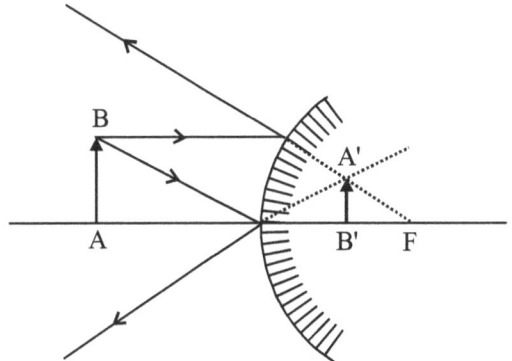

Convex mirror can be used as read&view mirrors in automobiles because it gives a wider field of view as the mirror is curved outward. it produces erect and diminished image of the traffic behind the driver of the vehicle.

(1 mark)

32. The factors on which strength of magnetic field depends:
(a) **Around a straight current carrying conductor**
   (i) Current *i.e.* it is directly propotional to the current flowing through the conductor.
   (ii) Distance from the wire : Strength of magnetic field is inversely proportional to the distance from the wire carrying current. (1½ marks)
(b) **Around a circular coil carrying current**
   (i) Current *i.e.,* it is directly proportional to the current flowing through the conductor.
   (ii) Radius of coil, it is inversely proportional to the radius of coil. (1½ marks)

OR

Fleming's Left Hand Rule: The direction of force which acts on the current carrying conductor placed in a magnetic field is given by Fleming's left hand rule. It states that if the forefinger, thumb and middle finger of left hand are stretched mutually perpendicular and the forefinger point along the direction of external magnetic field, middle finger indicates the direction of current, then thumb indicates along the direction of force acting on the conductor.

(2 marks)

Example: When an electron enters a magnetic field at right angles, the direction of force on electron is perpendicular to the direction of magnetic field and current according to this rule. (1 mark)

33. (a) **Diagram of human alimentary canal**

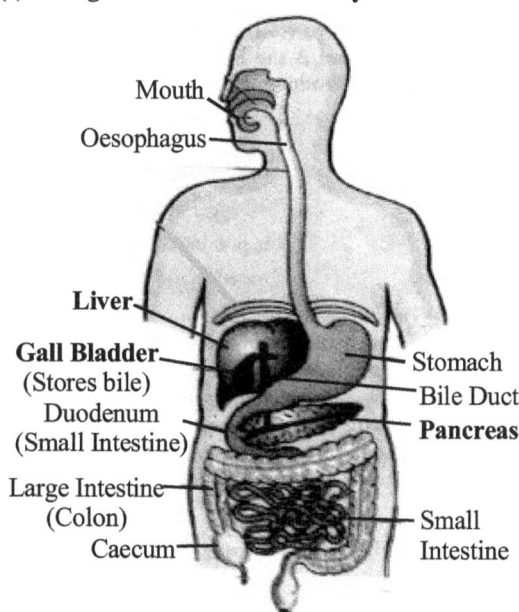

(1 mark)

(b) (i) **Role of Liver:** Decomposition of haemoglobin, formation and secretion of bile for emulsification of fat. Formation of urea, heparin, fibrinogen and prothrombin. Detoxification of chemicals and elimination of pathogens.

(ii) **Role of Pancreas:** Secretion of pancreatic juice having lipase, trypsin, and amylase, secretion of hormones, insulin and glucagon. (2 × ½ = 1 mark)

(c) (i) **Absorption of Digested Food:** Ileum part of small intesine.

(ii) **Absorption of Water:** Large intestine.

(2 × ½ = 1 mark)

34. Covalent bond formation involves sharing of electrons between bonding atoms which may be either same or different. (1 mark)

Covalency: The number of electrons contributed by an atom for sharing is known as its covalency. (1 mark)

Example:

(a) H(..)H ; H–H

(b) (Ö::Ö) ; O=O

(c) (:N:::N:) ; N≡N (1 × 3 = 3 marks)

OR

(a) $2CH_3COOH + 2Na \longrightarrow 2CH_3COONa + H_2 \uparrow$

(b) $2CH_3COOH + Na_2CO_3 \longrightarrow$
$\qquad 2CH_3COONa + CO_2 \uparrow + H_2O$

(c) $CH_3COOH + NaOH \longrightarrow CH_3COONa + H_2O$

(d) $CH_3COOH + C_2H_5OH \xrightarrow{conc. H_2SO_4}$
$\qquad CH_3COOC_2H_5 + H_2O$

(e) $CH_3COONa + NaOH \xrightarrow{CaO} CH_4 + Na_2CO_3$

(5 × 1 = 5 marks)

35. (a) Three growth hormones in plant are-
  (i) **Auxin:** It is synthesised in the young tip of roots and shoots. It promotes elongation and division of cell and root formation.
  (ii) **Gibberellins :** They help in the growth of the stem and flowers.
  (iii) **Cytokinins :** They promote cell division and delay leaf ageing. (3 × 1 = 3 marks)

(b) The ability of a plant to recognise change and respond to that change is termed as the sensitivity of the plant. Yet plants have no nervous system and no muscle tissue, they use electrical and chemical means to convey the information from one cell to another cell. The leaves of the sensitive plant (*Mimosa pudica*) folds up in response to touch. These leaf movements are independent of growth whereas, the directional movements of the shoot of a germinating seedling breaking through the soil is growth dependent. (2 marks)

36. (i) A coil of many circular turns of insulated copper wire wrapped closely in a cylinderical shape is called solenoid. (1 mark)

(ii) magnetic fields of a solenoid and a bar magnet are similar. (1½ marks)

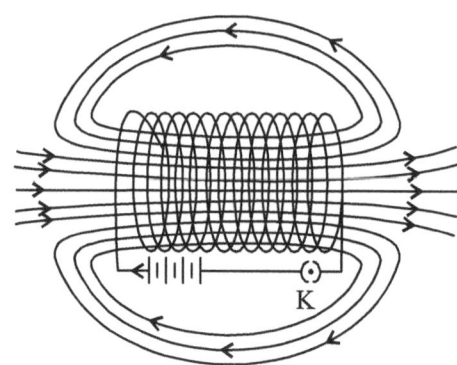

(iii) A small aluminium rod suspended horizontally from a stand using two connecting wires. Place a strong horse shoe magnet in such a way that the rod lies between the two poles with the magnetic field directed upwards. For this put the north pole of the magnet vertically below and south pole vertically above the aluminium rod. Now connect the aluminium rod in series with a battery, a key and a rheostat. Pass a current through the aluminium rod from one end to other. The rod is displaced towards left. The displacement of rod will be towards right, when the direction of current flowing through the rod is reversed. (2 ½ marks)

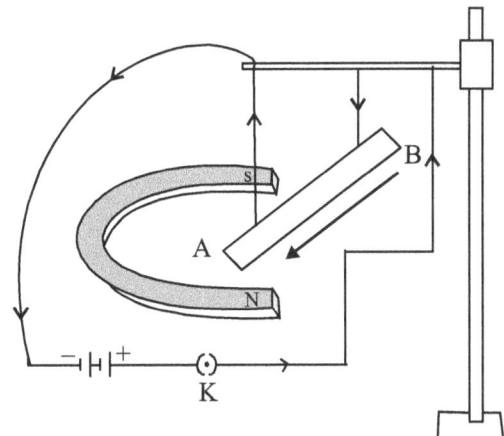

37. (a) (i) Graphite, one of the allotropes of carbon shows conducting property like metal. (1 mark)
   (ii) Polyrinyolchloride (PVC) is used as an insulating material. (1 mark)
   (b) Non-metals have tendency to accept electrons from other species and get reduced itself. This means that it oxidizes the other species and act as oxidizing agent. (2 marks)

   OR

   (b) P_2O_5 is an acidic oxide. It produces phosphoric acid on reacting with water.
   $P_2O_5 + 3H_2O \longrightarrow 2H_3PO_4$ (2 marks)

38. (i) The approximate length and thickness of kidney is 11 cm and 3 cm.
   (ii) Hilum allows the entry of blood vessels, lymph vessels and nerves to enter kidney.
   (iii) The correct order of processes that occur in urine formation is :
   Glomerular filteration → reabsorption → secretion.
   (iv) The correct order of toxicity is
   uric acid < urea < ammonia (4 × 1 = 4 marks)

39. (a) Among the given material kerosene refractive index, $\mu = 1.44$, water $\mu = 1.33$, mustard oil $\mu = 1.46$ and glycerine $\mu = 1.74$. Glycerine is most optically denser. Therefore, ray of light bend most in glycerine.
   (1 mark)
   (b) In medium B. (speed of light is higher in a rarer medium). (1 mark)
   (c) A stick partially immersed in water appears to be bent due to refraction of light. When a ray of light travels from water to air (i.e. denser to rarer medium) from the point O, then it bends away from the normal. On extending these refracted rays on other sides, the rays appear to meet at O'.
   The actual stick which is ABO appears to be as ABO'.

   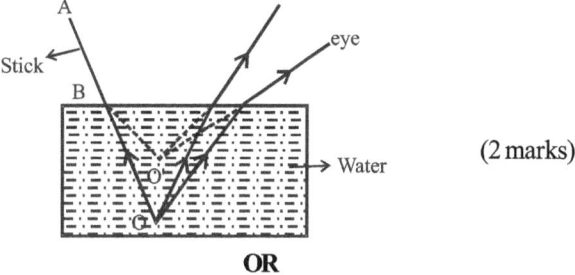
   (2 marks)

   OR

   (c) $^a\mu_g = 1.5$; $v = ?$; $c = 3 \times 10^8$ m/sec

   $a_{\mu_g} = \dfrac{c}{v} \Rightarrow v = \dfrac{c}{a_{\mu_g}} = \dfrac{3 \times 10^8}{1.5} = 2 \times 10^8$ m/sec

   (2 marks)

SAMPLE PAPER-2

1. **(a)** White silver chloride in sunlight turns to grey.
2. **(c)** Vanilla essence is an olfactory indicator. So, its smell is different in acid and basic media which can be detected easily by a visually impared student.
3. **(c)** Coal gas is obtained from destructive distillation of coal. Coal is allotropic form of carbon but not coal gas.
4. **(a)**
5. **(d)** Combustion of liquefied petroleum gas is a chemical change. As it is an irreversible reaction and new products (carbon dioxide and water vapours) are formed during the change. Also, a lot of heat is released during this reaction.
6. **(c)** Aqua regia is a 3:1 mixture of Conc. HCl and Conc. HNO_3.
7. **(d)** Calcium oxide (Lime, CaO) does not produce CO_2 gas when reacted with dilute acid while other given compounds are carbonates and hydrogen carbonates which can evolve CO_2 with dilute acids.
8. **(c)** Ozone is composed of three atoms of oxygen.

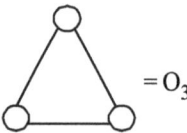

9. **(c)** Sometimes a few eipdermal cells in the vicinity of the gurad cells become specialised in their shape and size are known as subsididary cells or accessory cells.
10. **(c)** Involuntary activities such as breathing blinking, yawning, heart beat, digestion etc are controlled by mid brain and hind brain. (c) is hind brain and (d) is mid brain.
11. **(b)**
12. **(c)** Its phenotypic ratio will be 3:1
13. **(c)** If magnetic field lines are parallel and equidistant then it represents uniform magnetic field.
14. **(a)** To get the maximum resistance, all four resistors should be connected in series,

$$\therefore R = \frac{1}{2}\Omega + \frac{1}{2}\Omega + \frac{1}{2}\Omega + \frac{1}{2}\Omega = 2\Omega$$

15. **(a)** $Q = 150$ C, $t = 60$ sec so, $I = \frac{Q}{t} = \frac{150}{60} = 2.5\, A$

16. **(d)** The field consists of concentric circles centred on the wire according to Maxwell's Right Hand Grip Rule.

17. **(c)** Ammonium nitrate is salt of strong acid and weak base.
18. **(d)** The bulbs are usually filled with chemically inactive gases. Nitrogen and oxygen gases are inactive and are filled in order to prolong the life of the filament. Thus, in this case, assertion is incorrect but the reason is correct.
19. **(a)** The receptors receive the neurotransmitters. These neurotransmitters stimulate action potential in the postsynaptic cell. Thus, transmission of nerve impulses across a synapse is through the release of neurotransmitters by the axon.
20. **(b)** Both Assertion and Reason are correct but Reason is not a correct explanation of Assertion.
    The blood of an insect functions differently than the blood of a human. Insect blood, however, does not carry gases and has no haemoglobin which gives red colour to the blood.
21. Unsaturated hydrocarbons are more reactive due to the presence of $C = C$ and $C \equiv C$ bonds. These are the reactive sites in the unsaturated hydrocarbons. (2 marks)

    OR

    (i) Combination reaction are generally exothermic whereas decomposition reactions are endothermic. (1 mark)
    (ii) In a displacement reaction one element displaces another element from its compound, whereas in double displacement reaction two different atoms or group of atoms are exchanged. (1 mark)

22. By using two identical prisms, one placed inverted with respect to the other. (1 mark)

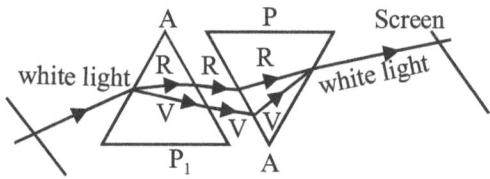

(1 mark)

OR

A rainbow is a band of seven colours extending from violet to red. It is formed by the combined effect of dispersion, reflection and refraction of the sunrays through raindrops. A rainbow is always formed in a direction opposite to that of the Sun, the water droplets act as a small prisms, they refract and disperse the sunlight, then reflect it internally and finally refract it again when it comes out of the raindrop. Due to dispersion of light and internal reflction, different colors reach the observer's eye. (2 marks)

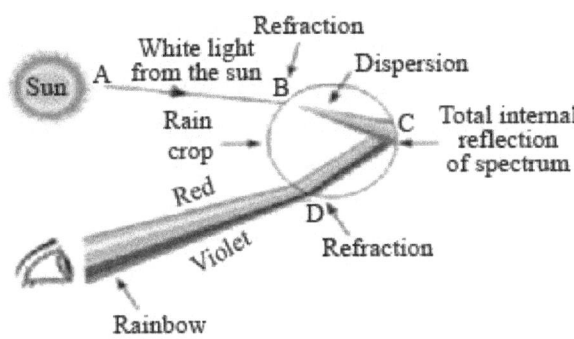

23. (i) Auxin (ii) Abscisic acid (1 + 1 marks)
24. (i) Plasma (1 + 1 marks)
    (ii) Haemoglobin present in RBCs.

25.
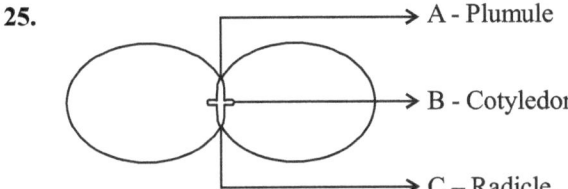

A - Plumule
B - Cotyledon
C – Radicle.

(½ + ½ + ½ marks)

Cotyledons store food reserves in the seed, Hence it supply nutrition to the developing embryo. (½ mark)

26. Leaf notches.
27. (a) $KOH + HCl \longrightarrow KCl + H_2O$
    (b) $2Al(OH)_3 + 3H_2SO_4 \longrightarrow Al_2(SO_4)_3 + 6H_2O$
    (c) $2KOH + H_2SO_4 \longrightarrow K_2SO_4 + 2H_2O$
    (1 × 3 = 3 marks)
28. (a) To obtain pure metal from an ore of high reactivity, following steps are involved :
    (i) Concentration of ore for removal of impurities.
    (ii) Electrolysis of molten ore, metal is obtained at cathode of the electrolytic cell. This metal obtained is pure metal e.g., Na, K, Mg, Ca. (2 marks)
    (b) Magnesium reacts with hot water to form magnesium oxide and hydrogen gas is evolved. As the bubbles of hydrogen gas stick to pieces of magnesium and become lighter which makes them float. (1 mark)
29. (i) A convex mirror forms an erect, virtual and diminished image of an object placed anywhere in front of it. Thus, convex mirrors enable the driver to view much larger traffic behind him that would not be possible by a plane mirror. (1½ marks)

(ii) A concave mirror is used as a shaving or make-up mirror because it forms an erect and enlarged image of the face when it is held closer to the face. (1½ marks)

30. (a) The man is suffering from diabetes mellitus. The hormone is insulin. (½ + ½ marks)
Endocrine gland which secretes insulin is pancreas.
    (b) The endorcrine gland that which secretes growth hormone is pituitary gland. (½ mark)
    (i) Deficiency of growth hormone causes **dwarfism**.
    (ii) Excess secretion of growth hormone causes **gigantism**.
31. (i) Ability of lens to converge or diverge the light rays. (1 mark)
    (ii) + ve sign → converging lens/convex lens (½ mark)
        – ve sign → diverging lens/concave lens (½ mark)
    (iii) S.I. unit of power is dioptre
         1 dioptre = 1/focal length (m) (1 mark)
32. (a) In figure (a) P – North Pole : Q – South Pole
              (b) R – North Pole : S – South Pole
    (2 marks)
    (b) Magnetic field lines always starts from North Pole and end at South Pole. (1 mark)

OR

The force experienced by a current-carrying straight conductor placed in a uniform field is
(i) maximum when the conductor is placed perpendicular to the magnetic field. (1½ marks)
(ii) minimum when the conductor is placed parallel to the magnetic field. (1½ marks)

33. **Transport of materials in xylem:** The movement of water and minerals absorbed by the plants root from the soil through xylem elements-tracheids and vessels are transported to other parts of the plants. Transpiration helps in upward conduction of material. (1½ mark)

Transport of materials in phloem: Food synthesized in the leaves is transported through sieve tubes of phloem tissues to other parts both upwards and downwards. It is bidirectional. Answer is same for both options. (1½ mark)

34. (a) n indicates number of carbon atoms and $2n$ indicates number of hydrogen atoms.
    (b) C_6H_{12}
    (c) C_3H_6
    (d) C_2H_4 $\begin{matrix} H \\ H \end{matrix} C=C \begin{matrix} H \\ H \end{matrix}$
    (e) Lower homologue – C_3H_6
        Higher homologue – C_5H_{10} (1 × 5 = 5 marks)

OR

(i) Soaps are sodium or potassium salts of fatty acids while detergents are sodium salts of sulphonic acid. (2 marks)

(ii) Soaps do not work well with hard water, acidic and saline water while detergents work well. Glycerol is the byproduct of soap industry. (3 marks)

$$\begin{array}{l} CH_2-O-COC_{17}H_{35} \\ | \\ CH-O-COC_{17}H_{35} + 3NaOH \longrightarrow \\ | \\ CH_2-O-COC_{17}H_{35} \\ \text{Triglyceride} \end{array} \begin{array}{l} CH_2OH \\ | \\ CHOH + 3C_{17}H_{35}COONa \\ | \\ CH_2OH \\ \text{Glycerol} \end{array} \text{Soap}$$

(2 marks)

35. Electric circuit: The closed path along which an electric current flows is called an 'electric circuit'. Electric cell, electric battery, electric generator are the devices that helps to maintain a potential difference across a conductor in a circuit are- (2 marks)

1 Volt: The potential difference between two points in an electric field is said to one volt if one joule of work has to be done in bringing a positive charge of one coulmb from one point to another. (1 mark)

$1 \text{ volt} = \dfrac{1 \text{ joule}}{1 \text{ coulomb}}$ or $1 \text{ V} = \dfrac{1 \text{ J}}{1 \text{ C}}$ (1 mark)

Work done $= V \times Q = 85 \times 2 = 170$ Joule. (1 mark)

36. (i) (1 marks)

Pollen Tube	Style
Pollen tube is the part of the male gametophyte in plant. It is a long tube like structure that takes the male gamete from the stigma to the ovules.	It is a part of the female reproductive organ, carpel. It connects the stigma to the ovary. It is made up of soft tissue which allows the pollen tube to grow downward towards the ovule.

(ii) **Binary fission in *Amoeba*:** A single cell divides itself into two daughter cell is known as binary fission, it can also occur in particular axis.

Multiple fission in *Plasmodium*: It is also a type of asexual reproduction in which a cell divides itself into many daughter cells simultaneously. It occurs in a definite orientation. e.g., yeast, malarial parasites. (1 mark)

(iii) **Regeneration** is of two types, in the first type, a part of the body that gets broken off or cut is regenerated. For example, lizards cast off their tails to escape predators and then regenerate them. The other type of regeneration involve to the capacity to give rise to an entire organism from a cut part. It is seen in small invertebrates such as *Planaria* and *Hydra*. (1 mark)

Fragmentation is also a type of asexual reproduction. It is the unintentional cutting up of the body of an organism in which each part grows into an organism. It is most commonly seen in some algae.

(iv) In *Hydra*, the cells divide rapidly at a specific site and develop as an outgrowth called a bud. These buds, while attached to the parent plant, develop into small individuals. When this individual becomes large enough, it detaches itself from the parent body to exist as an independent individual. (1 mark)

In the *Bryophyllum*, the leaves have small buds (as in potato). These buds are later converted into small plants which also have roots present on them. When these buds start growing further then the leaf becomes heavy and falls on the ground. Then the buds which are present on the leaf dumps into ground and form a new plant.

(v) **Vegetative propagation:** It is the ability of plants to reproduce by producing new plants from vegetative parts such as roots, stem, and leaves.

Spore formation: Spore formation is the mode of asexual reproduction in some organisms like fungi produce sporangia, which contains spores. The sporangia burst to release lots of spores and each of these spores germinates to produce a new individual. (1 mark)

37. (a) The reaction involved in the above experiement $MnO_2 + HCl \longrightarrow MnCl_2 + Cl_2\uparrow + 2H_2O$ (1 mark)

This is an example of redox reaction. (1 mark)

(b) The Cl_2 gas shows bleaching property with dry $Ca(OH)_2$. (1 mark)

$Ca(OH)_2 + Cl_2 \longrightarrow Ca(OCl)Cl + 2H_2O$ (1 mark)
Bleaching Powder.

OR

$MnO_2 + GHCl \longrightarrow MnCl_2 + Cl_2 + 2H_2O$ (1 mark)

MnO_2 gets reduced and chlorine in HCl gets oxidized. So, the given statement is incorrect. (1 mark)

Sample Paper-2 Solutions

38. Generally, in case of a prism (i), the formation of spectrum is shown below (2 marks)

(a)

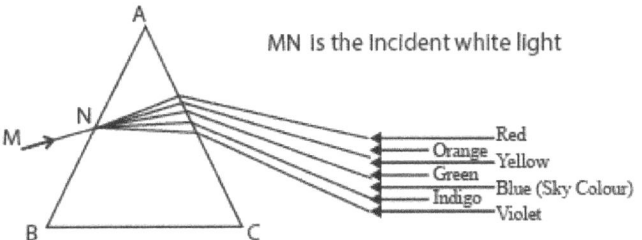

In the above figure, from top the third colour is yellow. But we can see that from bottom the third colour is blue (colour of sky). So, we can obtain the correct situation by inverting the prism. Thus the required orientations can be found in case (ii).

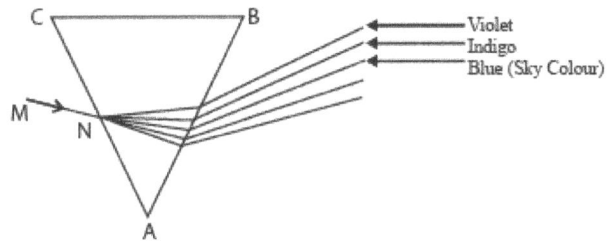

(b) Red (1 mark)
(c) Violet (1 mark)

OR

At noon, light is least scattred. (1 mark)

39. (i) The ozone layer absorbs 97-99% of UV radiation in the wavelength range 200 to 315 nm. (1 mark)

(ii) Disposable paper cups are generally used in trains for serving tea or coffee on daily basis. (1 mark)

(iii) Carbon dioxide is the main long-lived greenhouse gas in the atmosphere related to human activities. (1 mark)

(iv) Due to the depletion of the ozone layer increases risk in skin cancer. (1 mark)

SAMPLE PAPER-3

1. (c)
2. (d) Antacids contain weak base like $Mg(OH)_2$ and pH paper turns greenish blue for weakly basic compound.
3. (a)
4. (c)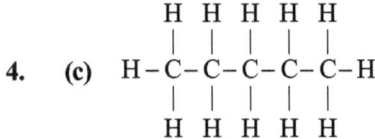

   Pentane has 16 covalent bonds
   (12C – H and 4C – C bonds)
5. (a) Cu does not produce hydrogen gas on reaction with hydrochloric acid. Cu is present below hydrogen in reactivity series, i.e. it is less reactive than hydrogen.
6. (a) $CaCO_3 \xrightarrow{\Delta} CaO + CO_2$
7. (b) $\underset{(A)}{HCl} + \underset{(B)}{Na_2CO_3} \longrightarrow \underset{(C)}{NaCl(aq)} + \underset{(D)}{CO_2 + H_2O}$

   $CO_2 + NH_3 + NaCl(aq) \longrightarrow \underset{\text{Baking soda}}{NaHCO_3} + NH_4Cl$

   Hence A & B are HCl and Na_2CO_3
8. (a) When we breathe in, we lift our ribs and flatten our diaphragm, and the chest cavity becomes larger as a result. Because of this, air is sucked into the lungs and fills the expanded alveoli.
9. (d)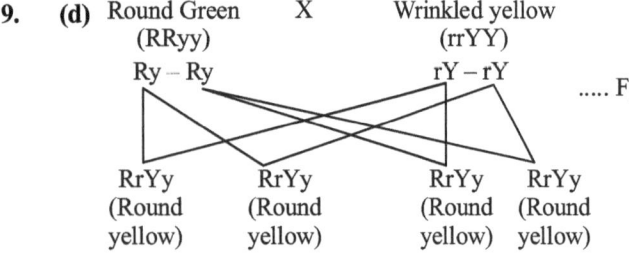

   Thus, in the first generation (F_1), all seeds would be round and yellow.
10. (d) The sequence of events that takes place in a reflex action is as follows–
    Receptor organ → Sensory neuron → CNS → Motor neuron → Effector muscle.
11. (c) The following step for this experiment are-
    (i) Take two healthy potted plants which are nearly the same size.
    (ii) Keep them in a dark room for three days.
    (iii) Now place each plant on separate glass plates. Place a watch-glass containing potassium hydroxide by the side of one of the plants. The potassium hydroxide is used to absorb carbon dioxide.
    (iv) Cover both plants with separate bell-jars.
    (v) Use Vaseline to seal the bottom of the jars to the glass plates so that the set-up is air-tight.
    (vi) Keep the plants in sunlight for about two hours.
    (vii) Pluck a leaf from each plant and check for the presence of starch as in the above activity.
12. (d) The given figure (d) shows self pollination. The transfer of pollen grains from anther to stigma is called pollination. It is of 2 types self pollination and cross - pollination. In self-pollination, the pollen grains transfer from anther to stigma on the same flower or another genetically similar flower as of the same plant.
13. (b)
14. (b) The rate of generation of heat, for a given potential difference is, $P = V^2/R$
15. (c) 25 cm
16. (c) 17. (c) 18. (b)
19. (c) Assertion is correct but Reason is incorrect. Success rate of test tube baby is less than 20%.
20. (a) Both Assertion and Reason are correct and the Reason is a correct explanation of Assertion.
    According to principle of segregation (first law of mendel), the two factors of a character which remain together in an individual do not get mixed up but keep their identity distinct and separate at the time of gametogenesis. Gametes carry a single factor or allele for a trait. The two Mendelian factors present in the F_1 plants segregate during gamete formation. The principle of segregation is called the principle of purity of gametes because segregation of the two Mendelian factors of a trait results in gametes receiving only one factor out of a pair. As a result gametes are always pure for a character.
21. A, because it is more acidic. [2 marks]

    OR

    Zn (Zinc) is most reactive and Cu (copper) is least reactive. [2 marks]
22. (i) Potential difference of 1 volt means the amount of work done when a unit charge moves from one point to the other point in an electric field. [1 mark]

Sample Paper-3 Solutions

(ii) First symbol is variable resistance and second is ammeter. Variable resistance changes the magnitude of current in the circuit, by variation in resistance. Ammeter is used to find current. (1 mark)

OR

Given, Radius (r)= 0.01 cm = 0.01×10^{-2} m.
Resistivity (ρ) = $50 \times 10^{-8} \Omega$ m.
Resistance (R) = 10Ω

As we know, $\quad [\because A = \pi r^2]$

$R = \rho \dfrac{l}{A} = \rho \dfrac{l}{\pi r^2}$ (1 mark)

$\Rightarrow l = \dfrac{R\pi r^2}{\rho} = \dfrac{10 \times 3.14 \times 0.01 \times 10^{-2} \times 0.01 \times 10^{-2}}{50 \times 10^{-8}}$

$= \dfrac{314 \times 10^{-4}}{50 \times 10^{-8} \times 10^5}$

Length $= \dfrac{6.28 \times 10^{-4}}{10^{-3}} = 0.628$ m. (1 mark)

23. (a) The menstrual cycle lasting 28- 30 days can be divided into four main phases :-
(i) Menstrual Phase. (ii) Follicular Phase.
(iii) Ovulatory Phase. (iv) Luteal Phase.

[4 × ¼= 1 mark]

(b)

	Menarche	Menopause
1.	It is the onset of menstruation is females.	It is the stoppage of menstruation in females.
2.	It occurs at age of 10 to 12 yrs.	It occurs at the age of 45 to 50 yrs.

[2 × ½ = 1 mark]

24. (a) **Phototropism:** It is the growth which responds to a light stimulus. The cells on the plant that are farthest from the light have a chemical called auxin that reacts when phototropism occurs.

Geotropism: The movement of plant part in response to gravity is called geotropic movement and the phenomenon involved is known as geotropism. When the tip of the stem grows away from the earth's gravitational forces, it is known as negative geotropism and when the root tips grow towards gravity, it is known as positive geotropism.
Stem shows negative geotropism and roots show positive geotropism.
In the figure below roots are positively geotropic while shoot part in negatively geotropic.

[2 × ½ = 1 mark]

Activity to demonstrate phototropism:
(a) (i) Fill a conical flask with water.
(ii) Cover the neck of the flask with a wire mesh.
(iii) Keep two or three freshly germinated bean seeds on the wire mesh.
(iv) Take a cardboard box which is open from one side.
(v) Keep the flask in the box in such a manner that the open side of the box face light coming from a window.
(vi) After two or three days, it can be noticed that the shoots bend towards light and roots away from light.
(vii) Now turn the flask so that the shoots are away from light and the roots towards light.
(viii) Leave it undisturbed in this condition for a few days.

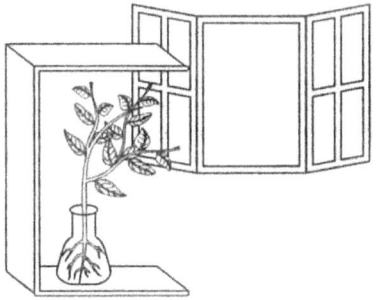

[1½ mark]

(b) Folding up of the leaves of *Mimosa* plant is an example of each. (½ mark)

25. A. **Anther :** It produces pollen granis.[1½ + ½ = 2 marks]
B. **Style :** It provides the path through which the pollen tube grows and reaches the ovary.
C. **Ovary:** It contains ovules and each ovule has an egg cell/female gamete. It develops into fruit after fertilization.

26. (i)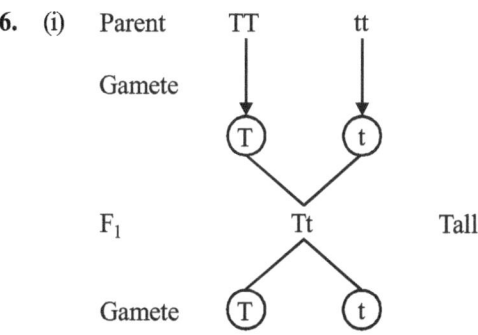

The dwarf trait of the plants does not gets expressed in the presence of the dominants tall trait.

    F_2 TT   Tt   tt   [1 mark]
        Tall Tall Dwarf

(ii) In the F_2 generation, both the tall and dwarf traits are present in the ratio of 3 : 1. This shows that the traits for both tallness and dwarfness are present in the F_1 generation, but the dwarfness, the recessive trait does not express itself in the presence of tallness the dominant trait. [1 mark]

27. (i) The colour of precipitate formed is yellow. The name of the compound is lead (II) iodide having the formula PbI_2. [1 mark]
(ii) $Pb(NO_3)_2$ (aq) + $2KI$(aq) $\longrightarrow$ PbI_2(s) + $2KNO_3$(aq)
                     yellow ppt. [1 mark]
(iii) Yes, it is a double displacement reaction. [1 mark]

28. (a) Fuel oil has higher calorific value than coal.
(b) Fuel oil produces less smoke than coal.
(c) Fuel oil is more efficient than coal. [3 × 1 = 3 marks]

OR

The property due to which an element exists in two or more forms, which differ in their physical and some of the chemical properties is known as "Allotropy" and the various forms are called "Allotropes".

Carbon exists in two allotropic form (i) crystalline (ii) amorphous. The crystalline forms are diamond and graphite whereas the amorphous forms are coal, charcoal, lamp black etc. [3 marks]

29. (i) No, Since, a charged particle at rest in magnetic field. It does not interact with magnetic field. [1 mark]
(ii) No, because, when current and field are parallel i.e. in the same direction magnetic force is zero. [1 mark]
(iii) Yes, because, the force is maximum when current and magnetic field are maximum. [1 mark]

30. (i) these are good conductors of electricity because having low resistance or low resistivity. [1 mark]
(ii) Very high melting point and high resistivity. [1 mark]
(iii) Low melting point. [1 mark]

31. (i) Capillaries [½ mark]
(ii) Refer to below figure.

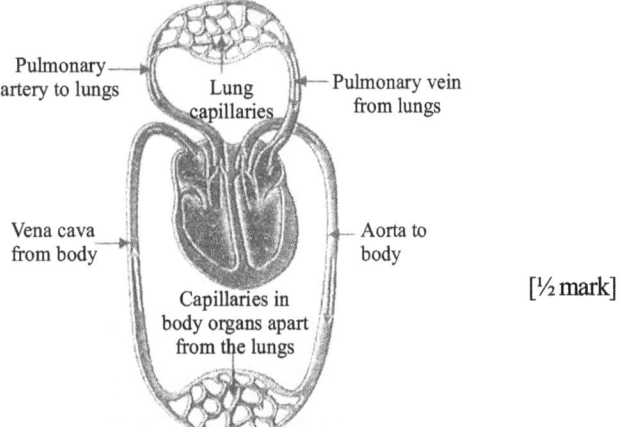

[½ mark]

Schematic representation of transport and exchange of oxygen and carbon dioxide

Overview:
(i) The smallest vessels have walls which are one-cell thick, called capillaries. Exchange of material between the blood and surrounding cells takes place across this thin wall. [1 × 2 = 2 marks]
(ii) Schematic representation of transport and exchange of oxygen and carbon dioxide.

32. (a)

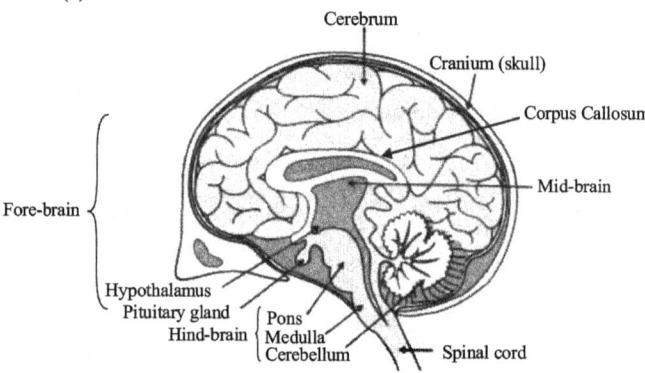

(b) Fore brain, [2 marks]

33. (i) The space around the magnet or currernt carrying conductor within which its influence i.e. force of magnetism can be felt by the magnetic field. [1 mark]
Magnitude and direction describe it completely. [1 mark]
(ii) It indicate that at the point of intersection, compass needle would point to two directions which is impossible. [1 mark]

OR

An electromagnet is a solenoid coil that attains magnetism due to flow of current. It works on the principle of magnetic effect of current. [1 mark]
(i) By suspending magnetised bar and identify its north and south poles.
(ii) By finding the polarity of electromagnet using the property-like poles repel. [2 × 1 = 2 marks]

34. (a) Ammonia (NH_3)
(b) Ethanol (C_2H_5OH)
(c) Sodium hydroxide (NaOH)
(d) Calcium oxide (CaO)
(e) Carbonic acid (H_2CO_3)   (1 × 5 = 5 marks)

OR

(a) $2HCl$ (aq) + $2Na$ (s) $\longrightarrow$ $2NaCl$(s) + H_2 (g)↑
(b) HCl (aq) + $NaOH$(aq) $\longrightarrow$ $NaCl$ (aq) + H_2O (l)
(c) Na_2CO_3(s) + $2HCl$ (aq) $\longrightarrow$ $2NaCl$ (aq) + H_2O(l) + CO_2 (g)↑
(d) $2HCl$ (aq) + Na_2O(s) $\longrightarrow$ $2NaCl$ (aq) + H_2O(l)
(e) $2NaOH$ (aq) + Zn(s) $\longrightarrow$ Na_2ZnO_2(aq) + H_2(g)↑

[1 × 5 = 5 marks]

Sample Paper-3 Solutions

35. Some examples of actions that are good for the global environment: reducing the quantity of nonfood items purchased; reuse items until they are no longer usable; buy used items rather than getting everything new. Recycling paper, plastic, glass, and metal use of reusable cloth bags when shopping. Plant trees and other native plants, especially those that help feed the native wildlife. Reducing water use by not leaving water running when brushing teeth, by adjusting the water level of washing machines to match the size of the load, and by using water-saving fixtures. Reducing fossil fuel use by choosing a gas-efficient car and by using household heating and air conditioning only as needed. Use of compact fluorescent light bulbs, and turning off lights that are not in use. Supporting organic farmers by purchasing organically grown food. Some examples of actions that are harmful for the global environment: Use of nonrecyclable products and products that are not from recycled sources. Driving alone rather than carpooling or taking public transportation. Use of a gas or electric-powered lawn mower. Make excessive purchases of non-essential items (gadgets, many sets of clothes, extra cars, vacation homes, etc.). Driving a low-mileage vehicle, such as a sport utility vehicle or truck, out of choice, not necessity. [5 marks]

36. We can choose any two of the following rays:
  (i) A ray parallel to the principle axis, after reflection, will pass through the principle focus of concave mirror.
  (ii) A ray passing through the principle focus of a concave mirror after reflection will emerge parallel to the priniple axis.
  (iii) A ray passing through the centre of curvature of a concave mirror after reflection is reflected back along the same path.
  (iv) A ray incident obliquely to the principle axis towards the pole of a concave mirror is reflected obliquely, making equal angles with the principal axis. [2 marks]

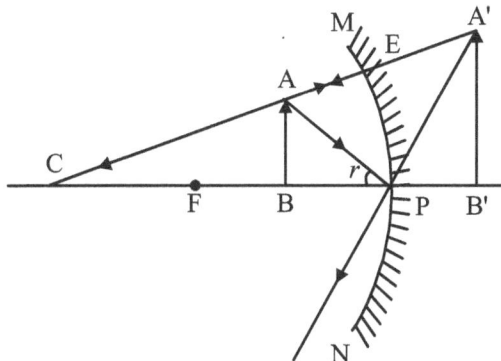

Rays which are choosen such that

Path of these rays after reflection:
  (i) A ray parallel to the principal axis after reflection, it will pass through the prinipal focus of a concave mirror or appear to diverge in case of a convex mirror.
  (ii) A ray passing through the centre of curvature of a concave mirror or appear to pass through the centre of curvature of convex mirror. after reflection, it is reflected back along the same path. [2 marks]

$f = -12$ cm, $u = -8$ cm

we know, $\dfrac{1}{f} = \dfrac{1}{v} + \dfrac{1}{u}$

$\dfrac{1}{v} = \dfrac{1}{f} - \dfrac{1}{u} = \dfrac{1}{-12} - \dfrac{1}{-(8)}$

$= \dfrac{3-2}{24} = \dfrac{1}{24} = 24$ cm

$v = +ve$, So image is virtual and is formed at a distance of 24 cm behind the mirror. [1 mark]

37. (a) (i) $Na(s) + H_2O(l) \rightarrow NaOH(aq) + H_2(g)$ [1 mark]
  (ii) $2Al(s) + 3H_2O(g) \rightarrow Al_2O_3(s) + 3H_2(g)$ [1 mark]
  (iii) $Zn(s) + H_2O(g) \rightarrow ZnO(s) + H_2(g)$ [1 mark]

  (b) Metals can be converted into thin sheet by hammering. This property is known as ductile. [1 mark]

  OR

  Gold is the most ductile metal. [1 mark]

38. (i) 120/80 mm Hg is normal blood pressure range. [1 mark]
  (ii) Less of approximately 10% of blood volume can occur without a decrease in blood pressure or cardiac output. [1 mark]
  (iii) The person C. [1 mark]
  (iv) This is because capillaries are less in diameter. [1 mark]

39. (a) Focal length = $\dfrac{\text{Radius of curvature}}{2}$ [1 mark]

  (b) (i) within focus, (virtual) (ii) at focus, (real) (iii) between C and F.(real) [2 marks]

  (c) (i) for real image → negative,
    (ii) for virtual image → positive [1 mark]

  OR

  Convex [1 mark]

SAMPLE PAPER-4

1. **(d)**
2. **(c)** Carbonic acid is a weak and so it does not react with metal.
3. **(b)** Formation of crystals by process of crystallization.
4. **(d)**
5. **(d)** Graphite and diamond show different physical and chemical properties. Diamond is colourless transparent substance. It does not conduct electricity. Graphite is greyish black. It is good conductor of electricity.
6. **(b)**
7. **(c)** The value of x, y, z are 8, 4, 4 respectively hence the reaction is
   $H_2SO_4 + 8HI \rightarrow H_2S + 4I_2 + 4H_2O$
8. **(b) Arteries** are blood vessels which carry blood coming from heart to various organs of the body. Blood flows inside the arteries with jerk due to pumping activity of the heart.
   Veins are blood vessels which carry blood from various parts of the body towards the heart. Blood flows smoothly and slowly inside veins.
   Pulmonary arteries carry deoxygenated blood from the heart to the lungs and **pulmonary veins** receive oxygenated blood from the lungs to the left atrium of the heart.
9. **(a)**
10. **(d)** The sperm releases from the testis, enters into epididymis which leads to vas deferens. Then sperms are transferred into the urethra.
11. **(b)** The yellow color is dominant aver green color. (1 mark)
12. **(b)**
13. **(a)** Real, inverted and same in size because object is at the centre of curvature of the mirror.
14. **(d)** $P = \dfrac{100}{-75} = -\dfrac{4}{3} D$
15. **(a)**
16. **(a)** A heating wire should be such that it produces more heat when current is passed through it and also does not melt. It will be so if it has high specific resistance and high melting point.
17. **(a)** Bases generate hydroxide ions in water hence water soluble bases are called alkalis.
18. **(c)** Alloys have higher resistivity than constituents metals.
19. **(a)** The digestion in stomach is taken care of by the gastric glands present in the wall of the stomach. These release hydrochloric acid, a protein digesting enzyme called pepsin, and mucus. The hydrochloric acid creates an acidic medium which facilitates the action of the enzyme pepsin.
20. **(a)** Both Assertion and Reason are correct and the Reason is a correct explanation of Assertion.
    The agents which help in pollination are wind, water etc. Petals of flowers are colourful and attract insects and birds which on the other hand, results in pollination.
21. Al is more reactive because it displaces Mn in this reaction.
    (2 marks)

    OR

    Corrosion is slow while combustion is fast process.
    (2 marks)
22. In sensitive plants like *Mimosa pudica* (touch me not), there is an electrical-chemical means to convey the information of touch from cell to cell. Plant cells change shape by changing the amount of water in them, resulting in swelling or shrinking.
    This type of movements in sensitive plant is totally different from the movement of a shoot towards light.

    A sensitive plant

    The movement of the plant (shoot and root) due to the influence of sunlight is called phototropism. In this movement, the cells of that part which are in direct contact of light shrink due to the transfer of water from these cells to the cells of opposite side. Thus, the plant part bends towards sunlight. It is called positively phototropic. It does not have the effect of sensation by electrical-chemical means.
    (2 marks)
23. Part A is stigma.
    Function : It is the terminal part of carpel, which may be sticky and helps in receiving the pollen grains from the anther of stamen during pollination part B is pollen tube.
    Function : The pollen tube grows out of the pollen grain through the style to reach the ovary.
    Part C is female germ cell. (1 + 1 = 2 marks)
    Function : It is female gametes which fuses with male gamete to form a diploid cell called zygote.

Sample Paper-4 Solutions

24. 10000 J. According to 10% law of energy in the form heat is lost and only 10% energy is available to the lower trophic level so, if lion has 100 J of energy, deer will have 100 × 10 → 1000 J and plant will have 1000 × 10 → 10,000 J of energy. (2 marks)

25. Laws of refraction of light:
(i) The incident ray, the refracted ray at the point of incidence and the normal all lies in the same plane for the two given mediums.
(ii) The ratio of sine of angle of incidence (*i.e.*, sin *i*) to the sine of angle of refraction (*i.e.*, sin *r*) is always constant for the light of given colour and for the given pair of media.

Mathematically, $\frac{\sin i}{\sin r} = $ constant $= n$ (½ × 2 = 1 mark)

The constant '*n*' is called refractive index of the second medium with respect to the first medium.
Absolute refractive index of the medium is given by

$$n = \frac{\text{Speed of light in vacuum (c)}}{\text{Speed of light in medium (v)}}$$ (1 mark)

OR

The power of a lens is defined as the reciprocal of its focal length (f) expressed in metres. SI unit of power is dioptre. One dioptre is defined as the power of a lens whose focal length is 1 metre. (1 mark)

Focal length of lens is positive 40 cm hence lens is convex and the lens of focal length negative (–20cm) is concave lens.
Power of lens of focal length (f = –20cm)

$$= \frac{1}{\frac{-20}{100}} = -5 \text{ dioptre}$$ (½ mark)

Power of lens of focal length (f = 40 cm)

$$= \frac{1}{\frac{40}{100}} = 2.5 \text{ dioptre}$$ (½ mark)

26. Aerobic respiration occurs in mitochondria of the cell.

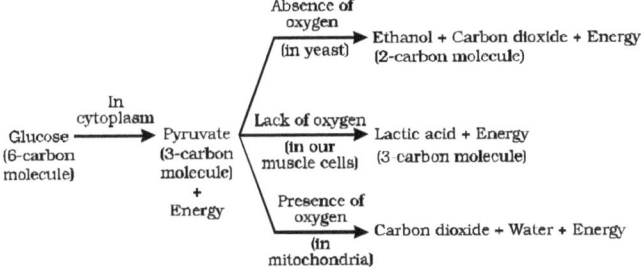

Break-down of glucose by various pathway (1 mark)

27. Reaction (iii) Shows oxidation and reduction both as in this reaction CuO is reduced to copper and H$_2$ is oxidised to H$_2$O. (1 mark)

$$\underbrace{CuO + H_2 \xrightarrow{\text{Oxidation}} Cu + H_2O}_{\text{Reduction}}$$ (½ mark)

Reaction (iv) shows both oxidation and reduction in which Na is oxidised and oxygen is reduced to form Na$_2$O. (1 mark)

$$\underbrace{4Na + O_2 \xrightarrow{\text{Oxidation}} 2Na_2O(s)}_{\text{Reduction}}$$ (½ mark)

28. The acids (HCl, HNO$_3$ etc.) have replaceable hydrogen atoms in their molecule and they release hydrogens ion (H$^+$) in aqueous solution. Since they release H$^+$ ion so they show acidic character. (1½ marks)
In their aqueous solution both the compounds alcohol (C$_2$H$_5$OH) and glucose (C$_6$H$_{12}$O$_6$) fail to release H$^+$ ions because of absence of replaceable hydrogen atom in their molecule. So, they do not show acidic properties in solution. (1½ marks)

29. If two many electrical appliances of high power rating are switched on at the same time, they draw large current from the circuit. This is called overloading. (1 mark)
If the live wire and neutral wire brought in contact to each other either directly or via conducting wire, the situation is called short circuiting. (1 mark)
To avoid risk of an elctrical shock, the metal body of the appliances is earthed. Earthing means to connect the metal case of the appliance to earth by a means of metal wire called earth wire. (1 mark)

30. (a)

PE – Incident ray   ∠i – Angle of incidence
EF – Refracted ray   ∠r – Angle of refraction
FS – Emergent ray   ∠e – Angle of emergence
∠A – Angle of the prism ∠δ – Angle of deviation (2 marks)

(b) When a narrow beam of white light passes through a prism, it emerges as a spectrum of all components of white light. (see the fig.)

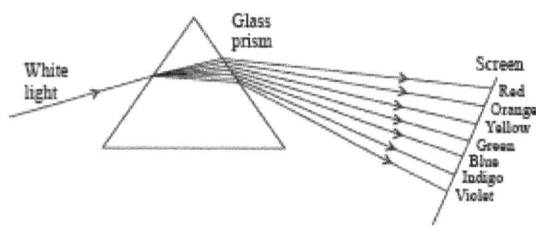

(1 mark)

31. (i) Rheostat —/\/\/\/\/—

(ii) Voltmeter —+(V)—

(iii) Electric bulb —◠— (1 × 3 = 3 marks)

OR

$R = R_1 + R_2 = 10 + 20 = 30\,\Omega$ (1 mark)

(i) From Ohm's law $V = IR$

$3 = I \times 30 \Rightarrow I = \dfrac{3}{30} = \dfrac{1}{10}$ Ampere or 0.1 A

(1 mark)

(ii) Potential difference across 10Ω resistor
$V = IR$
$= \dfrac{1 \times 10}{10} = 1$ volt. (1 mark)

32. (i) Ozone layer helps in shielding the Earth from the lethal UV radiation coming from the sun. If ozone layer gets depleted, UV radiation will directly reach the earth's surface and seriously affect the life on earth.

(iii) Ozone layer can be protected by:
  (a) Restriction in release of chlorofluorocarbons
  (b) Eliminating the pollutant nitrogen monoxide and carbon monoxide
  (c) Less usage of air conditioners

33. (a) **Xylem:**
  (i) Transport of water and mineral.
  (ii) Upward movement. (Unidirectional)
  Phloem:
  (i) Transport of food and hormones. (2 marks)
  (ii) Upward and downward movements (bidirectional).

(b) Transport of soluble food by phloem is define as translocation. (1 mark)

34. **Advantages**
  (a) It is very cheap.
  (b) It is readily available and is widely used in metallurgy.
  Disadvantages
  (a) It cannot be used for the reduction of metals which are very high in the activity series of metals like Na, K, Ca, Mg, Al, because these metals have more affinity for oxygen than carbon therefore carbon is unable to remove oxygen from these metal oxides and hence cannot convert them into free metals.

(b) Some traces of carbon left in the metals act as an impurity when we use carbon as a reducing agent.

(2½ × 2 = 5 marks)

OR

Metals are found in nature in the form of ores or minerals.
(1 mark)

Reaction with oxygen : When a metal combines with oxygen, it loses its valence electrons and forms positively charged metal ions (oxidation of metal). The atoms of oxygen accept the electrons lost by the metal and form negative oxide ions.

$Mg \longrightarrow Mg^{2+} + 2e^-$

$O + 2e^- \longrightarrow O^{2-}$

$Mg^{2+} + O^{2-} \longrightarrow MgO$ (2 marks)

Reaction with dil. acids: The metal replaces the hydrogen atom in the acid to form a salt.

$2Al(s) + 6HCl(aq) \longrightarrow 2AlCl_3(aq) + 3H_2(g)$ (2 marks)

35. Given,
$u = -40$ cm, $v = 40$ cm
From lens formula,

$\dfrac{1}{f} = \dfrac{1}{v} - \dfrac{1}{u}$

$= \dfrac{1}{40} - \dfrac{-1}{(-40)}$

Focal length, $f = +20$ cm
The positive sign of focal length shows that it is a convex lens.

Now, Magnification, $m = \dfrac{v}{u} = \dfrac{40}{(-40)} = -1$ (1 mark)

Thus, the image is real, inverted and same size as object.

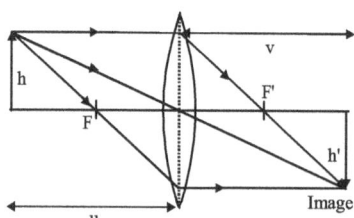

(1 mark)

If candle flame is shifted 25 cm toward the lens, then
u = −(40 − 25) = − 15 cm

then, $\frac{1}{20} = \frac{1}{u} - \frac{1}{(-15)} = \frac{1}{v} + \frac{1}{15}$

or v = − 60 cm

$m = \frac{v}{u} = \frac{-60}{-15} = 4$

Thus the image will be virtual, erect and enlarged. For this you can refer to the following diagram,

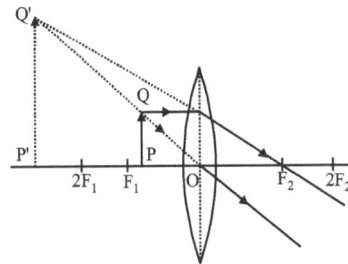

(1 mark)

36. (i) Mendel experimented on garden pea plant with selection of seven visible contrasting characters forming laws of inheritance. He selected and crossed homozygous tall pea plant with genotype TT and a homozygous dwarf pea plant with the genotype tt. F_1 generation consists only of tall plants having genotype Tt.

The expressed allele 'T' for tallness is dominant over the unexpressed allele t for dwarfness. Therefore, the trait of tallness is dominant while dwarfness is the recessive trait. Thus, Mendel's experiment showed that traits may be dominant or recessive.

(2½ marks)

(ii) In Mendel's experiment, different traits were tall and dwarf plant, round and wrinkled seeds. In F_2 (second) generation, some plants were tall with round seeds and others were dwarf with wrinkled seeds. Other combination was dwarf plants having round/wrinkled seed traits, that were independently inherited.

(2½ marks)

37. (a) 2, 3, 3 - Trimethylhexane (1 mark)
    (i) The volency of 'e' atom = 4 (½ mark)

Structure of methane: 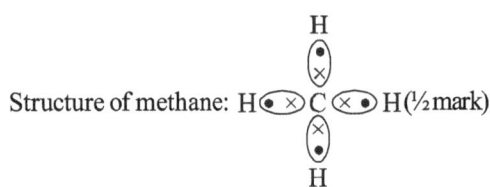 (½ mark)

(ii) Primary-5, secondary-2, tertiary-1, quaternary-1
(½ / 4 = 2 marks)

OR

(i) Chemical formula of butane: $CH_3CH_2CH_2CH_3$
(1 mark)

$$H \cdot \times C \times \times C \times \times C \times \times C \times \cdot H$$
(with H atoms above and below each C)
(1 mark)

(ii) In a hydrocarbon chain, the H-atom is sometimes replaced by other atoms or groups, which confer specific properties to the compound regardless of the length and nature of chain. This heteroatom or group of atoms is known as functional group. e.g. CH_3CH_2OH-Ethanol; CH_3-O-CH_3-Ether-Functional group: I-OH and -O-, respectively (1 mark)

38. (i) Water
(ii) Gravity
(iii) Light
(iv) B and C; Gravity and Light (Sunlight)

39. (a) Resistance of the heater be R.
New resistance of heater is R/2

Initial power = $\frac{V^2}{R}$ Final power = $\frac{V^2}{R/2} = 2\frac{V^2}{R}$

∴ Heat generated is doubled. (1 mark)

(b) It becomes four times. (1 mark)

(c) (i) Electric toaster
    (ii) Electric heater. (2 marks)

OR

(c) H = $I^2 Rt = 5^2 \times 20 \times 30 = 15000$ J, H = 15 kJ
(2 marks)

SAMPLE PAPER-5

1. (a) $-OH \Rightarrow$ alcohol; $-CHO \Rightarrow$ aldehyde
   $-COOH \Rightarrow$ Carboxylic acid; $>C=O \Rightarrow$ Ketone

2. (c) In this reaction, NH_3 is changing into NO. Removal of hydrogen from a substance is called oxidation. So, NH_3 is undergoing oxidation. O_2 is changing into H_2O. The addition of hydrogen to a substance is called reduction. So, O_2 is undergoing reduction.
   Also, it is a displacement reaction as H in NH_3 is getting displaced by oxygen.

3. (b) HCl and CCl_4 both are formed by sharing of electrons. HCl is a polar covalent compound while CCl_4 is a non-polar covalent compound.

4. (c) Carbonic acid is a weak and so it does not react with metal.

5. (d) Methane (CH_4), ethane (C_2H_6) and propane ($CH_3CH_2CH_3$) differ from each other by CH_2 group. Hence these are said to form a homologous series.

6. (a) The soap solution in water is not neutral and cannot be used to wash all kinds of fabrics.

7. (a) When quick lime react with water, a large amount of heat is released along with the formation of calcium hydroxide means this is an exothermic reaction. Similarly, the process of dissolving an acid or base in water is a highly exothermic reaction. While, evaporation of water and sublimation of camphor are endothermic reactions.

8. (d) Only 10% of the energy entering a particular trophic level of organisms is available for tranfer to the next higher trophic level according to 10% law. In this food chain, at the 4th trophic level, only 5 kJ energy is available to the snake. Thus, the energy available at the producer level will be 5000 kJ. (1 mark)

9. (b) Photosynthesis is a process by which green plants make their food from CO_2 and H_2O in the presence of sunlight. If we blow air into water in a beaker then air from mouth that contains CO_2 utilized in photosynthesis. Hence, O_2 production increases. (1 mark)

10. (c) Messages in the form of electrical signals carried by neurons are called electrical impulses or nerve impulses. The dendrites pick up the impulses from receptor and pass on to the cell body and finaling to the axonal end.
    At the axonal end, electrical impulse releases some chemicals which crosses the gap or synapse and start an impulse in dendrite of the next neuron. (1 mark)

11. (a) In asexual reproduction the offsprings are formed by the body parts of organism like in planaria, Hydra, etc.

12. (d) Mendel used round seed and green coloured pod which is dominant over wrinkled seed and yellow pod respectively.

13. (a)

14. (b) The primary reason why the colour red is used for traffic signals is that red light is scattered the least by air molecules. So, the red light is able to travel the longest distance.

15. (b)

16. (c) We know that, $R = \rho \dfrac{l}{A}$
    where, ρ = resistivity, l = length, A = area.
    For first and second conductor,
    $R_1 = \dfrac{\rho_1 l_1}{A_1}, R_2 = \dfrac{\rho_2 l_2}{A_2}$
    $\dfrac{R_1}{R_2} = \dfrac{\rho_1}{\rho_2} \dfrac{l_1}{l_2} \times \dfrac{A_2}{A_1} \Rightarrow \dfrac{R}{R} = \dfrac{\rho}{\rho} \times \dfrac{l}{2l} \times \dfrac{A_2}{A} \Rightarrow A_2 = 2A$
    [as given $R_1 = R_2 = R$, $l_1 = l$, $l_2 = 2l$, $\rho_1 = \rho_2 = \rho$ (same material)]

17. (d) Decomposition of vegetable matter into compost is an exothermic reaction.

18. (c) Distance of image from the optical centre is determined by $\dfrac{1}{u} + \dfrac{1}{v} = \dfrac{1}{f}$

19. (a) Both Assertion and Reason are correct and the Reason is a correct explanation of Assertion.
    According to principle of segregation (first law of Mendel), the two factors of a character which remain together in an individual do not get mixed up but keep their identity distinct and separate at the time of gametogenesis. Gametes carry a single factor or allele for a trait. The two Mendelian factors present in the F_1 plants segregate during gamete formation. The principle of segregation is called the principle of purity of gametes because segregation of the two Mendelian factors of a trait results in gametes receiving only one factor out of a pair. As a result gametes are always pure for a character.

Sample Paper-5 Solutions

20. **(b)** Both Assertion and Reason are correct but Reason is not a correct explanation of Assertion.

    Lichens are sensitive to SO_2 level in air. Increased released of SO_2 from auto-mobiles and other sources causes their depletion. Delhi has more air pollution due to increased vehicles, this lichens do not grow here.

21. Hydrogen ion concentration will increase. (2 marks)

    OR

    Non-metals cannot supply electrons to convert H^+ to $H_2(g)$ whereas metals can give electrons to form H_2
    $$2H^+ + 2e^- \rightarrow H_2(g).\qquad \text{(2 marks)}$$

22. The finger like projections in small intestine are villi.
    Function of villi are: (1 marks)
    (i) Villi are richly supplied with blood vessels which take the absorbed food to each and every cell of the body.
    (ii) They absorb water and they increase the surface area for the absorption of food. (1 mark)

23. The hormone which regulates carbohydrates, protein and fat metabolism in our body is thyroxine. (½ mark)
    It is secreted by the thyroid gland. (½ mark)
    Iodised salt in diet is important because it contains iodine, which is essential for the synthesis of thyroxine hormone by the thyroid gland. In case, iodine is deficient in our diet, there is a chance of suffering from goitre. (1 mark)

24. The principle of segregation is called as first law of heredity. This principle states that a pair of contrasting factor or gene remains together and separate at the time of gamete formation. (2 marks)

25. Person is suffering from long-sightedness or hypermetropia hence, lens to be used is a convex lens of suitable focal length.
    Here, $u = -25$ cm, $v = -1.5\,m = -150$ cm, $f = ?$, $P = ?$
    By lens formula,
    $$\frac{1}{f} = \frac{1}{v} - \frac{1}{u} = \frac{1}{-150} + \frac{1}{25} = \frac{-1+6}{150} = \frac{5}{150} = \frac{1}{30}$$
    $\therefore f = +30$ cm $= 0.3$ m (1 mark)
    Power $(P) = \dfrac{1}{f\,(\text{in m})} = \dfrac{1}{0.3} = \dfrac{10}{3} = +3.33$ D. (1 mark)

    OR

    Hypermetropia is a defect of the eye in which parallel rays are focused behind the retina and a person unable to see nearby objects distinctly. This defect can be corrected by using a convex lens of appropriate power.

    Hypermetropic eye and its correction

    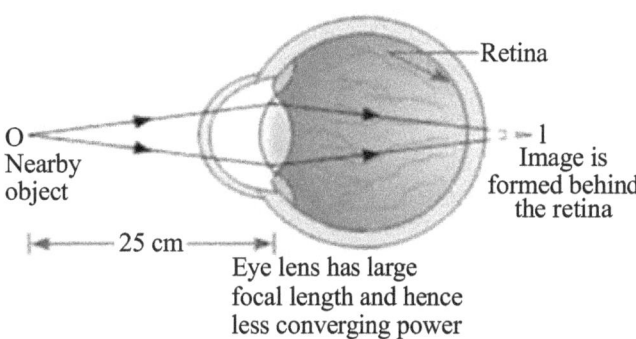

    (2 marks)

26. Two functions of testes are:
    (i) Testes produce sperms.
    (ii) Testes produce male sex hormone called testosterone. (2 marks)

27. A is carbon, B is carbon monoxide and C is carbon dioxide. ($1 \times 3 = 3$ marks)

28. (i) 2-hydroxy-propan-1-oic acid (1 mark)
    (ii) Ethyl ethanoate (1 mark)
    (iii) But-1, 2-diol (1 mark)

29. (a) (i) Positively phototropic – Shoot
        (ii) Negatively geotropic – Shoot (1 mark)
    (b) Root (1 mark)
    (c) Shoot tip (1 mark)

30. (i) Ozone layer helps in shielding the Earth from the lethal UV radiation coming from sun. If ozone layer gets depleted, UV radiation will directly reach the earth's surface and seriously affect the life on earth. (1½ marks)
    (ii) Ozone layer can be protected by:
    (a) Restriction in release of chlorofluorocarbons
    (b) Eliminating the pollutant nitrogen monoxide and carbon monoxide
    (c) Less usage of air conditioners (1½ marks)

31. (i) He should use a concave miror, because it forms a real image on the same side of the mirror. (1 mark)
    (ii) Given, $u = -12$ cm, $= -48$ cm
    Magnification, $m = -v/u = -(-48)/(-12) = -4$
    The munus sign of magnification shows that the image formed is real and inverted. (½ mark)
    (iii) The image is formed at a distance of 36 cm from the object. (½ mark)

(iv)

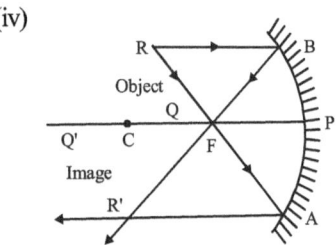

(1 mark)

In this case, the image is formed beyond the centre of curvature. This image is real, inverted and enlarged.

32. Ray diagram to find the position and size of the image formed.

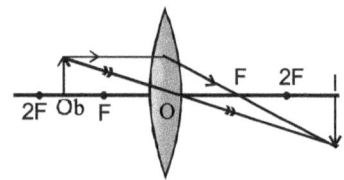

(1 mark)

Here, focal length, f = 20 cm, u = –30 cm, h_0 = 4 cm

Using, lens formula, $\dfrac{1}{f} = \dfrac{1}{v} - \dfrac{1}{u} \Rightarrow \dfrac{1}{20} = \dfrac{1}{v} - \dfrac{1}{(-30)}$

∴ Image distance, v = 60 cm   (1 mark)

The image formed is real and inverted.

The ratio of size of the image to the size of the object

$\dfrac{h_1}{h_0} = \dfrac{v}{u} = \dfrac{60}{30} = 2$ (1 mark)

33.

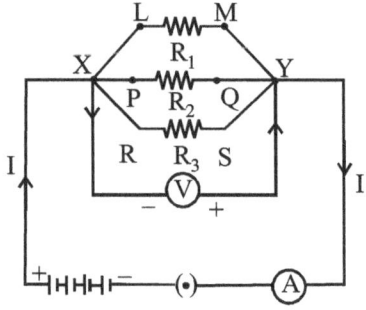

(1 mark)

It is observed that the total current I, is equal to the sum of the separate currents through each branch of the combination.

$I = I_1 + I_2 + I_3$ ......(i)

Let R_P be the equivalent resistance of the parallel combination of resistors.

By applying Ohm's law to the parallel combination of resistors, we have

$I = \dfrac{V}{R_p}$ ......(ii)

On applying Ohm's law to each resistor, we have

$I_1 = \dfrac{V}{R_1}, I_2 = \dfrac{V}{R_2}, \text{ or } I_3 = \dfrac{V}{R_3}$ ......(ii)   (1 mark)

From eqns (i), we have

$\dfrac{V}{R_p} = \dfrac{V}{R_1} + \dfrac{V}{R_2} + \dfrac{V}{R_3}$

or $\dfrac{1}{R_p} = \dfrac{1}{R_1} + \dfrac{1}{R_2} + \dfrac{1}{R_3}$ (1 mark)

Thus, we may conclude that the reciprocal of the equivalent resistance of a group of resistances joined in parallel is equal to the sum of the reciprocals of the individual resistances.

OR

(i) **Applications of heating effect of electricity:**
(a) This effect of electricity is used in electrical heating appliances like geyser, heater, iron, etc, - all these appliances contain nichrome wire which has very high resistance.
(b) Heating effect of electricity is also used in bulbs. The bulb contains tungsten filament which has very high resistance due to which large amount of heat is produced which causes emission of light.
(c) Heating effect is also used for making fuse wire because when heat is produced, fuse wire melts which disconnects the household circuit with the main electricity board. The fuse wire is a thin wire of high resistance. When high voltage or electricity (due to short circuit) enters into the main electricity board, large amount of heat is produced due to which the fuse wire melts and the whole household circuit gets disconnected from the main electricity board.

(1½ marks)

(ii) Energy of fans = n × P × t = 5 × $\dfrac{40}{1000}$ × 10 = 2 kWh.

Energy of bulbs = n × P × t = 4 × $\dfrac{100}{1000}$ × 6 = 2.4 kWh.

Total energy consumed in 25 days
= 25 × (2 + 2.4) = 25 × 4.4 = 110 kWh.
Total cost of bill = 0.30 × 110 = ₹ 33   (1½ marks)

Sample Paper-5 Solutions

34. The four ions involved are Na^+, CO_3^{2-}, Ca^{2+} and Cl^- when a solution of Na_2CO_3 is mixed with a solution of $CaCl_2$. The combinations of the Na^+ and Cl^- and the Ca^{2+} and CO_3^{2-} produce the compounds NaCl and $CaCO_3$. If both of these compounds are soluble, no reaction occurs. In this case, however, $CaCO_3$ is insoluble. Thus, a reaction occurs that we can illustrate with a balanced reaction written in molecular form. (2 marks)

$$Na_2CO_3(aq) + CaCl_2(aq) \longrightarrow CaCO_3(s) + 2NaCl(aq)$$
(1 mark)

The above equation can be written in total ionic form:

$$2Na^+(aq) + CO_3^{2-}(aq) + Ca^{2+}(aq) + 2Cl^-(aq)$$

$$\longrightarrow CaCO_3(s) + 2Na^+(aq) + 2Cl^-(aq) \quad \text{(1 mark)}$$

The net ionic equation will be:

$$Ca^{2+}(aq) + CO_3^{2-}(aq) \longrightarrow CaCO_3(s) \quad \text{(1 mark)}$$

OR

(a) $CaCO_3 \longrightarrow CaO + CO_2$
(b) $4Na + O_2 \longrightarrow 2Na_2O$
(c) $2H_2O_2 \longrightarrow 2H_2O + O_2$
(d) $2Al + 2H_3PO_4 \longrightarrow 2AlPO_4 + 3H_2$
(e) $Ca(OH)_2 + 2HCl \longrightarrow CaCl_2 + 2H_2O$
(f) $3Mg + N_2 \longrightarrow Mg_3N_2$
(g) $2C_2H_6 + 7O_2 \longrightarrow 4CO_2 + 6H_2O$
(h) $Mg_3N_2 + 6H_2O \longrightarrow 3Mg(OH)_2 + 2NH_3$
(i) $2H_2S + O_2 \longrightarrow 2S + 2H_2O$
(j) $2BF_3 + 6NaH \longrightarrow B_2H_6 + 6NaF$ (½ × 10 = 5 marks)

35. (i) **Binary fission :** (a) *Amoeba*
(b) **Binary fission :** Two daughter cells. (1 mark)
Multiple fission : Many daughter cells are formed
(c) Asexual reproduction is a type of reproduction in which offsprings are produced from a single parent. (1 mark)
(ii) In *Amoeba*, splitting of two cells during division can take place in any plane. (1 mark)
In *Leishmania*, binary fission occurs in definite orientation in accordance to the whip like structure. (1 mark)

36. (a) The rod get displaced on passing current through it because a force is exerted on the rod when it is placed in a magnetic field. (1 mark)
(b) Fleming's left hand rule determines the direction of the force on the conductor AB. (1 mark)

According to this rule, stretch the thumb, forefinger and middle finger of your left hand such that they are mutually perpendicular. If the first finger points in the direction of magnetic field and the second finger in the direction of current, then the thumb will point in the direction of motion or the force acting on the conductor. (1 mark)

(c) (i) If the polarity of the magnet and the direction of current both are reversed, the rod gets displaced towards the right.
(ii) Two devices that use current carrying conductors and magnetic field are electric motor and electric generator. (1 × 2 = 2 marks)

OR

Pattern of magnetic field lines produced around a current carrying straight conductor held vertically is shown in the figure below.
Also indicated the direction of field lines as well as the direction of current flowing through the conductor.

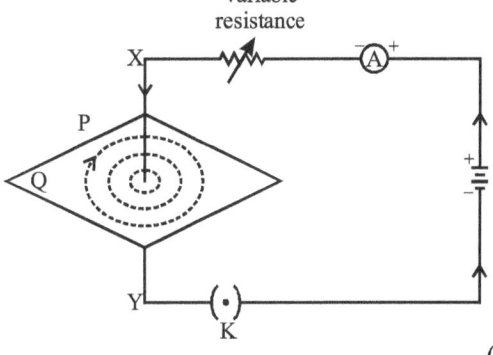

(5 marks)

37. (a) A few bases dissolved in water are known as alkali
(i) Action on indicators: An alkaline solution turns red litmus into blue and pink phenophthalein into colurless solution (1 mark)
(ii) Bases produce hydroxyl ($-OH^-$) ion in aqueous medium and reacts with acid (1 mark)
(b) A storng base dissociates completely in aqueious medium land a weal bases dissocates paritally. Therefore, of the concentration of strong base increses the production of OH– increases and the soltuion becomes strongly basic.
Wheras the dissociation of a weak base in solution depends on the concentration of the base. As the concentration decreses the degree of dissociation and eventually, production of OH– increases.
Therefore, the concentration and degree of dissociation both these parameters required to define the strength of basicity. (2 marks)

OR

(i) $Ba(OH)_2 \rightarrow Ba^{2+} + 2OH^-$;
(ii) $Ca(OH)_2 \rightarrow Ca^{2+} + 2OH^-$

Both of the compound have two replacable hydroxyl ions.

(1 mark)

$$\underset{\text{Base}}{\overset{\ominus}{N}H_2} + \underset{\text{Acid}}{H_3O^+} \longrightarrow \underset{\substack{\text{Conjugate} \\ \text{acid}}}{NH_3} + \underset{\substack{\text{Conjugate} \\ \text{base}}}{H_2O}$$

(1 mark)

38. (a) A combination of electrical devices connected by conducting wires is called an electric circuit. (1 mark)

(b) Its S.I unit is ampere. If one coulomb of charge flows through a conductor in one second, then the amount of current flowing is said to be 1 ampere. (2 marks)

(c) Charge on one electron $= 1.6 \times 10^{-19}$ C

∴ 1.6×10^{-19} C charge carried by 1 electron

∴ 1 C charge carried by

$= \dfrac{1}{1.6 \times 10^{-19}} = 6.25 \times 10^{18}$ electrons (1 mark)

OR

(c) It means that 1 joule of work is done in carrying one coulomb charge between the two given points.

(1 mark)

39. (i) Taenia (tapeworm) is an example of parasite. (1 mark)

(ii) Heterotrophic nutrition is the mode of nutrition where the organism is unable to prepare its food and hence, depends upon plants or other organisms for nutrition.

(1 mark)

(iii) Mushroom is an example of the organism that exhibits saprotrophic mode of nutrition. (1 mark)

(iv) Autotrophs are capable of converting carbon dioxide into sugar via photosynthesis. (1 mark)

SAMPLE PAPER-6

1. (a) The ability of metals to be drawn into thin wire is known as ductility.
2. (d) C_4H_8 belongs to C_nH_{2n} series.
3. (c) Acids are those chemical substances which have a sour taste and turn blue litmus solution to red.
4. (d) $4FeSO_4 \longrightarrow 2Fe_2O_3 + 4SO_2 + O_2]$
5. (a) Factual
6. (a) Our stomach produces hydrochloric acid (pH < 7) which helps in digesting our food.
7. (d)
8. (b) Tiny pores (called stomata) present on the surface of the leaves. Massive amounts of gaseous exchange takes place in the leaves through these pores for the purpose of photosynthesis.
9. (b)
10. (c) A convex lens of focal length 5 cm. (Because its magnification is more than others as it is inversely proportional to the focal length $\left(m = \frac{v}{f} - 1\right)$).
11. (c)
12. (c) Focal length of a lens, F = 25 cm
    $f = 0.25$ m
    $P = \frac{1}{f} = \frac{1}{0.25} = 4D$
13. (b) Phloem is a permanent complex tissue of the plant that helps in the transportation of food. Sieve tubes and companion cells are the two components of phloem tissue that transport food bidirectional.
14. (c) A complete set of chromosomes inherited as a unit from one parent is known as genome.
15. (a) Mendel's law of segregation state's that allele pairs separate or segregate during gametic formation and randomly unite at fertilisation.
16. (c) puberty starts in boys in between 10 and 13 and continues to grow till 16.
17. (a) $H_3PO_4 \rightleftharpoons H_2PO_4^- + H^+$
    $H_2PO_4^- \rightleftharpoons H^+ + HPO_4^{2-}$
    $HPO_4^{2-} \rightleftharpoons H^+ + PO_4^{3-}$
    Similarly, bases which give two or more than two hydroxyl ions per molecule are known as polyacidic bases.
18. (d) The resistance depend on the material of which it is made and can be expressed as:
    $R = \rho L / A$
    where
    R = resistance (ohm)
    ρ = resistivity coefficient (ohm m)
    L = length of wire (m)
    A = cross sectional area of wire (m²)
    The factor in the resistance which takes into account the nature of the material is the resistivity.
19. (a) In many plant species, the growth of axillary meristems in inhibited by the primary shoot or primary inflorescence. This phenomenon is generally known as apical dominance. Auxin has an inhibitory effect on the growth of axillary buds.
20. (b) Ventricles have thicker walls than auricles because they have to pump blood to different organs and the pressure with which the blood flows through them is more than the auricles. While valves are present in the heart to prevent backflow of the blood.
21. NaOH and Cl_2 are the products that are formed in a chlor-alkali process. (2 marks)

    OR

    The molecular formula of two consecutive members of this series is CH_3Cl (chloromethane) and C_2H_5Cl (chloroethane). (2 marks)
22. The importance of transpiration :
    (i) Ascent of sap- Transpiration makes possible for the water to be raised from the xylem of the roots to the top of the plant by producing suction force (Transpiration pull).
    (ii) It helps in removal of excess of water.
    (iii) It causes cooling effect.
    (iv) It helps in absorption and distribution of salts.
    $(4 \times 1½ = 2 \text{ marks})$
23. The flow of electric charges across a cross-section of a conductor in unit time constitutes an electric current. Electrons. $(1 + 1 = 2 \text{ marks})$

    OR

    (a)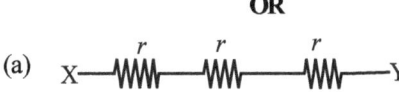

    (b)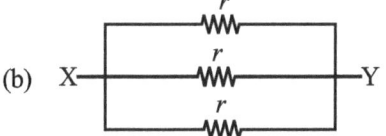

    (c)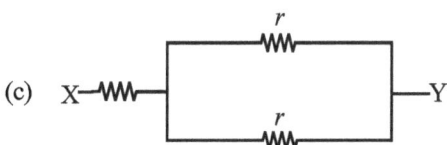

(d)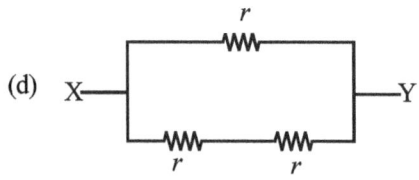

(i) Circuit (a) have maximum resistance
(ii) Circuit (b) have minimum resistance (½ × 4 = 2 marks)

24.

	Phototropism		Geotropism
(i)	In this process, the growing plant bends towards light.	(i)	In this process, the plant bends towards gravity.
(ii)	Stem is positively phototropic.	(ii)	Stem is negatively geotropic.
(iii)	Root is negatively phototropic.	(iii)	Roots are positively geotropic.

(1 + 1 = 2 marks)

25. (i) Auxin (ii) Abscisic acid   (1 + 1 = 2 marks)

26. The male reproductive part of an angiospermic plants is stamen and female is called carpel. It is located in the flower. Male reproductive part consist of two parts–

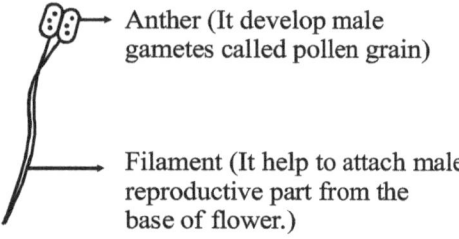

Anther (It develop male gametes called pollen grain)

Filament (It help to attach male reproductive part from the base of flower.)

(1 + 1 = 2 marks)

OR

– Puberty is the phase in humans, when a boy or girl reach to their sexual maturity.   (1 mark)
– Two changes that are common to both boys and girls in early teenage years are–
 (i) Releasing of hormones.
 (ii) Growth of public hair, facial hair and increasing in height.   (2 × ½ = 1 mark)

27. The reaction in which single reactant breaks down into two or more simpler product is known as decomposition reaction. When a reaction is carried out in the presence of heat is called thermal decomposition reaction.

$CaCO_3(s) \xrightarrow{Heat} CaO(s) + CO_2(g)$

When a decomposition reaction is carried out by electric current, it is called as electrolytic decomposition.

$2H_2O(l) \xrightarrow{Electric\ current} 2H_2(g) + O_2(g)$ (3 marks)

28. (a) C_5H_{12} (C_nH_{2n+2})
 (b) C_2H_4 (C_nH_{2n})
 (iii) C_5H_{10} (C_nH_{2n})   (1 × 3 = 3 marks)

29. (a)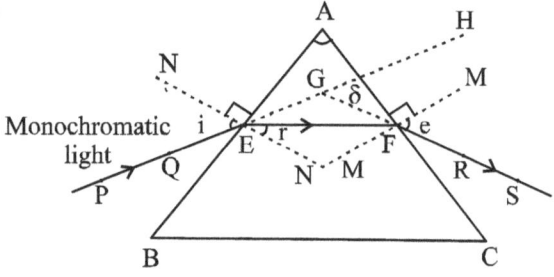

PE – Incident ray   ∠i – Angle of incidence
EF – Refracted ray   ∠r – Angle of refraction
FS – Emergent ray   ∠e – Angle of emergence
∠A – Angle of the prism   ∠δ – Angle of deviation

(2 marks)

(b) When a narrow beam of white light passes through a prism, it emerges as a spectrum of all components of white light. (see the fig.)

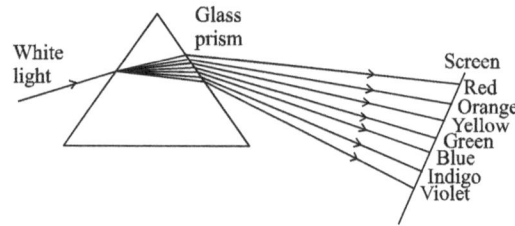

(1 mark)

30. (i) The graph show that V ∝ I   (1 mark)
 (ii) It states that the current passing through a conductors is directly proportional to the potential difference across its ends, provided the physical conditions like temperature, density, etc, remain unchanged. This is ohm's law.   (1 mark)
 (iii) **Slope of graph gives** resistance of a conductor and its unit is Ohm (Ω).   (1 mark)

OR

Given, The resistance of conductor $R1_1 = 4Ω$
The resistance of conductor $R_2 = 20Ω$
(i) The total resistance of the circuit
 $R = R_1 + R_2$ (series combintion)
 $R = 4 + 20 = 24Ω$ (1 mark)
(ii) Now by ohm's Law, The current through the circuit,

$V = IR \Rightarrow I = \dfrac{V}{R} = \dfrac{6}{24} = \Rightarrow = 0.25$ Amp.   (1 mark)

Sample Paper-6 Solutions

(iii) The potential difference across the two terminals of the battery = 6V.
$V_1 = I \times R_1$
$= 0.25 \times 4 = 1V$ (Potential difference across the conductor R_1)
$V_2 = I \times R_2$
$= 0.25 \times 20 = 5V$ (Potential difference across the conductor R_2) (1 mark)

31. When *Planaria* is cut into many pieces, each piece grows into a complete organism; this regeneration process is carried out by specialized cell or regenerative cell; which proliferate; develop and differentiate into various cell types and tissues.

Regeneration is not same as reproduction as most of the organisms would not normally depend on being cut up to be able to reproduce. (3 marks)

32.

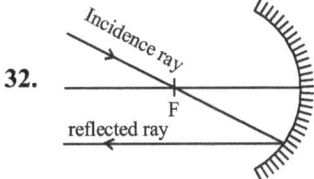
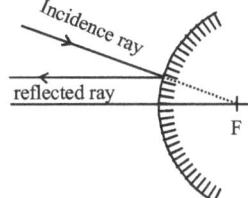

(1 × 3 = 3 marks)

33. (i) Green stem   Purple Stem
Parent – GG   gg
            ↓   ↓
gamete – G   g
                    ↓
f_1 Gen –   Gg   (green stem)

f_1 progeny must be like their dominant parent with green stemmed tomato plant. (1 mark)

(ii) f_2 Gen

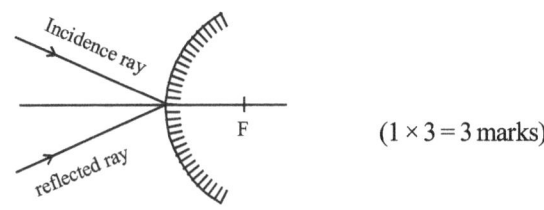

Phenotype ratio → GG : Gg : Gg : gg
                    ⎵⎵⎵⎵⎵⎵   ⎵⎵
                    green stem purple stem

Hence, the Ratio for green stem and purple stem is 3:1 respectivily. (1 mark)

(iii) The above observation show law of dominances. (1 mark)

34. (a) (i) An electropositive element is the one that has tendency to lose electrons and form positively charged ion. Metals like Na, Mg, K, Ca, Fe lose electrons and form positively charged ion. Due to this, metals are called electropositive elements. (1 mark)

(ii) Aluminium is a reactive metal and reacts readily with moisture and water. On reaction, it forms a layer of aluminium oxide (Al_2O_3), which acts as a non-penetrating layer and protects aluminium from being corrode. (1 mark)

(b) When zinc metal is placed in solution of mercuric chloride, Zn displaces mercury and a shining silvery surface is formed because zinc is more reactive than mercury.
$Zn(s) + HgCl_2(aq) \longrightarrow ZnCl_2(aq) + Hg(l)$
When zinc metal is placed in $MgSO_4$ solution, no reaction takes place because Zn is less reactive than Mg, therefore, it cannot displace Mg from $MgSO_4$. (3 marks)

OR

(a) X — Na;   Y — NaOH;   Z — H_2

$2Na(s) + 2H_2O(l) \longrightarrow 2NaOH(aq) + H_2(g) + Heat$
(1+1=2 marks)

(b) Gold and platinum are the two metals that do not corrode easily. (1 mark)

(i) Corrosion of some metals is an advantage. For example: a thin impervious layer of aluminium oxide forms a protective layer which protects the aluminium metals underneath from further damage. (1 mark)

(ii) Corrosion of metal is a serious problem. For example: corrosion of iron in the presence of oxygen and air leads to formation of brown solid known as rust. It causes damage to car bodies, bridges, ships, iron railings and all objects made of metals (specially iron). (1 mark)

35. (i) **Alternating Current:** If the current changes direction after equal intervals of time i.e. periodically change its direction and magnitude, it is called alternating current. The positive and negative polarities of AC are not fixed.

Direct Current: If the current always flows in the same direction i.e. magnitude and direction does not vary with time, it is called direct current. It can be obtained from a cell or a bettery. The positive and negative polarities of DC are fixed for long distance transmission. AC is preferred as it caused minimum loss of energy during transmission. (2 marks)

(ii) Source of AC current - electric generator.
Source of DC current - electric cell. (1 mark)

(iii) Frequency of alternating current in India is 50 Hz. (1 mark)

(iv) (a) Alternating current reverse its direction periodically but direct current always flow in one direction.
(b) AC electric power can be transmitted over long distances without much loss of energy while DC not. (1 mark)

36. In the ecosystem, there is continuous and unidirectional flow of energy. The energy from the sun through the various energy levels finally reaches the tertiary consumers. These various energy levels are joined by a food chain. Many food chains overlap and form a food web. (2 marks)

Loss of energy at different levels

Trapped energy is fixed in the form of complex organic compounds and is used by herbivorous and carnivorous animals. But the energy does not terminate or end here. When the organism dies, then the dead body gets mixed with the soil. Indirectly it can be said that the complex energy rich compounds from the dead body are now utilized by decomposers or scavangers, and then ultimately energy is released back into nature after decomposition. Thus, we see at every level, organisms make use of energy and as a result of use of energy when life activity occurs then energy is lost and therefore, supply of energy is continuously required from the sun. (3 marks)

37. (a) $2C_8H_{18}(l) + 25O_2(g) \longrightarrow 16CO_2(g) + 18H_2O(g)$
 'X' 'Y'
(½ + ½ = 1 mark)
Thus is an exothermic oxidation reaction. (1 mark)

(b) Nitrogen acts as an inert gas since it has triple bonds which are covalent in nature. The nature of bond is very strong. So, it requires a large amount of energy to break apart two 'N' atoms and take part in the combustion reaction under normal atmospheric condition.

Note : In chemistry laboratory, nitrogen gas is used to make reaction atmosphere inert. But, for sensitive reaction, helium gas is used for creating inert atmosphere (2 marks)

OR

(b) Limited supply of air leads to partial combustion of fuel. As a result, carbon monoxide (CO) gas is produced and black smoke is created.

$C_3H_8(g) + \frac{3}{2}O_2(g) \longrightarrow 3CO(g) + 4H_2(g)$

(Partial combustion)

$C_3H_8(g) + 5O_2(g) \longrightarrow 3CO_2(g) + 4H_2(g)$

(Complete combustion) (2 marks)

38. (i) Contraction of ventricle region is responsible for generating blood pressure.

(ii) 120/80 mm Hg.

(iii) When the decrease in blood volume is greater than 10% the blood presure on decrease at higher %.

(iv)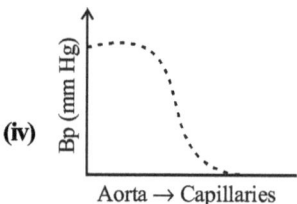

39. (a) Focal length, f = –50 cm (concave lens)
Now, Power,

$$P = \frac{1}{f \text{ (in metre)}} = \frac{1}{-\frac{50}{100}m} = -\frac{100}{50} = -2$$ (1 mark)

Thus, the power of this concave lens is –2 dioptres

(b) $\frac{1}{v} - \frac{1}{u} = \frac{1}{f}$

$v = -32$ cm, $f = 8$ cm,
∴ $u = -32/5$
Now $m = v/u = 5$ (1 mark)

(c) A healthy human eye can see the objects at infinity distinctly. So far point is infinity. The eye can also see the nearly objects beyond 25 cm. (2 marks)

OR

The lens used for correcting the disease is concave lens

$P = -\frac{1}{\text{far point (metre)}} = -\frac{1}{80 \text{ cm}} = \frac{-100}{80}$

$= -1.25$ D. (2 marks)

SAMPLE PAPER-7

1. **(d)** Because it can furnish H⁺ ions in solution.
2. **(c)**
3. **(b)** Graphite is an allotrope of carbon which is a non-metal, it is a good conductor of electricity.
4. **(d)** Y is chlorine which is a non-metal. Z is magnesium which is a metal. X is neon which is an inert gas as it has complete octate.
5. **(d)**
6. **(c)** Isomers have same molecular formula, molecular weight and molecular composition but different chemical properties and structural formulae because the properties are based on the position of atoms.
7. **(a)** The soap solution in water is not neutral and cannot be used to wash all kinds of fabrics.
8. **(c)** Correct order for the urine formation is
   Glomerular filtration → reabsorption → secretion
9. **(c)** According to Rayleigh's law, scattering $\propto \dfrac{1}{\lambda^4}$ $\lambda_{Red} > \lambda_{Blue}$ so red light is least scattered in the atmosphere.
10. **(d)**   11. **(b)**   12. **(a)**
13. **(d)** Oxygen-rich blood from the lungs comes to the thin-walled upper chamber of the heart on the left, the left atrium. The left atrium relaxes when it is collecting this blood. It then contracts, while the next chamber, the left ventricle, relaxes, so that the blood is transferred to it. When the muscular left ventricle contracts in its turn, the blood is pumped out to the body. De-oxygenated blood comes from the body to the upper chamber on the right, the right atrium, as it relaxes. As the right atrium contracts, the corresponding lower chamber.
14. **(d)**
15. **(a)** Fertilisation does not lead to clone formation.
16. **(d)** Homozygous red flower RR and homozygous white flower. When it is crossed it will form pink flower.
17. **(d)** A reducing agent is a substance which oxidises itself but reduces others *i.e.,* looses electrons.
18. **(c)** Magnetic field inside a long solenoid is uniform. This magnetic field magnetises the iron bar.
19. **(a)** Cerebrum is the largest part of the brain and is composed of right and left hemispheres. It performs higher functions like interpreting touch, vision and hearing, as well as speech, reasoning, emotions, learning and fine control of movement. It is responsible for intelligence, memory and judgement.
20. **(a)** Both Assertion and Reason are correct and the Reason is a correct explanation of Assertion.
    Mendel used a number of contrasting visible characters of garden peas, produced progeny from them, calculated the percentage of tall or short progeny. He was the first person to make use of his knowledge of science and mathematics and keep a count of individuals exhibiting a particular trait in each generation. This helped him to arrive at the laws of inheritance/heredity.
21. Combustion reaction: It is a reaction between a substance and oxygen with releasing energy in the form of heat or light.
    $$C + O_2 \xrightarrow{heat} CO_2 + heat \qquad \text{(2 marks)}$$
    OR
    When milk changes into curd there occures a decrease in pH. It happens because of the fact that lactose (a carbohydrate) present in milk gets converted into lactic acid (an acid). As more of acid is formed, the pH of medium decreases (i.e., it becomes more acidic)   (2 marks)
22. Cerebrospinal fluid (CSF) is a clear colourless bodily fluid produced in the choroid plexus of the brain. It acts as a cushion or buffer for the cortex, providing a basic mechanical and immunological protection to the brain inside the skull and serves a vital function in cerebral autoregulation of cerebral blood flow.   (2 marks)
23. Gonads are primary sex organs. Male gonads is testes and female gonad is ovary.   (1 + 1 marks)
24. The angle between the extended incident ray and the emergent ray is called the angle of deviation.   (1 mark)
    This is because the different colours travel through a glass prism at different speeds.   (1 mark)

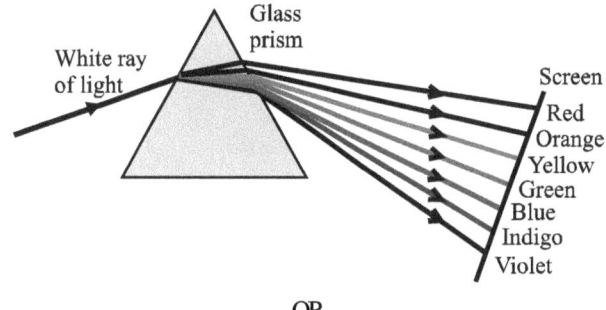

    OR
    There is nearly no atmosphere for the astronauts as they are flying high in sky. So there is no scattering of light. This is why the sky appear dark to the astronauts.
    (2 marks)
25. The loss of energy at each step is so great that very little usable energy remains after four trophic levels. (2 marks)
26. No, because mothers have a pair of X-chromosomes. All children will inherit an 'X' chromosome from their mother regardless of whether they are boys or girls.   (2 marks)
27. Aqua-regia is a freshly prepared mixture of 1 part of concentrated nitric acid and 3 parts of concentrated hydrochloric acid.   (1 mark)
    Properties:
    (i) It is highly corrosive   (1 mark)
    (ii) Aqua-ragia can dissolve all metals.   (1 mark)
28. Petroleum was formed by slow decomposition of sea plants and animals. These plants and animals were buried under the Earth's crust millions of years ago. They got covered by layers of sedimentary rocks which cut off the supply of air. In the absence of air, these fossils undergo

a slow chemical change due to high temperature and pressure and then turned into new form, known as petroleum. It is also known as crude oil. (3 marks)

29. The earth wire is connected to a metallic plate deep inside the earth. which provides a low resistance conducting path for the current. In this way, the metallic body of appliance is connected to the earth, Hence, any leakage of current to the meetallic body of appliance keeps the potential to that of earth i.e. the earth wire allows the current to flow into the earth The user might not get a severe electric shock on touching such an appliance. Earth wire has green insulation, so it can be identified. (3 marks)

30. The valves (i.e. bicuspid and tricuspid) are present between auricles and ventricles. Their presence stops the back flow of blood. When ventricles contract, the valves get closed and it helps to maintain the unidirectional flow of blood. (i.e.the blood does not go back into auricles). (2+1 marks)

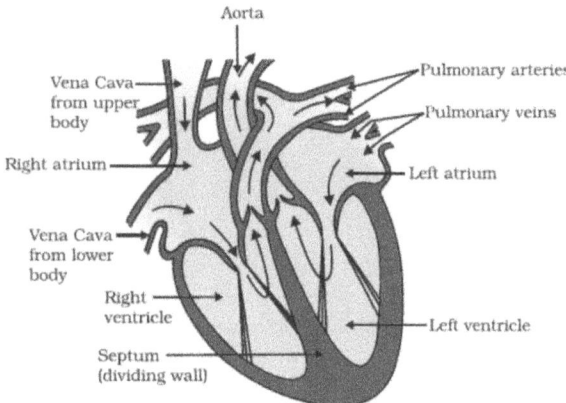

31. Figure shows the setting of the iron filings.

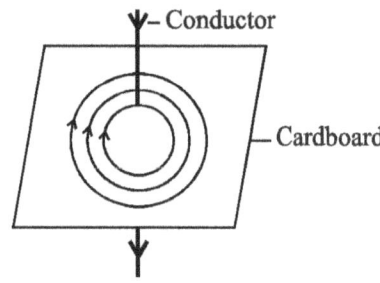

(1 mark)
(i) The shape of distribution of iron filings remains unchanged but they get arranged upto a larger distance from the conductor when the strength of current is increased. This is because on increasing the strength of current, the strength of the magnetic field is increased and it is effective upto a larger distance from the conductor. (1 mark)
(ii) Magnetic field strength is increased so the iron filings get arranged upto a larger distance. (1 mark)

32. It will bend towards the normal because the velocity of light decreases as it enters into water. Here, air is a rarer medium and water is denser medium.So, light ray will bend towards normal. (3 marks)

OR

(i) Converging
(ii) Simple microscope and telescope (½ mark)
(iii) In this case,
(a) Reflected rays are divergent , therefore image A_1B_1 is formed behind the mirror.
(b) Image is virtual and erect.
(c) Size of image A_1B_1 is larger than object AB. (see the fig.)
(1½ marks)

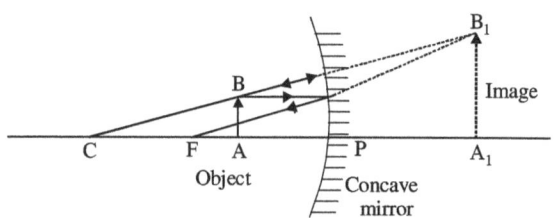

(1 mark)

33. Energy present in Grass = 20000 J

Justification : According to the ten percent law of energy in a food chain, only ten % of energy is transferred to the next trophic level. Thus, the energy keeps on decreasing by 10% of each level.

Explanation:

Energy available to grass = 20000 J

Energy available to grass hopper
= 10% of 20000 = 2000 J

Energy available to frog = 10% of 2000 = 200 J

Energy available to snake = 10% of 200 = 20 J

Energy available to peacock = 10% of 20 = 2 J

hence, justified. (3 marks)

34. (a) $Fe_2O_3(s) + 2Al(s) \longrightarrow Al_2O_3(s) + 2Fe(s)$
Iron(III)oxide Aluminium   Aluminium oxide Iron

(b) $AgNO_3(aq) + NaCl(aq) \longrightarrow$
Silver nitrate Sodium chloride

$AgCl(s) + NaNO_3(aq)$
Silver chloride Sodium nitrate

(c) $Cl_2(g) + 2KI(aq) \longrightarrow 2KCl(aq) + I_2(s)$
Chlorine Potassium iodide Potassium chloride Iodine

(d) $CuO(s) + Mg(s) \longrightarrow MgO(s) + Cu(s)$
Copper oxide Magnesium Magnesium oxide Copper

(e) $Cu(s) + 2AgNO_3(aq) \longrightarrow Cu(NO_3)_2(aq) + 2Ag(s)$
Copper Silver nitrate Copper nitrate Silver

(1 × 5 = 5 marks)

OR

(a) $Si_2H_6 + 8H_2O \longrightarrow 2Si(OH)_4 + 7H_2$

(b) $C_2H_6 + Cl_2 \longrightarrow C_2H_5Cl + HCl$

Sample Paper-7 Solutions

(c) $B_4H_{10} + \frac{11}{2}O_2 \longrightarrow 2B_2O_3 + 5H_2O$

(d) $3H_2 + N_2 \longrightarrow 2NH_3$

(e) $CS_2 + 3O_2 \longrightarrow CO_2 + 2SO_2$

(f) $N_2O_5 \longrightarrow N_2O_4 + \frac{1}{2}O_2$

(g) $KNO_3 \longrightarrow KNO_2 + \frac{1}{2}O_2$

(h) $NH_4NO_3 \longrightarrow N_2O + 2H_2O$

(i) $NH_4NO_2 \longrightarrow N_2 + 2H_2O$

(j) $2NaHCO_3 \longrightarrow Na_2CO_3 + H_2O + CO_2$

(½ × 10 = 5 marks)

35. (a) (i) Bifocal lenses are used to correct the defect when a person suffers from both the defects of vision myopia and hypermetropia. (1 mark)
  (ii) Bifocal lens is made by using two lenses in one eyepiece. Convex lens of appropriate focal length is positioned below while concave lens of appropriate focal length is positioned above. (1 mark)

(b) We know that, Power of lens(P) = 1/f
Or, f = 1/P (1 mark)
So, focal length (f) of lens for near vision
= 1/3 = +0.33m (1 mark)
And focal length of lens for distant vision
= – 1/3 = – 0.33m. (1 mark)

36. (a) Hormones are the chemical substances which coordinate and control the activities of living organisms and also their growth. The term hormone was introduced by Bayliss and Starling. (1 mark)

(b) **Characteristics of Hormones.** (Any four)
  (i) Hormones are the secretions of endocrine glands or tissues.
  (ii) They are poured directly into the blood and carried throughout the body by blood circulatory system.
  (iii) Hormones have their effect at the sites different from the sites where they are made. So, they are also called 'chemical messengers.'
  (iv) They act on specific tissues or organs called 'target organs.'
  (v) They coordinate the activities of the body and also its growth.
  (vi) They are secreted in extremely minute quantities.
  (vii) Chemically, hormones may be polypeptides and proteins, amino acids and their derivatives or steroids.
  (viii) Hormones help the body to cope with emergency demands such as infection, trauma, dehydration, starvation, haemorrhage and extreme temperature.
  (ix) They generally slow in their actions.

(4 × ½ = 2 marks)

(c) The hormone required for the following are as follows:
  (i) Functioning of mammary glands – Prolactin.
  (ii) Regulation of calcium and phosphate in blood – Calcitonin.
  (iii) Lowering of blood glucose – Insulin.
  (iv) Development of moustache and beard in human male – Testosterone. (4 × ½ = 2 marks)

37. (a) Raw materials for preparing $NaHCO_3$:
$NaCl, H_2O, CO_2, NH_3$ (1 mark)
$CaCl + H_2O + CO_2 + NH_3 \longrightarrow NaHCO_3 + NH_4Cl$ (1 mark)

(b) The compounds used as antacids —
$NaHCO_3, Ca(OH)_2, Mg(OH)_2$, cimetidine; all are mild basic in nature.
But NaOH cannot be used as it is corrosive in nature. (2 marks)

OR

(b) Backing powder mainly contain, sodium bicarbonate and a weak acid, generally tartaric acid. It is used to increase the volume of bakery products such as cakes. (2 marks)

38. (i) It is because yellow colour is dominant over green colour.
(ii) The work of mendel was more quantitative.
(iii) All the offspring will be tall.
(iv) Option A is correct.

39. (a) (i) In series (ii) In parallel. (1 mark)
(b) Because it is safer as the current in it is smaller. Also large number of electric bulbs connected in series can be controlled with just one switch. (1 mark)
(c) The equivalent resistance of resistors connected in parallel is less than even the smallest resistance connected in parallel, so, large current is obtained in the circuit for the same potential difference. So resistances are connecting in parallel. (2 marks)

OR

(a)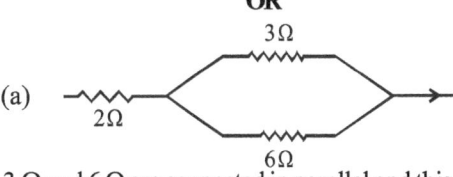

3 Ω and 6 Ω are connected in parallel and this combination is connected in series to 2 Ω resistor to get an equivalent resistance of 4Ω. (1 mark)

(b)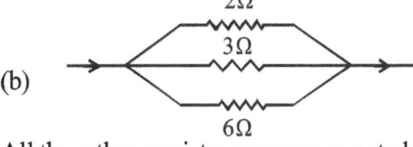

All these three resistances are connected in parallel to get an equivalent resistance of 1 Ω. (1 mark)

SAMPLE PAPER-8

1. **(d)** A chemical equation represents energy change during a reaction.
2. **(c)** Common salt (sodium chloride) is used as a raw material for making a large number of chemicals such as washing soda, baking soda and chlorine gas. Chlorine gas obtained during electrolysis of aqueous NaCl (brine) is used for making bleaching powder.
3. **(b)** From the properties of the element given in the question, it is clear that the element is sodium (Na).
4. **(d)** Butane and isobutane have same chemical formula but different arrangement of atoms and have different structure.

$$H-\underset{H}{\overset{H}{C}}-\underset{H}{\overset{H}{C}}-\underset{H}{\overset{H}{C}}-\underset{H}{\overset{H}{C}}-H \quad , \quad H-\underset{H}{\overset{H}{C}}-\underset{\underset{H-\underset{H}{\overset{H}{C}}-H}{|}}{\overset{H}{C}}-\underset{H}{\overset{H}{C}}-H$$

(Butane) (Isobutane)

5. **(c)**
6. **(b)** $Zn + 2HCl \longrightarrow ZnCl_2 + H_2$
   Hydrogen gas burns with a pop sound.
7. **(b)** The decomposition of water during electrolysis gives hydrogen and oxygen gases in the ratio 2 : 1 by volume.
   $$\underset{\text{Water}}{2H_2O(l)} \xrightarrow{\text{Electric current}} \underset{\text{Hydrogen}}{2H_2(g)} + \underset{\text{Oxygen}}{O_2(g)}$$
8. **(c)** The colour of Y is red the colour used to paint the danger signal. When white ray of light passes through a prism it disperses into seven colours VIBGYOR. Red colour deviates or bends the least.
9. **(a)** The accumulation of harmful chemicals with an increase in trophical level is known as biological magnification.
10. **(a)** Scattering of light is not enough at such heights.
11. **(d)** Fuse wire should be such that it melts immediatley when strong current flows through the circuit. The same is possible if its melting point is low and resistivity is high.
12. **(a)** Good ozone is found in the upper part of the atmosphere called stratosphere and it acts as a shield absorbing ultraviolet radiation from the Sun.
13. **(c)** Both sperm and ova contain 23 chromosomes, total 46 chromosomes.
14. **(d)** Sex determination in humans is due to the two types of chromosomes (X & Y) in males.
15. **(c)** Increases heavily
16. **(a)**
17. **(b)** Electric wires are made up of copper metal because metal are good conductor of electricity.
18. **(a)** Both Assertion and Reason are correct and the Reason is a correct explanation of Assertion.
    The male urethra is lined by pseudostratified epithelium.
19. **(b)** When a light ray passes through denser medium from a rarer it undergoes refraction.
20. **(c)** Bowman's capsule which is found in kidney, accomodates one glomerulus, and is lined by flat cells. Some of which have fine pores to allow passage of materials filtered out of a glomerulus.
21. In pure state, metals have a shining surface. (2 marks)

    OR

    Glucose is oxidised to produce energy used by cells. (2 marks)
22. The main organs of human digestive system involved in the process of digestion of food, *i.e.*, starting from mouth in the correct order are as follows:
    Mouth → Oesophagus → Stomach → Small intestine (consisting of duodenum, jejunum and ileum) → Large intestine (consisting of caecum, colon and rectum). (1 mark)

    - **Digestion of carbohydrate:** Carbohydrate digestion begins in the buccal cavity, as human saliva contains an enzyme ptyalin or salivary amylase which hydrolyses starch into the disaccharides, maltose, isomaltose and small dextrins. (1 mark)

    OR

    (a) Digestion of fat occurs in duodenum and jejunum parts of small intestine with the help of enzyme lipase that acts on emulsified fat to form fatty acids and glycerol. (1 mark)
    (b) Small intestine is lined by epithelium which is specialised to absorb food. It has structure to increase its absorbing surface area several times. (1 mark)
23. Mendel took pea plant in his experiment with tallness and shortness trait produced progeny in F_1 generation there is no halfway characteristic *i.e*, plant of F_1 generation will show-tallness and dwarfness both. But for F_2 generation when F_1 progeny gametes combine together both the traits will show their separate identity in 3 : 1 ratio in which 70% offsprings will show dominant characters while 25% offsprings will show recessive characters. (2 marks)

Sample Paper-8 Solutions

24. As here $u = -0.25$ m and $f = 1/P = (1/3)$ m,

from lens formula $P = \dfrac{1}{f} = \dfrac{1}{v} - \dfrac{1}{u}$,

we have $3 = \dfrac{1}{v} - \dfrac{1}{-0.25}$

or $\dfrac{1}{v} = 3 - 4 = -1$ m

i.e. $v = -1$ m (1 mark)

i.e., the lens shifts the object from 25 cm to 1 m for clear vision, i.e., his near point is 1m. So in absence of glasses, he must hold the newspaper at a distance of 1m away from his eyes for clear vision. (1 mark)

OR

Let x be the distance of the actual far point from the eye and hence from the concave lens placed close to the eye. The rays coming from infinity, after refraction through the concave lens, appear to come from the far point F.

$\therefore$ $u = -\infty, v = -x, f = ?$

By lens formula,

$\dfrac{1}{f} = \dfrac{1}{v} - \dfrac{1}{u} = \dfrac{1}{-x} - \dfrac{1}{-\infty} = -\dfrac{1}{x} + 0 = -\dfrac{1}{x}$ (1 mark)

$\therefore$ Required focal length, $f = -x$

Required power, $P = \dfrac{1}{f} = -\dfrac{1}{x}$

The negative sign shows that the correcting lens is a concave lens. (1 mark)

25. The units which make up the nervous system are called neurons.
(i) End of dendrite tip of nerve cell.
(ii) Dendrite $\to$ cell body $\to$ axon to its ends.
(2 × 1 = 2 marks)

26. During asexual reproduction the traits which are present in the previous generation will remain the same with very minor differences. On this basis, the trait which are present in high percentage will be arising earlier i.e. trait 'B' having existence of 60% is likely to have arose earlier. (2 marks)

27. (a) Carbonate salt: Sodium carbonate: Na_2CO_3
(b) Chloride salt: Potassium chloride: KCl
(c) Copper salt: Copper sulphate: $CuSO_4$
(d) Sodium salt: Sodium sulphate: Na_2SO_4
(e) Nitrate salt: Ammonium nitrate: NH_4NO_3
(f) Sulphate salt: Ammonium sulphate: $(NH_4)_2SO_4$
(½ × 6 = 3 marks)

28. (a) (i) Ethanol (½ mark)
  (ii) Ethanoic acid (½ mark)
  (iii) Ethene (½ mark)
(b) (i) 2-methylpropanoic acid (½ mark)
  (ii) Ethyl ethanoate (½ mark)
  (iii) But-1, 2-diol (½ mark)

29. It the image formed by a mirror for all positions of the object in front of it is always virtual, erect and diminished, the mirror is convex (1 mark)

A convex mirror forms only virtual images for all positions of the ral object. The image is always virtual, erect, amaller that the object and is located between the pole and the focus.

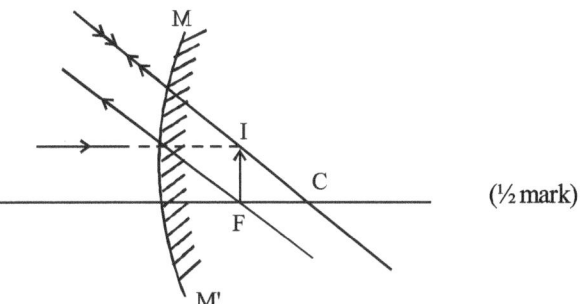
(½ mark)

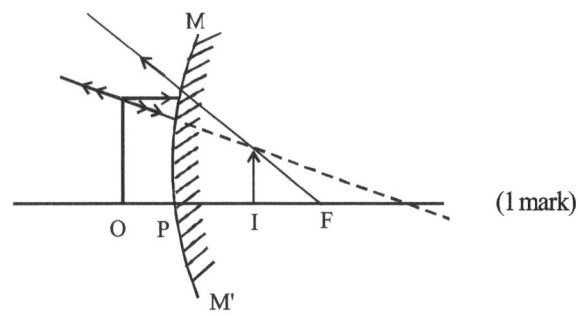
(1 mark)

Power $= -\dfrac{1}{f}$

$10 = \dfrac{-1}{f}$

$f = \dfrac{-1}{10} = -0.1$ m (1 mark)

30. (i) 1 Kilowatt-hour = 1000 watt × 1 hour
= 1000 watt × 3600 sec.
= 3.6×10^6 watt-sec = 3.6×10^6 joules. (1 mark)

(ii) $P = 2000$ W, $t = 1$ hr. $E = ?$

$E = n \times P \times t = 1 \times \dfrac{2000}{1000} \times 1 = 2$ kWh. (1 mark)

T.E. = $30 \times 2 = 60$ kWh. (1 mark)

31. As per 10% law of energy (1942), the energy available decreases by 90% with the rise of trophic level. 2000 J of energy available at the producer or T_1 level will provide only 2J of energy to second order carnivores (T_4). Therefore, an ecosystem cannot have food chains of several steps.

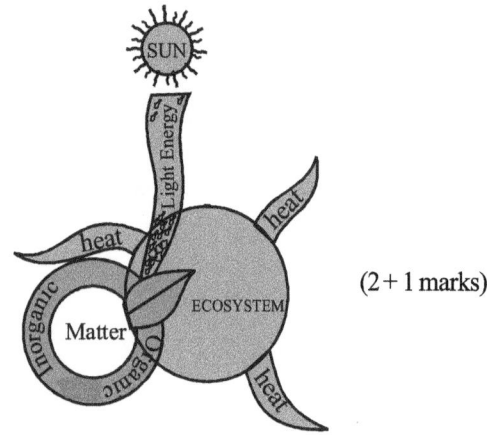

(2 + 1 marks)

32. (i) Length of conductor : It is directly proportional to the length of conductor. (1 mark)
(ii) Area of cross-section : It is inversely proportional to the area of cross-section. (1 mark)
(iii) Nature of a material. (½ mark)
(iv) Temperature of the conductor. (½ mark)

OR

(i) Power, P = VI = 5 × 0.5 = 2.5 Watt (1 mark)
(ii) Resistance, $R = \dfrac{V}{I} = \dfrac{5}{0.5} = 10\Omega$ (1 mark)
(iii) Energy consumed, W = P×t = 2.5 × 4 × 3600
    = 36000 = 3.6×10⁴ J (1 mark)

33. (a) Three growth hormones in plant are-
(i) Auxin: It is synthesised in the young tip of roots and shoots. It promotes elongation and division of cell and root formation.
(ii) Gibberellins : They help in the growth of the stem and flowers.
(iii) Cytokinins : They promote cell division and delay leaf ageing. (1½ marks)

(b) The ability of a plant to recognise change and respond to that change is termed as the sensitivity of the plant. Yet plants have no nervous system and no muscle tissue, they use electrical and chemical means to convey the information from one cell to another cell. The leaves of the sensitive plant (*Mimosa pudica*) folds up in response to touch. These leaf movements are independent of growth whereas, the directional movements of the shoot of a germinating seedling breaking through the soil is growth dependent. (1½ marks)

34. (a) Calcium carbonate gives CO_2 gas when reacts with HCl.
$CaCO_3 + 2HCl \rightarrow CaCl_2 + CO_2 + H_2O$
CO_2 turns lime water milky when passed through it because of the formation of $CaCO_3$. When CO_2 so formed, is passed through lime water, lime water turns milky because of the formation of $CaCO_3$.
$CO_2 + Ca(OH)_2 \rightarrow CaCO_3 + H_2O$
On electrolysis of brine, Cl_2 gas is deposited over anode which gives calcium oxychloride on passing over slaked lime. $CaOCl_2$ is used in disinfecting the drinking water.
$Ca(OH)_2 + Cl_2 \rightarrow CaOCl_2 + H_2O$
Therefore,
→ Metal carbonate 'X' is $CaCO_3$. (1 mark)
→ Solution 'Y' is lime water. (1 mark)
→ Gas 'G' is chlorine gas. (1 mark)
→ Dry 'Y' is dry $Ca(OH)_2$ (dry slaked lime).
→ Compound 'Z' is $CaOCl_2$ (bleaching powder). (1 mark)

(b) The chemical formula of plaster of paris is $CaSO_4 \cdot \dfrac{1}{2} H_2O$. (1 mark)

OR

(a)

Substance	Action on Litmus Paper
Dry HCl gas	No change
Moistened NH₃ gas	Turns red to blue
Lemon juice	Turns blue to red
Carbonated soft drink	Turns blue to red
Curd	Turns blue to red
Soap solution	Turns red to blue

(½ × 6 = 3 marks)

(b) (i) It is done to prevent the formation of lactic acid which spoils the milk. (1 mark)
(ii) When milk boils, micro-organisms are destroyed and fermentation to lactic acid does not take place easily. Thus, milk takes long time to set as a curd. (1 mark)

35. Representation of the magnetic field path along which an imaginary free north pole would tend to move. The tangent at any point on the magnetic field line gives the direction of the magnetic field at that point. (1 mark)
(i) Emerge at north pole and merge at south pole. Inside the magnet, the direction of field lines is from south pole of magnet to its north pole and are closed curves.
(ii) field lines are crowded at the points where the magnetic field is stronger, and vice-versa.

(iii) No two magnetic field lines can intersect each other, If intersects there will be two direction of field, which is impossible. (2 marks)

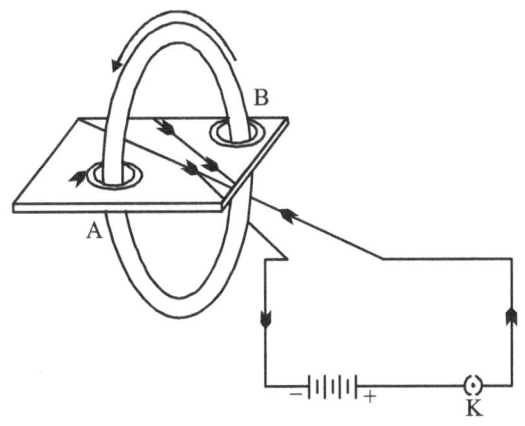

(2 marks)

36. (i) The organ that produces sperms and secretes male hormones is testis. The hormone secreted by testis is testosterone.

Function of testosterone include:
(a) Stimulation of sperm production. (1 mark)
(b) Stimulation of the development of secondary sexual characters in males. (1 mark)
(c) Development, maturation and functioning of accessory sex organs like vas deferens and seminal vesicles. (1 mark)

(ii) Fallopian tubes (1 mark)

(iii) The embryo gets nourishment from the mother's blood with the help of a special tissue called placenta. This tissue is embedded in the uterine wall, containing villi on the embryo's side of the tissue. On the mother's side blood spaces are present which surround the villi. This provides a large surface area for glucose and oxygen to pass from the mother to the embryo. (1 mark)

37. (a) Corrosion is a natural process of deterioration of a metal or material with the reaction of surrounding which results into the production of more stable form such as oxide, hydroxide or sulphide.
e.g. Iron gets corrodded in presence of water and oxygen and forms brown coloured iron oxide. (2 marks)

(b) The methods of preventing corrosion –
(i) Painting/ Oiling/ Galvanizing/ Chrome plating/ making alloys.

(ii) The best way to prevent rusting of iron is making the iron article as cathode. This method is known as cathodic protection.
Note : Saline water accelerates the formation of rust as it is highly conducting. (2 marks)

OR

(b) (i) The iron metal at the bottom of ship is connected with more reactive metal like Mg than iron. This is called cathodic protection. (1 mark)
Zn is the best metal for metal plating on iron article as it has higher oxidation potential than Ni, Cu, Sn. The process of coating of iron surface with zinc is known as galvanization.
Note : Galvanized iron sheets maintain their lusture due to the formation of protective layer of basic zinc carbonate. (1 mark)

38. (i) This indicates the presence of starch.
(ii) Destarched leaves, strips of black paper and iodine solution.
(iii) The plant with the leaves exposed to light of a lamp, a night before the experiment.
(iv) Alcohol, iodine and water. (4 × 1 = 4 marks)

39. (a) Benzene (1 mark)
(b) Medium in which speed of light is less is known as optically denser medium and the medium in which speed of light is more is optically rarer medium. (1 mark)

(c) (i) **Statement of first law of refraction :** The incident ray, the normal to the transparent surface at the point of incidence and the refracted ray, all lie in one and the same plane. (1 mark)

(ii) **Statement of second law of refraction :** The ratio of sine of angle of incidence to the sine of the angle of refraction is constant and is called refractive index of the second medium with respect to the first medium. It is represented by the symbol $_1\mu_2$ i.e., $\dfrac{\sin i}{\sin r} = {_1\mu_2}$

($_1\mu_2$ means refractive index of second medium with respect to the first medium) (1 mark)
This law is called Snell's law.

OR

(c) $^a\mu_g = 1.5$; v = ? ; c = 3 × 10^8 m/sec

$^a\mu_g = \dfrac{c}{v} \Rightarrow v = \dfrac{c}{^a\mu_g} = \dfrac{3 \times 10^8}{1.5} = 2 \times 10^8 \text{ m/sec}$

(2 marks)

SAMPLE PAPER-9

1. **(c)** Calcium chloride is a good dehydrating agent so calcium chloride ($CaCl_2$) will absorb moisture from the gas (HCl).

2. **(d)** $2Pb(NO_3)_2 \xrightarrow{\Delta} 2PbO + 4NO_2 + O_2$

3. **(d)** When one or more reactant(s) react to form new substance(s) with entirely different properties, the reaction is called chemical reaction.
   In option (d), copper reacts with oxygen to form copper oxide (chemical reaction).

   $\underset{\text{Copper wire}}{2Cu} + O_2 \xrightarrow{\Delta} \underset{\text{Copper oxide}}{2CuO}$

4. **(c)** C_4H_9OH and $C_5H_{11}OH$ represent homologous series in increasing order of C atoms, other two also represent homologous series, but in decreasing order because they differ from each other by a CH_2 group.
   $CH_3CH_2CH_2CH_2OH$, $CH_3CH_2CH_2CH_2CH_2OH$

5. **(c)** Conc. HCl and conc. HNO_3 in 3 : 1 ratio form aqua-regia.

6. **(b)** 7. **(b)** 8. **(d)** 9. **(b)** 10. **(b)**

11. **(c)** The strength of magnetic field lines inside a long current carrying straight solenoid same at all points because the magnetic field lines are straight, equi-spaced and parallel to the axis of solenoid and thus uniform magnetic field exist inside the solenoid.

12. **(a)** The normal systolic and diastolic pressure is about 120/80 mmHg.

13. **(c)** Correct direction of flow of electrical impulses is as follows:
    Impulse → Dendrite → Cell body → Axon → Release of chemicals that cross synapse → Dendrite of next neuron

14. **(a)** Offsprings have greater similarity because only one parent is involved in asexual reproduction thus, no gametes formation. Asexual reproduction is based on mitosis i.e., division of a nucleus into two identical daughter nuclei. Each daughter nucleus has similar genetic make up because of replication of parentals DNA. The new offsprings produced are called clones.

15. **(c)** The figure is showing low of independent assortment.

16. **(a)** A is refer for copper T and is for B is for implants.

17. **(c)** Suspension of calcium hydroxide $Ca(OH)_2$ is used in white wash. It reacts with CO_2 in air to form a thin layer of calcium carbonate ($CaCO_3$) on the walls which gives shiny white finish after two or three days.

18. **(c)**

19. **(a)** Both Assertion and Reason are correct and the Reason is a correct explanation of Assertion.
    9 purple and 7 white flowers are obtained in sweet pea (*Lathyrus odoratus*).

20. **(b)** Both Assertion and Reason are correct but Reason is not a correct explanation of Assertion.
    Mammals have a well-developed respiratory system.

21. Hydrogen gas is liberated when an acid reacts with a metal. (1 mark)
    During reaction of zinc with dilute hydrochloric acid, colourless gas (H_2) with pop up sound is evolved.
    $2HCl + Zn \longrightarrow ZnCl_2 + H_2 \uparrow$ (1 mark)

    OR

    (i) Non-metals do not donate electron, they cannot supply electrons so as to convert H^+ ion to $H_2(g)$. (1 mark)
    (ii) Like metals, it has properties to lose an electron to form positive H^+ ion. (1 mark)

22. Sino-atrial node also called pace maker because it determines the rate of heart beat by determining the rate of discharge of cardiac impulse. (2 marks)

23. We should have to drink plenty of water, eat healthy food perform exercise and not take stress to avoid accumulation of harmful chemicals in our body. We should eat more vegetables i.e. cruciferous vegetables (such as broccoli, cauliflower, etc.) than meat. (2 marks)

24. (i) For getting a resistance of 13.5 Ω, the two resistors should be connected in parallel and one in series with them.
    The equivalent resistance of the two resistors in parallel, R_p is given by

    $\dfrac{1}{R_p} = \dfrac{1}{9} + \dfrac{1}{9} = \dfrac{2}{9} \Rightarrow R_p = 4.5\,\Omega$ (½ mark)

    Now, the equivalent resistance of R_p and 9 Ω in series is given by

    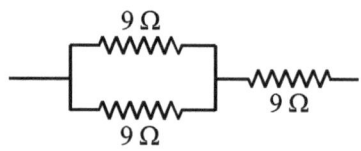

    $R = R_p + 9 = 4.5 + 9 = 13.5\,\Omega.$ (½ mark)

Sample Paper-9 Solutions

(ii) To get a resistance of 4 Ω, two resistors should be connected in series and one is parallel to them.

The equivalent resistance of the two resistors in series is given by

$R_p = 9\,\Omega + 9\,\Omega = 18\,\Omega$ (½ mark)

Now, the equivalent resistance of R_p and 9 Ω in parallel is given by

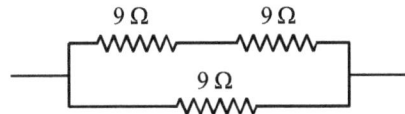

$\dfrac{1}{R} = \dfrac{1}{R_p} + \dfrac{1}{9} = \dfrac{1}{18} + \dfrac{1}{9} = \dfrac{1+2}{18} = \dfrac{3}{18} = \dfrac{1}{6}$

R = 6Ω (½ mark)

OR

(a) **Joule's Law of Heating:** It states that the amount of heat produced in a conductor is

(i) directly proportional to the square of current passing through it, i.e., $H \propto I^2$ .... (i)

(ii) directly propotional to the resistance of conductor, i.e., $H \propto R$ .... (ii)

(iii) directly proportional to the time for which current passed, i.e., $H \propto t$ .... (iii)

Combining (i), (ii) and (iii). $H \propto I^2 Rt$.

Here, constant of proportionality is 1.

∴ $H = I^2 Rt$ joule (1 mark)

(b) Resistance of first lamp = R_1
Resistance of second lamp = R_2

$R = \dfrac{V^2}{P}$, $R_1 = \dfrac{220 \times 220}{100} = 484\,\Omega$

$R_2 = \dfrac{220 \times 220}{60} = \dfrac{2420}{3}\,\Omega$

They are connected in parallel

$\dfrac{1}{R} = \dfrac{1}{R_1} + \dfrac{1}{R_2} = \dfrac{1}{484} + \dfrac{3}{2420}$ (½ mark)

$R = \dfrac{484 \times 2420}{3\left(484 + \dfrac{2420}{3}\right)} = \dfrac{605}{2}\,\Omega$

∴ $I = \dfrac{V}{R} = \dfrac{220 \times 2}{605} = \dfrac{8}{11}\,A$

I = 0.727 A

i.e., current drawn by two bulbs, I = 0.727 A.

(½ mark)

25. (a) If only one pair of contrasting characters is taken. f_1 generation either shows tall or short characterstic, as it follows law of dominance where only dominant character expres itself. (1 mark)

(b) Short plant have recessive trait. (½ mark)

(c)

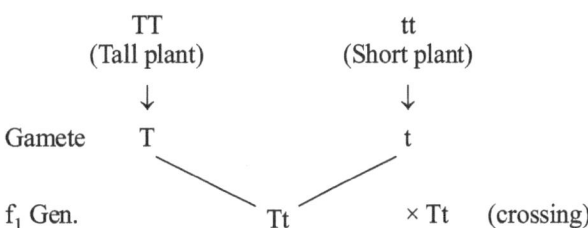

Phenotype Ratio → 3 : 1 (½ mark)

26. The chemical compound released by stimulated cells for control and coordination in plants are called plant hormones or phytohormones. (1 mark)

Auxin - controls growth

Gibberellins - helps in growth of stem (1 mark)

Cytokinin - promotes cell division (any two)

Abscisic acid - Inhibits growth, wilting of leaves

27. A solenoid is a long coil of wire wrapped in many turns. When a current passes through it, it creates a nearly uniform magnetic field inside. (1 mark)

Pattern of magnetic field lines of

(i) A current carrying solenoid

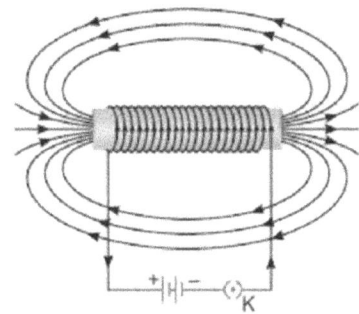

(½ mark)

(ii) A Bar magnet-

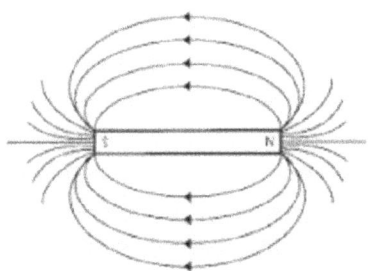

(½ mark)

Two distinguishing features between the two fields:

Solenoid	Bar Magnet
(1) It produces very strong magnetic field.	(1) It produces weak magnetic field.
(2) Its strength can be changed by changing current or turns.	(2) Its strength cannot be changed.

(1 mark)

OR

Electric short circuit occurs when
(i) a current of value more than its rating passes through a wire;
(ii) the live wire touches with the earth or neutral-wire;
(iii) the insulation of the wires is weak;
(iv) over load is provided in the circuit. (3 marks)

28. (a) A strong acid in aqueous solution ionises to a large extent thereby producing a high concentration of hydrogen ions. For example, HCl, H_2SO_4 and HNO_3. Whereas, a weak acid ionises partially in aqueous solution to a smaller extent and contain ions as well as molecules. For example, acetic acid, carbonic acid and formic acid. (1½ marks)

(b) Strong acids are those which ionize completely in solution. For example, H1, H_2SO_4. A concentrated acid has more moles of acid per litre of its solution as compared to a dilute acid. For example, Conc. H_2SO_4 has more moles of acid per litre of its solution as compared to dilute H_2SO_4. (1½ marks)

29. Light is formed of different colours which travel at their own speed inside a prism. Due to which the light bend the through different angles with respect to the incident ray, as they pass through a prism. The red light bends the least while the violet most causing dispersion this can be explained by the fact that light of different colours having different wavelengths has different velocities while travelling in a medium $v_m = n\lambda_m$. (1 mark)

Newton showed that the reverse of dispersion of light is also possible. If we kept two prisms close to each other one in erect position and the other in an inverted position. The light get dispersed when passes through the first prism. The second prism receives all the seven coloured rays from first prism and combines into original while light i.e., recombine the different colour of spectrum & hence gives white light. This proves that white light is made of seven colours. (1 mark)

Diagram:

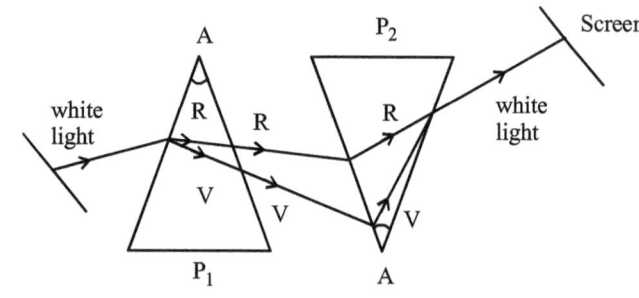

(Dispering Prism) (Recombination Prism)

(1 mark)

30. (i) *Planaria* on being cut into many pieces, each piece regenerates into a new individual. (1 mark)

(ii) When *Bryophyllum* leaf falls on the wet soil, the buds that are developed in the notches along the leaf will develop into new plants via a process known as vegetative propagation. (1 mark)

(iii) when the matured sporangia of *Rhizopus* burst open, it releases spores which germinate into new mycelium in moist conditions. (1 mark)

31. (i) As magnification is negative, the image formed by mirror is real.
Hence, it is a concave mirror. (1 mark)

(ii) Magnification $m = -v/u = -1$
$\therefore u = v = -50$ cm
Distance of the image from the object
$v - u = -50 - (-50) = 0$ cm (1 mark)

(iii) By using mirror formula:
$1/f = 1/v + 1/u$
$= 1/(-50) + 1/(-50) = -1/25$
$\therefore f = -25$ cm (½ mark)

(iv)

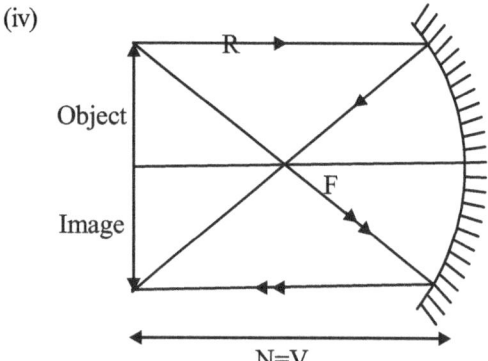

(½ mark)

Sample Paper-9 Solutions

32. Ozone is molecule which contains three atoms of oxygen (O_3). It is highly poisonous gas present on the upper layer of the atmosphere. (½ + ½ = 1 mark)

Formation of ozone – The UV radiations split some molecular oxygen (O_2) apart into free oxygen atoms (O + O). These atoms then combine with molecular oxygen to form ozone.

$$O_2 \xrightarrow{UV} O + O$$
$$O + O_2 \longrightarrow O_3 \text{ (Ozone)}$$ (2 marks)

33. On heating, $FeSO_4$ crystals lose water and anhydrous $FeSO_4$ is formed, so colour of crystals changes to white. On further heating, $FeSO_4$ decomposes to form SO_2, SO_3 and a brown iron oxide. (2 marks)

$$FeSO_4 \cdot 7H_2O \xrightarrow{Heat} \underset{\text{(white) (anhydrous form)}}{FeSO_4} + 7H_2O$$ (½ mark)
$$\underset{\text{(white)}}{2FeSO_4} \xrightarrow{Heat} \underset{\text{(brown)}}{Fe_2O_3} + SO_2 + SO_3$$ (½ mark)

34. (a)

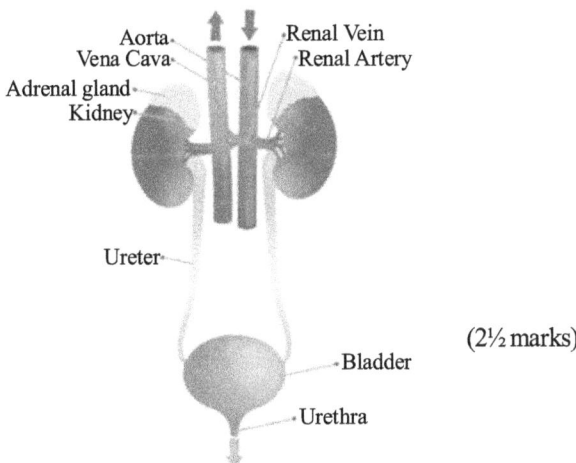

(2½ marks)

(b) Each kidney has large numbers of these filtration units called nephrons packed close together. Some substances in the initial filtrate, such as glucose, amino acids, salts and a major amount of water, are selectively re-absorbed as the urine flows along the tube. The amount of water re-absorbed depends on how much excess water there is in the body, and on how much of dissolved waste there is to be excreted. The urine forming in each kidney eventually enters a long tube, the ureter, which connects the kidneys with the urinary bladder. Urine is stored in the urinary bladder until the pressure of the expanded bladder leads to the urge to pass it out through the urethra. (2½ marks)

35. (i) **To find out the total resistance of a circuit in which 3 resistances are connected in series :**

3 resistances – R_1, R_2 and R_3 are connected in series and put in a circuit as shown in figure. The circuit has cell of voltage 'V' which supplies current I ampere.

When current I flows through the circuit, it remains same in each resistance but PD gets distributed in these three resistances, i.e., V_1, V_2, V_3 across R_1, R_2, R_3 respectively.

According to Ohm's law, **V = IR**

Therefore, V_1 (across resistance R_1) = IR_1
V_2 (across resistance R_2) = IR_2
V_3 (across resistance R_3) = IR_3
Since, $V = V_1 + V_2 + V_3$

$\Rightarrow IR = IR_1 + IR_2 + IR_3$
$\Rightarrow IR = I(R_1 + R_2 + R_3)$
$\Rightarrow R = R_1 + R_2 + R_3$ (1 mark)

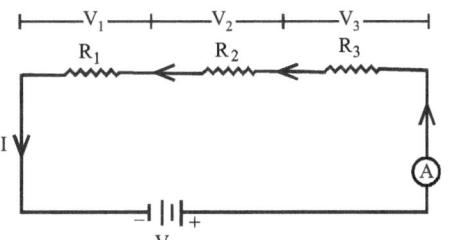

(1 mark)

Conclusion : It means if two or more resistances are connected in series then the total resistance of the circuit is equal to the sum of individual resistances. Therefore if 'n' resistances are connected in series then total resistance is,

$R = R_1 + R_2 + R_3 + \ldots\ldots\ldots + R_n$.

(ii) $R_1 = 5\,\Omega$, $R_2 = 10\,\Omega$, $R_3 = 15\,\Omega$, $I = 1\,A$

(a) $\dfrac{1}{R'} = \dfrac{1}{R_2} + \dfrac{1}{R_3} = \dfrac{1}{10} + \dfrac{1}{15} = \dfrac{3+2}{30} = \dfrac{5}{30}$

$R' = \dfrac{30}{5} = 6\,\Omega$

$R = R_1 + R' = 5 + 6 = 11\,\Omega$ (1 mark)

Now, $V = IR = 1 \times 11 = 11\,V$

(b) $V_1 = IR_1 = 1 \times 5 = 5\,V$.

Therefore, $V_2 = V - V_1 = 11 - 5 = 6\,V$ (1 mark)

(c) $V_2 = I_1 R_2 \Rightarrow I_1 = \dfrac{V_2}{R_2} = \dfrac{6}{10} = 0.6\,A;$

$I_2 = \dfrac{V_2}{R_3} = \dfrac{6}{15} = 0.4\,A$ (1 mark)

36. An alloy is a homogeneous mixture of two or more metals or a metal and a non-metal.
    (a) Brass is an alloy of Cu and Zn.
    (b) Bronze is an alloy of Cu and Sn.
    (c) Solder is an alloy of Pb and Sn.
    Brass is used for making cooking utensils, screw, nuts, bolts wires etc.
    Bronze is used for making cooling pipes, utensils, statues.
    Solder is used for welding electric wires. (5 marks)

    OR

    (a) Mercury (Hg)　　(b) Aluminium
    (c) Amphoteric　　(d) No, its a neutral gas
    (e) Acidic　　($5 \times 1 = 5$ marks)

37. (i) Water (1 mark)
    (ii) Gravity (1 mark)
    (iii) Light (1 mark)
    (iv) B and C; Gravity and Light (Sunlight) (1 mark)

    OR

    (i) Like all organism, plant defect and respond to stimuli in their environment.
    (ii) This is due to stimulus of gravity.

38. (a) Reaction in which an atom or group of atoms are replaced by other atom or group of atoms without causing any change in the structure of remaining part of the molecule is known as substitution reaction.
    Example: $CH_4 + Cl_2 \rightarrow CH_3Cl + HCl$ (1 mark)
    (b) (i) $CH_2 = CH_2 + H_2 \rightarrow CH_3 - CH_3$; Addition reaction (1 mark)
    (ii) $C_2H_6 + O_2 \rightarrow 2CO_2 + 3H_2O$; Combustion reaction (1 mark)

    OR

    (b) (i) While a compound reacts with oxygen in a combustion reaction a great amount of heat is generated. This is why combustion reactions are exothermic reactions. (1 mark)
    (ii) $CH_3CH_2OH \xrightarrow[\text{or Acidified } K_2Cr_2O_7, \Delta]{\text{Alkaline } KMnO_4, \Delta} CH_3COOH$

    In the conversion of ethanol to ethanoic acid oxygen gets added to the product. So the reaction is oxidation reaction and these substances ($KMnO_4$ or $K_2Cr_2O_7$) are known as oxidizing agents. (1 mark)

39. (a) (i) A ray passing through the optical centre, is displaced but not deviated. But in thin lenses the displacement is very small which can be neglected. (1 mark)
    (ii) Optical centre of a lens can be within the lens or outside, depending on the nature of lens.
    ($½ \times 2 = 1$ mark)
    (b) $f = 20$ cm (convex lens) $= 0.2$ m,
    $P = \dfrac{1}{f} = \dfrac{1}{0.2} = 5$ diopter (1 mark)
    (c) $P = 4D$, $P = \dfrac{1}{f} \Rightarrow 4 = \dfrac{1}{f} \Rightarrow f = \dfrac{1}{4} = 0.25$ cm (1 mark)
    $f = (0.25 \times 100)$ cm $= 25$ cm
    It is a convex lens ('f' is + ve) (1 mark)

    OR

    (i) $f = -2$ m
    $P = \dfrac{1}{f} = \dfrac{1}{-2} = -0.5$ dioptre (1 mark)
    (ii) When the focal length of a lens is one metre then the power of lens is called one dioptre. (1 mark)

SAMPLE PAPER-10

1. **(b)** The reaction represents a neutralisation reaction in which base (NaOH) reacts with an acid (HNO$_3$) to form salt (NaNO$_3$) and water (H$_2$O).

2. **(c)** Aqueous solution of A is basic while that of B is acidic. Therefore A has pH greater than 7 and B has pH less than 7.

3. **(c)** Zinc is more reactive than tin (zinc is above tin in reactivity series) so it will react with organic acids (present in food) to form poisonous compounds. To avoid this food cans are coated with tin and **not** with zinc.

4. **(a)** Ca(OH)$_2$ + CO$_2$ → CaCO$_3$ + H$_2$O

5. **(c)** Conversion of liquid to gas is endothermic process.

6. **(a)** Calcium (Ca) combines with oxygen to form calcium oxide (CaO) which has a high melting point and dissolves in water to form Ca(OH)$_2$.

7. **(c)**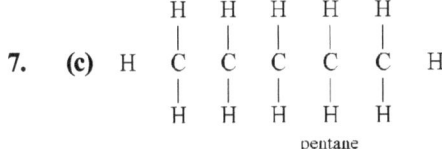
pentane

8. **(b)** The danger signals are red in colour because among all other colours, red colour is scattered the least by smoke or fog. So, it can be easily seen from a distance even in fog or smoky environment.

9. **(d)** The pathway of nerve impulse in a reflex action is called the reflex arc. A reflex action is an involuntary action in response to a stimulus e.g., coughing, sneezing etc. The specific pathway followed is given below:

   Stimulus → Receptors → (Sensory neurons) → Spinal cord → (Motor neurons) → Effector (Muscle/Gland) → Response

10. **(b)** In a rectangular glass slab, the emergent rays are parallel to the direction of the incident ray, as the extent of bending of the ray of light at the opposite parallel faces air-glass and glass-air interface of the rectangular glass slab is equal and opposite.
    This is why the ray emerges are parallel to the incident ray.

11. **(c)**

12. **(d)** Wrinkled and green are specific characters because they are different from parents and are recessive.

13. **(d)**

14. **(d)** Decomposers are present at the final level in a food web. They breakdown dead and decaying organic matter (plants and animals) and convert into nutrients in the soil. They naturally increase the decomposition process and therefore used in natural biocomposting.

15. **(d)** Removal of prostate gland will come the sperm to be reacted with the acid urine in the urethra.

16. **(a)** The genotypic ratio will be 1 : 2 : 1. The probably of having aa is 25% in F$_2$ generation.

17. **(b)** Both Assertion and Reason are correct but Reason is not a correct explanation of Assertion.
    Carbon dioxide and methane are commonly known as greenhouse gases because they are responsible for greenhouse effect.

18. **(b)** The blood of an insect functions differently than the blood of a human. Insect blood, however, does not carry gases and has no haemoglobin which gives red colour to the blood.

19. **(a)** Clouds are generally white as larger particles like dust and water drops scatter light of all colours, almost equally and all the colours reach our eyes equally and combine to form white light.

20. **(a)** The correct IUPAC name for the compound is 2, 4-dimethyl hexane not 3, 5 dimethyl hexane.

21. Transpiration refers to the evaporative loss of water by plant. The importance of transpiration are as follows:
    (a) It creates transpiration pull for absorption and transport of water and mineral from xylem of roots to the top of the plant.
    (b) It supplies water for photosynthesis.
    (c) It transport minerals from soil to all parts of the plant.
    (d) It regulates temperature of the leaves. (2 marks)

    OR

    In heart, the valves (i.e. bicuspid and tricuspid) are present between auricles and ventricles. Their presence stops the back flow of blood. When ventricles contract, the valves get closed and it helps to maintain the unidirectional flow of blood. (i.e., the blood does not go back into auricles).
    (2 marks)

22. (i) To pass signal from receptors to brain. (½ mark)
    (ii) Bony box which protects our brain. (½ mark)
    (iii) Bony structure that protects the spinal cord. (½ mark)
    (iv) To transmit signal from brain or spinal cord to effector organ. (½ mark)

23. The sexually transmitted disease (STD) are a group of communicable disease that are transmitted mainly by sexual contacts. STDs are also called as Veneral Disease (V.D). STDs are caused by bacteria, viruses, protozoa and fungi. (1 + 1 = 2 marks)

24. (i) Mendel experimented on garden pea plant with selection of seven visible contrasting characters forming laws of inheritance. He selected and crossed homozygous tall pea plant with genotype TT and a homozygous dwarf pea plant with the genotype tt. F$_1$ generation consists only of tall plants having genotype Tt.
    The expressed allele 'T' for tallness is dominant over the unexpressed allele t for dwarfness. Therefore, the trait of tallness is dominant while dwarfness is the recessive trait. Thus, Mendel's experiment showed that traits may be dominant or recessive.

(ii) In Mendel's experiment, different traits were tall and dwarf plant, round and wrinkled seeds. In F_2 (second) generation, some plants were tall with round seeds and others were dwarf with wrinkled seeds. Other combination was dwarf plants having round/wrinkled seed traits, that were independently inherited.

(1 + 1 = 2 marks)

25. Type of mirror used in:
   (i) **Headlights of a car :** Concave mirror
   Concave mirror is used because light from the bulb placed at the focus of it gets reflected and produces a powerful parallel beam of light to illuminate the road.
   (ii) **Solar furnace:** Concave mirror
   Cancave mirror has the property to concentrate the sunlight coming from sun along with heat radiation at its focus. As a result, temperature at its focus increases and the substance placed at the focal point gets heated to a high temperature. (1 × 2 = 2 marks)

   OR

   (i) Convex lens   (ii) Convex lens
   (iii) Convex lens   (iv) Concave lens
   (½ × 4 = 2 marks)

26. (i) In white washing, quick lime reacts with water to form slaked lime. (½ mark)
   $CaO + H_2O \longrightarrow Ca(OH)_2 + Heat$ (½ mark)
   Quick Slaked
   lime   lime
   (ii) Silver bromide, when exposed to light decomposes to silver and bromine. (½ mark)
   $2AgBr(s) \xrightarrow{Sunlight} 2Ag(s) + Br_2(g)$ (½ mark)
   Silver bromide   Silver   Bromine

   OR

   Covalent bonds are formed by sharing of electrons whereas ionic bonds are formed by transfer of electrons e.g. KCl. In KCl, ionic bond is present.

   $K^{\bullet} \quad {}^{x}_{x}Cl^{x}_{x} \longrightarrow K^+ \quad Cl^- \longrightarrow KCl$ (1 mark)

   In CH_4, covalent bond is present. (1 mark)

27. (i) Scattering of light – Phenomenon of spreading of light (diffused reflection) by minute particles in a medium. (1 mark)
   (ii) The sky appears blue because the blue colour of sunlight scatters much more strongly than the red colour by particles in atmosphere/air due to its shorter wavelength. (2 marks)

28. (i) Photo decomposition of silver chloride takes place which results in formation of silver and colour changing to grey. (1 mark)
   $2AgCl \rightarrow 2Ag + Cl_2$
              (grey)
   (ii) Copper undergoes oxidation and black coloured copper oxide is formed.
   $2Cu + O_2 \rightarrow 2CuO$ (1 mark)

   (iii) Zinc is more reactive than copper so it displaces copper from its solution and colour of the solution changes from blue to colourless.
   $Zn(s) + CuSO_4(aq.) \rightarrow Cu(s) + ZnSO_4(aq.)$ (1 mark)

29. (i) One end of current carrying solenoid behaves as a magnetic north pole, while the other behaves as the south pole. Like in bar magnet, the field lines emerge from one end and merge into another. So, there is either a convergence at S-pole or a divergence from N-pole of magnetic field lines near the ends of solenoid. (1 mark)
   (ii) A current carrying solenoid behaves like a bar magnet. We know that a freely suspended bar magnet aligns itself in the north-south direction. Hence, it rests along north-south direction when suspended freely. (1 mark)
   (iii) Fuse of lower rating will blow off immediately (and require frequent replacements). Fuse of higher rating will not break the circuit, even in case of higher load. So, burnt out fuse should be replaced by another fuse of identical rating for electrical safety. (1 mark)

   OR

   $P = \dfrac{V^2}{R}$ (1 mark)

   $2 \times 10^3 = \dfrac{220 \times 220}{R} \Rightarrow R = \dfrac{220 \times 220}{2 \times 10^3}$ (1 mark)

   $I = \dfrac{V}{R} = \dfrac{220 \times 2 \times 10^3}{220 \times 220} = \dfrac{100}{11} = 9.09 A$

   At this stage, due to very high value of current, oven will be damaged. (1 mark)

30. In a prism the refraction of light takes place at the two slant surfaces. The dispersion of white light occurs at the first surface of prism where its constituent colours are deviated through different angles. At the second surface, these split colours suffer only refraction and they get further separated. But in a rectangular glass block, the refraction of light takes place at the two parallel surfaces. At the first surface, although the white light splits into its constituent colours on refraction, but these split colours on suffering refraction at the second surface emerge out in form of a parallel beam, which give an impression of white light. (3 marks)

31. 1. Fertilization is the process of fusion of sperm with ovum. It is internal in human beings.
   2. During copulation (mating or coitus), the sperms are released in the vagina near the lower end of the uterus.
   3. Millions of sperms are released in the vagina, and they actively swim with the help of their tails and pass into the uterus.
   4. From the uterus, they reach the oviduct (fallopian tube).
   5. If there is an egg in the oviduct, it gets fertilised only by one sperm. (If copulation has taken place during ovulatory period i.e., middle of menstrual cycle).
   6. When the sperm unites with ovum, zygote is formed.
   7. The absence of menstruation indicates fertilisation (after copulation).

8. After fertilisation, the embryonic development of zygote starts in the fallopian tube (pregnancy starts). The embryo reaches the uterus and gets attached to its thickened inner wall. This attachment of the embryo with the uterus is called implantation.

9. After implantation, a special tissue develops between the embryo (foetus) and uterine wall called as placenta. It is richly supplied with blood.

10. Function of placenta : It provides all the basic needs of foetus till birth such as nutrition, respiration, excretion with the help of maternal body.

11. The growth or development of foetus inside the uterus till birth is known as gestation. On completion of gestation, the birth of fully grown and developed foetus taken place. This is known as parturition.

12. The duration of pregnancy, on an average lasts 280 days or 40 weeks from the 1st day of the last menstrual cycle.

13. The average weight of newborn should be 3.5 Kg After 40 weeks of gestation. (3 marks)

32. (i) In a food chain the energy always moves progressively through the various trophic levels and is no longer available to the organisms of the previous trophic level/energy captured by the autotrophs does not go back to the solar input. (1 mark)
    (ii) Pesticides are used in agriculture for crop protection. When washed away/down into the soil/water bodies absorbed by plants/producers. (1 mark)
    (iii) Upon consumption, they enter into our food chain and being non - biodegradable, these chemicals get progressively accumulated in our body. (1 mark)

33. (i) The bond which is formed by loss and gain of electron is called ionic or electro-valent bond. (½ mark)
    (ii) M.P. and B.P. of ionic compounds are high. (½ mark)
    (iii) Ionic compounds are soluble in water but not in organic solvents. (1 mark)
    (iv) Ionic compounds are good conductors of electricity. (1 mark)

34. (i) To find out the total resistance of the circuit when three resistances are connected in parallel:

    Let the three resistances R_1, R_2 and R_3 be connected in parallel across the two ends A and B. This combination is connected to a battery of 'V' volt which supplies a current 'I'. Since these three resistances are across the same points A and B i.e. why they have same PD i.e. 'V' volt.

    But the current gets divided into I_1, I_2 and I_3 through R_1, R_2 and R_3 respectively.
    According to Ohm's law,
    $V = IR \Rightarrow I = \dfrac{V}{R}$ (1 mark)

    Current I_1, (flowing through R_1) = $\dfrac{V}{R_1}$

    Current I_2, (flowing through R_2) = $\dfrac{V}{R_2}$

    Current I_3 (flowing through R_3) = $\dfrac{V}{R_3}$

    Since, $I = I_1 + I_2 + I_3$
    Therefore, $I = \dfrac{V}{R}$

    $\dfrac{V}{R} = \dfrac{V}{R_1} + \dfrac{V}{R_2} + \dfrac{V}{R_3}$

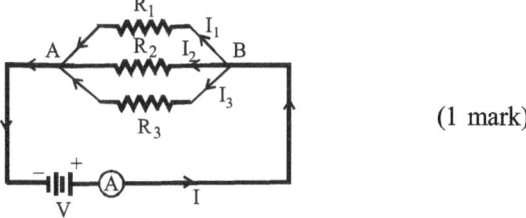

(1 mark)

    $\Rightarrow \dfrac{V}{R} = V\left[\dfrac{I}{R_1} + \dfrac{I}{R_2} + \dfrac{I}{R_3}\right]$

    $\Rightarrow \dfrac{I}{R} = \dfrac{I}{R_1} + \dfrac{I}{R_2} + \dfrac{I}{R_3}$ (1 mark)

    If two or more resistances are connected in parallel, then the reciprocal of total resistance is equal to sum of reciprocals of individual resistance.

    (ii)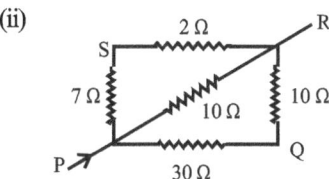

    $R_1 = 7\,\Omega$, $R_2 = 2\,\Omega$, $R_3 = 10\,\Omega$,
    $R_4 = 30\,\Omega$, $R_5 = 10\,\Omega$, $V = 6\,V$

    Now, R_1 and R_2 are in series,
    $R' = R_1 + R_2 = 7 + 2 = 9\,\Omega$
    Also, R_4 and R_5 are in series,
    $R'' = R_4 + R_5 = 30 + 10 = 40\,\Omega$

    Now, R', R'' and R_3 are in parallel,
    $\dfrac{1}{R} = \dfrac{1}{R'} + \dfrac{1}{R''} + \dfrac{1}{R_3}$ (1 mark)

    $\Rightarrow \dfrac{1}{R} = \dfrac{1}{9} + \dfrac{1}{40} + \dfrac{1}{10}$

    $\Rightarrow \dfrac{1}{R} = \dfrac{40 + 9 + 36}{360} = \dfrac{85}{360}$

    $\therefore R = \dfrac{360}{85} = 4.23\,\Omega$

    $V = IR \Rightarrow I = \dfrac{V}{R} = \dfrac{6}{4.23} = 1.41\,A$ (1 mark)

35. (i) The pathway taken by nerve impulses in a reflex action is called the reflex arc: (2½ marks)

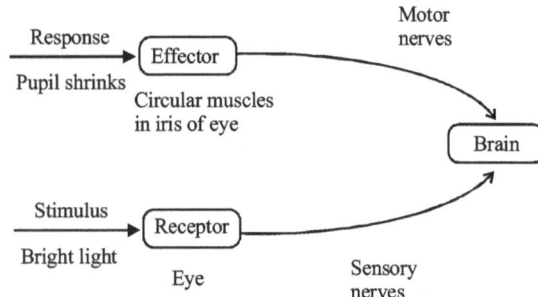

(ii) **Auxin**: It promotes elongation and division of cell and root formation.
Gibberellins: They help in the growth of stem.
Cytokinins: They promote cell division and delay leaf ageing.
Abscisic acid: It prevent wilting of leaves.
(2½ marks)

36. (a)

S. No.	Properties of baking powder	Uses
(i)	On heating releases CO_2 gas.	Baking industry
(ii)	Alkaline in nature, neutralises excess acid in stomach.	Antacid
(iii)	When it reacts with acid, it releases CO_2 gas which can extinguish fire.	Soda-acid fire extinguisher

(1 × 3 = 3 marks)

(b) Acid + Metal $\longrightarrow$ Salt + Hydrogen
e.g., 2HCl + 2Na $\longrightarrow$ 2NaCl + $H_2 \uparrow$
H_2SO_4 + 2Na $\longrightarrow$ Na_2SO_4 + $H_2 \uparrow$
HNO_3 + Na $\longrightarrow$ No hydrogen gas (1 mark)
Nitric acid does not release hydrogen gas when it reacts with metals. This is because nitric acid is strong oxidising agent. Nitric acid reacts only with magnesium and manganese to evolve hydrogen gas.
Mg + 2HNO_3 $\longrightarrow$ $Mg(NO_3)_2$ + $H_2 \uparrow$
Mn + 2HNO_3 $\longrightarrow$ $Mn(NO_3)_2$ + $H_2 \uparrow$ (1 mark)

OR

(a) Salts, having the same positive or negative radicals, are said to belong to the same family. (1 mark)
(b) It is because HCl and HNO_3 ionise in aqueous solution whereas ethanol and glucose do not ionise in aqueous solution. (2 marks)
(c) When a weak acid is added to a concentrated solution of hydrochloric acid, the solution becomes more acidic because it increases the hydronium ion concentration of the solution. (2 marks)

37. (i) Taenia and leech.
(ii) Heterotrophic nutrition is a mode of nutrition in which organisms depend upon other organisms for food to survive.
(iii) fungi (like Mushroom)
(iv) Autotrophic mode helps to fix carbondioxide into sugar by the process of hotosynthesis.
(4 × 1 = 4 marks)

38. (a) Esterification reaction (1 mark)
(b) $CH_3COOH + CH_3CH_2OH \xrightarrow{Acid}$
   Ethanoic acid   Ethanol

$$CH_3 - \underset{\underset{O}{\|}}{C} - O - CH_2 - CH_3$$
   Ester
(1 mark)

Esters are used in making perfumes and as a flavouring agent. (1 mark)
(c) Reverse reaction is known as saponification reaction because it is used in the prepration of soap. (2 marks)

OR

The soap molecules have two parts:
(i) long chain hydrocarbon which is not solible in wate buit soluble in oil; it is known as hydrophobic part.
(ii) ionic part consists of Na+ or K+salts of carboxybates ion, which is soluble in water; it is known as hydrophilic part.

While the soap solutions comes in contact with the oily dirt the hydrophobic part interacts with oil and the ionic part faces outwards to interact with water. Thus, the soap micelle helps in dissolving the dirt in water and acts as cleansing agent. (2 marks)

39. (a) Alloys have high resistivity in comparison to pure metals. Also alloys do not oxidise readily at high temperatures but pure metals do. Therefore, alloys are used for making coils of electric toasters and electric irons rather than a pure metal. (1 mark)
(b) According to the Joule's law of heating effect
$H = I^2RT$ and $H \propto R$
Because the resistance of heating element is very high. So more heat is developed, hence it glows. But the cord has very low resistance, so it does not glow.
(2 marks)
(c) The rate at which energy is delivered by a current is called the power which is given by P = VI
Thus, the potential difference (V) determine the power delivered by a current. (1 mark)
(d) V = 220V, R = 40 Ω
$V = IR \Rightarrow I = \dfrac{V}{R} = \dfrac{220}{40} = 5.5 A$ (1 mark)

www.ingramcontent.com/pod-product-compliance
Lightning Source LLC
LaVergne TN
LVHW070537070526
838199LV00075B/6797